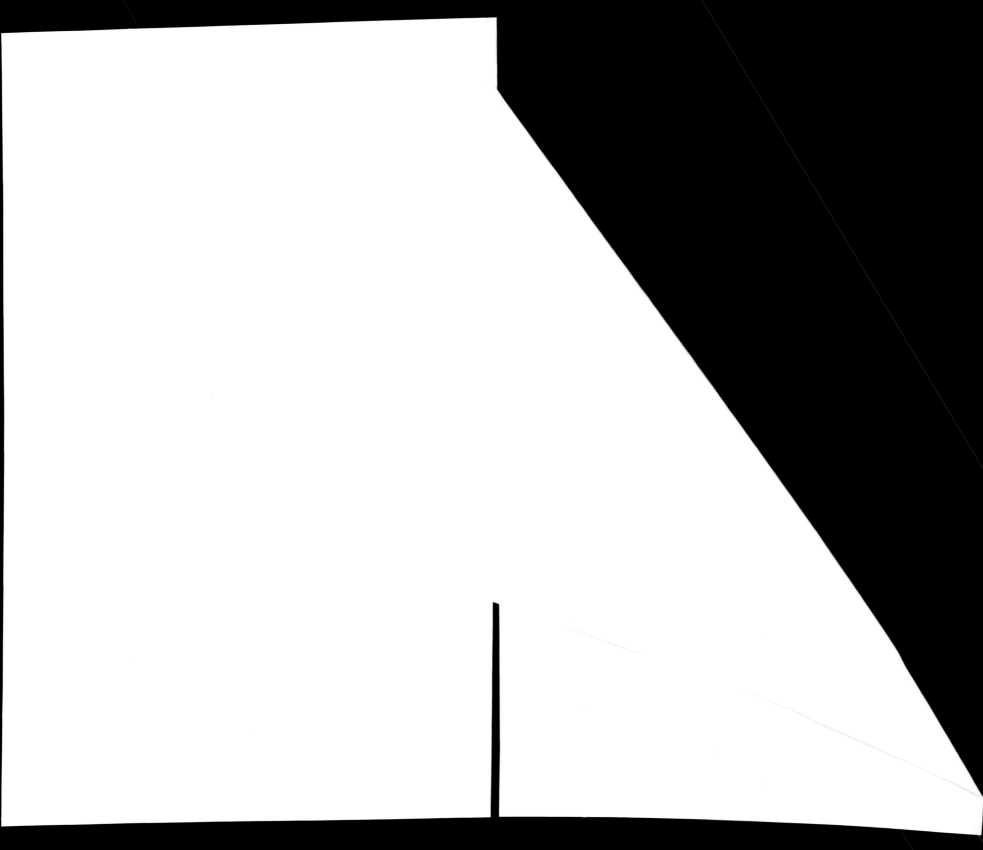

Controlling the Money Supply

D. H. Gowland

Routledge
Taylor & Francis Group

First published in 1982
Second edition 1984
by Croom Helm Ltd

This edition first published in 2013 by Routledge
2 Park Square, Milton Park, Abingdon, Oxon, OX14 4RN

Simultaneously published in the USA and Canada
by Routledge
711 Third Avenue, New York, NY 10017

Routledge is an imprint of the Taylor & Francis Group, an informa business

© 1982, 1984 David Gowland

Publisher's Note
The publisher has gone to great lengths to ensure the quality of this reprint but points out that some imperfections in the original copies may be apparent.

Disclaimer
The publisher has made every effort to trace copyright holders and welcomes correspondence from those they have been unable to contact.

A Library of Congress record exists under LC control number: 84186151

ISBN 13: 978-0-415-85485-6 (hbk)
ISBN 13: 978-0-203-74070-5 (ebk)

Controlling the Money Supply

Second Edition

DAVID GOWLAND

CROOM HELM
London & Canberra

©1982 David Gowland
Second edition © 1984
Croom Helm Ltd, Provident House, Burrell Row,
Beckenham, Kent BR3 1AT
Croom Helm Australia, PO Box 291,
Manuka, ACT 2603, Australia

British Library Cataloguing in Publication Data

Gowland, David
  Controlling the money supply. – 2nd ed.
  1. Money supply – Great Britain – History –
  – 20th century
  I. Title
  332.40941   HG939.5
  ISBN 0-7099-1170-X

Printed and bound in Great Britain
by Billing & Sons Limited, Worcester.

CONTENTS

PREFACE

This book is intended as a successor to *Monetary Policy and Credit Control* (Croom Helm, 1978). Some of the material is a revised version of material included in the earlier work, for example Chapter 6 of the new work follows Chapter 3 of the earlier work fairly closely. However, most of this book is new material. Some of the material in the earlier work has been omitted, especially the sections on monetary policy in other countries and on banking supervision. Many other arguments have been abbreviated, to make room for the new material. Accordingly, I have frequently referred back to the earlier work, using the abbreviated form MPCC. The *Bank of England Quarterly Bulletin* has been abbreviated in the notes to *Bulletin*.

Note to Second Edition

Chapters 1–10 have not been altered from the first edition, but Chapter 11 has been added.

1 INTRODUCTION

1.1 Introduction

In 1970, monetary policy was viewed as an esoteric subject of minor importance and of interest only to a few specialist economists. Thus, for example, the Nuffield study of the 1970 General Election included a 47-page survey of events from 1966-9, which though largely devoted to economic affairs did not include a single mention of monetary policy.[1] None of the nine chapters of 'The Labour Government's Economic Record 1964-70' was devoted to monetary policy and there was only one reference to any monetary topic in the index (money supply, p. 297).[2] By 1981, it was widely believed that the 'monetarism' of the Conservative government, led by Mrs Thatcher, was its major hallmark. Almost every speech by an opposition leader denounced 'monetarism' and Mr Healey's alleged tainting with monetarism was said to be a major reason why he was defeated by Mr Foot in the September 1980 Labour leadership election. In 1971 a new regime of monetary control was inaugurated – *competition and credit control* – with scarcely a mention outside the City pages. In September 1980 a visit by Professor Brunner to Mrs Thatcher to discuss monetary control topped the news headlines on Radios 1 and 2. One of the purposes of this book is to consider this extraordinary change and the events which brought it about.

Moreover, whilst monetary policy was becoming a matter of public attention, the modus operandi of monetary control was changed. In 1970 a long-established regime of ceilings on bank credit was the means of monetary control. In 1971 this was replaced by the 'new approach' to competition and credit control which put major emphasis on the impact of interest rates on bank lending. In 1973-4 this was scrapped and a new 'new approach' introduced. In 1979-80 the incoming Conservative government dropped some of the key features of this regime, especially the ceiling on bank deposits. They introduced an interim regime whilst a consultation process considered alternative modus operandi. A number of changes followed in 1980-1, but it is clear that no final solution has been achieved. This provides a classic case study of the techniques of monetary control and an opportunity to consider the theory of monetary control in the light of experience. This book has two purposes. The first is to provide a theory of alternative

1

techniques of monetary control (Chapters 2-4). The other is to describe, analyse and assess monetary policy in the UK from 1971-81, with special attention being paid to the changing mechanisms of control. The remainder of this introduction is devoted to the essential background needed for a study of monetary policy in the UK, and to a summary of some of the main themes of the book.

Initially attention is devoted to an analysis of the environment in which monetary policy-makers operate. In particular, the politics of monetary control cannot be ignored. Views about the very desirability of monetary policy are dependent on political attitudes. The choice of techniques of monetary control is certainly as much a political as a technical decision. Furthermore the workings and impact of monetary policy are influenced by political forces. Such political factors even extend to the definition of money. The appropriate definition of money is obviously essential to the conduct of monetary policy, but it is impossible to define money 'correctly'. Money is a theoretical construct devised by economists. It may not exist in the real world. Certainly it does not correspond to any particular statistical artefact, such as M_1 or M_3. It is a sobering thought that the New York Federal Reserve Bank has over 30 different definitions of 'the money supply'. Moreover, any attempt to control a financial aggregate will almost inevitably distort it and make it a less good measure of 'money' (1.3). The implication seems to be that multiple targets are necessary. Implicitly or explicitly, every act of monetary policy must assume some view of monetary theory, so it is necessary to examine the relationship between monetary policy and monetary theory. Finally, the implications of an open economy are considered (1.4).

Section 1.5 of the Introduction summarises the analysis presented in Chapter 2 about the causes of monetary expansion and the alternative techniques of monetary control. Some general conclusions about monetary control follow. Section 1.6 is devoted to explanation and proof of a vital but frequently ignored point: *the UK has never had a textbook reserve ratio system*. Section 1.7 summarises the main developments in UK monetary policy from 1971-80 with various conclusions which seem to follow from this analysis, and the following sections are devoted to discussion of a number of specific issues which are relevant to monetary policy in the UK. Finally an overall view of the choice facing the UK authorities is presented.

1.2 The Politics of Monetary Control

Politics and monetary policy have always been closely intertwined. This relationship emerges in the illogical link between swings to the right and upsurges of interest in monetarism, which continued in the late 1970s.[3] There was a spate of 'born-again' monetarism as one distinguished academic convert described it.[4] Ironically but confusingly, many of the converts went on to rediscover Keynesianism and to abandon monetarist beliefs for other creeds without being willing to drop the monetarist label. The choice between monetary and fiscal policy or between techniques of control is a highly political act. Another example of this was the link between support of some forms of monetary base control and 'right-wing' views in 1980-1.

Political factors are crucial to monetary policy in other ways. The single most important brute fact in UK monetary policy has been the building society constraint. While not necessarily logical, nor even correct, there is an accepted belief among politicians in the UK, as in the US and Australia, that higher mortgage rates are unpopular. The consequence is that there was an extreme unwillingness on some occasions to raise rates. Similarly, the need to protect building societies has inhibited a vigorous bid for personal savings as a means of financing budget deficits at least until 1981.[5] This perceived political need to maintain the structure of housing finance has been a major obstacle to the widespread issue of index-linked bonds. This is paradoxical since indexed mortgages, with very low cash outlays in the early years of a mortgage, would probably be popular.

Banks are highly sensitive political animals, and in the UK the 'big four' High Street banks have always put political factors high in their utility functions. In particular they have shown an astonishingly acute fear of nationalisation. They are reluctant to raise rates for many reasons, but politics is certainly one. In 1973 this was a major embarrassment to the monetary authorities as they strove to force bank lending rates up. It has been argued in self-defence by one banker that the then prime minister persuaded them to keep rates down, but Heath denies this.[6] In any case it illustrates further the intensely political nature of interest rates; can one imagine a prime minister lobbying to frustrate the workings of fiscal policy in this way? The switch from Bank Rate to MLR in 1972 (p. 109) was another political act in that the objective was to raise interest rates without the TUC being aware of the change in policy stance. In brief, political factors cannot be ignored in analysing any decision in monetary policy. This does not mean that vote-catching is the major aim of monetary policy nor that total cynicism about the authorities' motives is fair. In fact both Healey and Howe have aggressively pursued policies they believed to be unpopular. The point is that monetary policy should not be analysed in a vacuum which ignores political reality.

1.3 The Definition of Money

Macroeconomic textbooks and even research articles invariably assume that money is a uniquely defined set of assets. Consequently, they can concern themselves with the effects of a change in the money supply. In this book another crucial issue is considered: how can and should money be controlled? However, before either can be studied, an even more basic question has to be considered: what is money and can it be measured? Even at the level of high theory the issue has not been settled.[7] More relevantly, insuperable problems arise in trying to translate the theoretical concept into practice. Money can be defined as a means of payment, yet there is no asset which is always acceptable as a means of payment, not even currency. Virtually all assets are *sometimes* acceptable in payment: to take an extreme example, 'Bunker' Hunt recently paid some of his obligations to Englehard Metal with an area of the Beaufort Sea.

Moreover, unused credit facilities are a means of payment. An example of growing importance is undrawn credit card limits. Yet such facilities are not only impossible to measure but challenge the general notion that money is an asset. Even if we restrict the definition to the traditional 'assets acceptable in payment of debts', many ambiguities still arise. The usual answer of economists has been to seek an empirical definition of money as in Friedman's famous adage 'money is whatever does the work of money' (i.e. whatever is most closely related to income). A similar empirical definition is offered by the neo-Keynesian Tobin in his model.[8] These definitions lead one into a minefield of econometric problems. Most fundamentally of all, the definition need not be stable over time; indeed if monetary policy is active, it is unlikely to be stable. Money is an asset which has a specific influence on the holder, so that, in particular, if he holds an increased quantity of it he would dispose of the excess in a predictable manner, e.g. buy real assets. The policy significance of money holdings depends on the attitude of the holder. An asset is money if and only if it induces holders to spend it. Thus 'moneyness', like beauty, lies in the eye of the beholder. This attitude is likely to vary over time. Moreover, the observation of a variable may distort it. Certainly the attempt to control it will lead to the production of substitutes. This danger is especially great when (direct) quantity controls are used. To control is indeed to distort. This is sometimes called Goodhart's law.

The attempt to control may distort in various ways. Official action has changed the nature and structure of some assets, and created distinctions which did not exist before. For example, in the UK it would not otherwise matter to a bank whether it took a deposit (of given maturity) from another bank or from an equally creditworthy manufacturing company. In the US, Chase Manhatten would not care whether it took a deposit from Ford of Detroit or its wholly owned subsidiary, Ford of Dagenham. Because of the definitions of money used in the two countries both decisions are crucial to bank Treasurers. Banks are given incentives to change behaviour by the regulations and definitions. In the US a bank would prefer to have as its liability one $100,000 Certificate of Deposit rather than four certificates each worth $25,000, as CDs over $50,000 are not money. The private sector faces both price incentives to change behaviour as a result of the official definition and the banks' response and possible quantity constraints if the aggregate is controlled. Thus there will be an incentive to substitute out of 'money'. Finally and crucially, private sector expectations will depend on the movement of the controlled aggregate and behaviour will adjust accordingly.

In practice, money is normally defined as privately held currency plus bank deposits. In a textbook this seems precise enough. In practice, there are a number of problems. First, it is not clear what a bank is. Secondly, in textbooks, all bank deposits are demand or sight deposits and usually assumed not to pay interest. If some bank deposits are interest-bearing or time deposits are they money? Thirdly, should foreign-held or public sector deposits be included? Finally, what about deposits in foreign currencies held by residents? (All of these are assumed away in textbooks.)

For generations, a stock joke in banking textbooks was the definition of a bank: a body which carried out the business of banking, while banking was what a bank did.[9] Since the 1979 Banking Act such cracks are no longer merited; a bank is legally defined but in no less tautologous a fashion. It is not clear which institutions are banks and which are not since institutions lie along a spectrum. The Midland Bank is a bank, the gas board NEGAS is not, but many institutions have some aspects of a bank and some of a non-bank. It is impossible to draw a line between a bank and a non-bank. Moreover, even if it were possible, the fact that one was controlling the institutions on one side of the divide would create a very strong incentive for the institutions on the other side to expand. This is true of all direct controls and quantity controls. It is less true of interest rate controls. Even here, however, while the problems of inequity and evasion can be avoided, distortion of statistics is inevitable. The interest rate movements generated by an attempt to control one definition of money will generate switches of assets involving others.

Similar problems arise in specifying a maturity of asset: some holders of seven-day deposits do not view them as money whereas other people regard a three-month deposit as money. The question of whether to include interest-bearing deposits is equally vexed. On the one hand, many demand deposits pay implicit interest and some pay explicit interest, e.g. Co-operative Bank current accounts did at one time. Does it matter whether the interest paid is implicit or explicit? Surely any sight or demand deposit is 'money': what can be more liquid, what can be more likely to burn a hole in the pocket of the holder? On the other hand, once interest-bearing deposits are included it is virtually impossible to make any clear-cut distinction since the gradations are too fine. Why not include Treasury Bills or building society deposits, for example? There is no answer except to say that only a minority of the holders of these assets regard them as money whereas a majority of holders of overnight inter-bank deposits view them as money. Nevertheless these magnitudes could change and are likely to do so whenever an attempt is made to control any monetary aggregate. Hence its significance will alter. Then there is the problem of how to treat the following bank deposits:

(a) non-resident holdings of the native currency;

(b) resident holdings of foreign currency deposits; and

(c) public sector deposits.

The 'right' answer is that it is an empirical question. The US includes (a), the UK does not; (b) was included in M_3 in the UK but is excluded from $\pounds M_3$. Public sector deposits are in $\pounds M_3$ and M_3 but not in M_1 in the UK, and are in none of the official US definitions of money.

Any believer in monetary control is in the position that Tobin once ascribed to Friedman: that one wishes to control money but does not know what it is. This, however, is not as devastating an indictment as it sounds. There is a similar lack of agreement about the measurement of fiscal policy, of protection and virtually all other forms of economic policy. There is a relatively simple answer.[10] One should monitor (and set targets for) all possible financial aggregates, from the very narrow 'money base' to the very broad PSL_2. If all move in line then there is no problem. Sometimes they will deviate in a predictable, systematic fashion. M_3 always grows faster than $£M_3$ when sterling is weak and slower when it is strong. Again this is easily dealt with by the authorities. If one of the two deviates from its target, this indicates that the exchange rate is not at its expected level. In this case the authorities need to consider whether or not to alter their target (see 8.4). If monetary aggregates deviate in an unpredictable fashion then it is necessary for the authorities to ask why. The reason should reveal whether it is a growth in the underlying level of 'money' or some freak event. A primary target for whatever is the best possible measure of money accompanied by subsidiary targets for everything else can solve all problems. So would an index combining the alternative measures of money, as proposed by Gordon Pepper.

1.4 Monetary Theory and Monetary Policy

It may seem rather trite but it is nevertheless important to say that any act of monetary policy must make some explicit or implicit assumption about monetary theory. For example, to seek to control any measure of money must presume that in some way this will influence behaviour. It is even the case that the choice of a suitable definition of money assumes some theory about the workings of the economy, e.g. about substitution between assets. One of the factors that should influence the choice of techniques is how it is thought money influences income. Any judgement about money policy has to be rooted in some view of monetary theory. Policy cannot be analysed or judged outside some theoretical framework.

1.5 An Open Economy

Those who are responsible for monetary policy can never forget that they operate in an open economy. Those who analyse policy also have to remember this. Overseas flows are major determinants of the money supply. The balance of payments is a target of or a constraint upon macroeconomic policy. A balance of payments deficit will on the one hand reduce the money supply and on the other may lead to a lower monetary target. Sometimes the overseas flows act to counter the objectives of domestic monetary policy. An inflow may well be induced by a reduction in Domestic Credit Expansion (DCE) for example. There are two especially important aspects of an open economy that will influence UK monetary policy in the 1980s. The first is that the greatest threat to the successful working of either direct controls or a reserve base is the possibility of moving banking deals overseas. A bank may arrange to book both lending and deposits abroad; certain UK banks, for example, already make it a condition of some standby credit facilities that the borrower must accept a loan in the currency and financial centre of the bank's choice. This protects the bank against either direct controls or the tax element of a reserve base system. The borrower will then have to convert the loan into sterling and use this for his UK purposes. In effect he will have to persuade some UK citizen to accept an external deposit. This is unlikely to be difficult: US citizens often held deposits with foreign branches of US banks in the 1960s.[11] Alternatively, the UK banks may ask UK citizens to place deposits with their overseas branches in order to avoid the effects of a return of the IBELs ceiling and the tax element of a reserve base system. Either way the effect of UK citizens holding foreign deposits would be to weaken monetary control and to distort UK money supply data so that a rational policy became less likely. Moreover, two developments have radically altered the whole nature of the impact of overseas forces on domestic developments. The first is the growth of the Eurocurrency market. The other new feature is that because of North Sea oil the overseas constraint on UK economic policy has disappeared.[12] In 1978, for example, the UK did not have to deflate whereas in the 1950s or 1960s such a boom would have had to be curtailed very quickly because of the consequences for the balance of payments. In fact the pound now appears to be a 'strong' rather than a 'weak' currency. The change in the environment in which monetary policy operates is of enormous importance. For the first time since Gresham enumerated his other law it is no longer necessary 'to make credit scant in Lombard Street to raise the exchange for England'.[13]

1.6 Techniques of Control

Any method of control of the money supply must involve interference with the process of money creation. An understanding of the process of money creation is necessary for the analysis of the techniques of control. There are five primary causes of money creation:

(1) the PSBR

(2) a fall in non-bank private sector lending to the public sector

(3) a rise in bank lending to the non-bank private sector

(4) an acquisition of foreign currency assets purchased with sterling by the public sector

(5) a rise in banking sector net claims on foreigners.

It is crucial to distinguish a primary, direct effect from either a secondary or indirect one. Government spending (if not financed by taxation or debt sales) *must* cause an equal rise in the money supply as a primary, direct effect. This *will* involve a rise in bank claims on the public sector. This *may* induce banks to lend more to the private sector, which is likely in a reserve base system. In this case the government spending has had a direct impact on the money supply and a secondary impact, by inducing bank lending i.e. another direct effect. The two must not be conflated into one nor must it be thought that the effect of changes in the PSBR on the money supply depends on such indirect effects.

All magnitudes can be controlled by:

(a) price methods.

(b) quantity controls (rationing).

(c) interfering with the efficiency of those producing it; in monetary control this is the reserve base system.

To control the money supply, these methods can be applied to either the asset or the liability side of the banks' balance sheet, that is to either the supply of or the demand for money. By a process of substitution, flow-of-funds analysis (p. 25), the following relationships are derived:

$$\Delta \text{Money} = \Delta \text{Deposits (residents') } + \Delta \text{ Currency (non-bank} \qquad (1)$$
$$\text{private sector}$$
$$\text{holdings)}$$
$$= \text{PSBR} + \Delta \text{ Bank lending to non-bank private sector} \qquad (2)$$
$$- \Delta \text{ private lending to public sector} \pm \text{overseas}$$
$$\text{impact on money supply}$$

Here (1) represents the demand side and (2) the supply side. Any of the three methods of control can in principle be applied to any of the six aggregates involved. In practice, currency holdings are not directly manipulated. Altogether this leads to 17 methods of controlling money:

(a) price effects on deposits;

(b) quantity effects on deposits;

(c) price effects on bank lending;

(d) quantity effects on bank lending;

(e) price effects on (non-bank) private lending to the public sector;

(f) quantity effects on private lending to the public sector;

(g) variation of the PSBR;

(h) price effects on the overseas impact;

(j) quantity effects on the overseas impact;

(k) varying the size of the reserve base;

(l) variations in the reserve ratio;

(m) regulation Q;

(n) a tax on banking;

(p) licensing;

(q) 100 per cent reserve ratio banking;

(r) restricting bank competition.

All of these are analysed in Chapters 2-4. However, there are a number of general points that emerge from this analysis.

(1) Although (a), (c), (e), (f) and probably most of the others involve a change in interest rates, one cannot talk about interest rates as a method of control without some qualification. It is vital to ask *which* interest rate, since each aggregate is affected by a different one. Furthermore, it is often *relative* interest rates which determine the money supply.

(2) All quantity controls are likely to lead to inefficiency, inequity, evasion and to a distortion of official statistics that renders the rational conduct of monetary policy more difficult.

(3) Reserve base control is in some ways a half-way house between quantity and price effects. This is because one can rank the three groups of control as follows:

(a) level of interest rates for a given money supply —

highest : price effects (interest rates)

second : reserve base

lowest : quantity control.

(b) Likelihood of evasion and distortion —

highest : quantity control

second : reserve base

lowest : price effects.

(4) The crucial problem is to develop a system of control designed to deal with a world of uncertainty and human, fallible policy-makers. In other words it is necessary to devise a system which minimises the cost of mistakes. The regime of monetary control must be such that errors can be corrected quickly and at the lowest possible cost to the goal variables: inflation, output and unemployment.

1.7 Reserve Ratios in the UK

It is surprising how widespread is the view that monetary policy in the UK has relied upon a textbook reserve base/minimum reserve system; i.e. one in which the authorities alter the reserve base and multiple contraction or expansion of credit occurs, by an amount depending on the inverse of the reserve ratio. In fact the UK authorities have never used such a system; indeed they have fought hard to prevent such a system being introduced. Ever since Thornton first described the mechanism, authors have been denying its relevance to the UK. In the nineteenth century, Bagehot explained that this was not the way the UK banking system operated.[14] Fluctuations in the ratio of gold and/or notes to deposits held by banks were so large that no credit multiplier model made sense. Modern research has confirmed this view for both the eighteenth and nineteenth century.[15]

In the 1920s the banks observed, or pretended to, an 11 per cent cash ratio. Widespread window-dressing meant that this could not be used as a tool of monetary policy, even if the authorities had wanted to, which they did not. The evidence to the Macmillan Committee of Lord Norman, Governor of the Bank 1920-44, and McKenna, ex-Chancellor and Chairman of the Midland Bank, is very clear on this point. The report of the Macmillan Committee is equally clear-cut;[16] its membership included Keynes, Lord Bradbury, McKenna and Ernest Bevin. It is possible that confusion has arisen because the banks had a variety of ratios chosen or imposed for other purposes. In the 1950s and 1960s there were two, an 8 per cent cash ratio and a 30 per cent, later 28 per cent, liquidity ratio. The Radcliffe Report denied that these worked like the textbook ratios.[17]

Crucially, the Governor of the Bank made it plain that the 12½ per cent liquid assets ratio introduced as part of *competition and credit control* was not a textbook reserve ratio. Instead its purpose was to influence interest rates:

> It is not to be expected that the mechanism of minimum reserve ratio and Special Deposits can be used to achieve some precise multiple contraction or expansion of bank assets. Rather the intention is to use our control over liquidity, which these instruments will reinforce, to influence the structure of interest rates. The resulting change in relative rates of returns will then induce shifts in the current portfolios of both the public and the banks.[18]

The same message was repeated in 1980 in the Consultation Document *Monetary Control.*

> The RAR was never designed to serve as an officially controlled monetary base through which the pyramid of credit created by the banks might be directly limited. Instead, in conjunction with Special Deposits, the RAR was regarded as an element in the control of short-term interest rates.[19]

Indeed it would be absurd for the Bank to have explained why it did not want a reserve base system if it had already had one. Reserve ratio models are of relevance in analysing choice within a bank portfolio model. However, at present in the UK, ratios are either imposed by the banks themselves or are for prudential purposes or a minor weapon to influence interest rates. A reserve base system may be introduced, or it may not, but the significance of the decision cannot be understood unless it is appreciated how revolutionary a step it would be.

1.8 Monetary Policy in the UK

There have been three major reappraisals of monetary policy in the UK in the 1970s, in 1971, 1973 and 1979-80. As a result there have been four distinct regimes of monetary policy within a decade. This is unique. This decade has also included one of the sharpest accelerations in monetary growth, a successful deceleration and an avowedly monetarist policy, so 1971-80 has not been without incident. In the late 1960s, the authorities relied upon ceilings on bank lending to control monetary growth. These appeared to succeed in so far as M_3 growth was relatively stable, at 6-8 per cent p.a. Moreover, the Jenkins squeeze of 1968-9 seemed to suggest that financial policy was successful in its primary aim, which was to improve the balance of payments. However, the authorities were not content with their apparent success. They became ever more worried that their ceilings were being evaded on a very large scale. Such evasion inevitably leads to inequity and a distortion of official statistics which makes the rational conduct of policy impossible. Moreover, even if they work, ceilings lead to resource misallocation.

In 1971 the authorities accepted the implication of this analysis. They resolved to control money by use of the price mechanism. In financial markets, this meant by the use of interest rates, and of interest rates alone. The authorities rejected all means of control other than the effect of interest rates on bank lending. For various reasons, all other bank assets and liabilities were regarded as being immune to or exempt from monetary policy. Thus in the brave new world of the 'new approach' to *competition and credit control*, the authorities would manipulate the system so as to produce the desired rate of interest on bank loans. This, in turn, would ensure that the demand for bank lending was at a level that would ensure the optimal level of money, credit, liquidity and all other financial aggregates. The competition and credit control era, 1971-3, was a disaster. This was partly due to inherent defects in the system and partly due to official unwillingness to use the only weapon they had left — interest rates. M_3 grew by 60 per cent in 27 months. Largely in consequence, inflation tripled, to 28 per cent. Property and house prices rocketed. The whole financial system went through a classic boom and bust cycle.

In late 1973, it became necessary to control monetary growth for both political and economic reasons. Interest rates were too low, especially in real terms, to do this. The authorities were not prepared to raise them for a mixture of reasons, good and bad. In consequence, the new approach was unceremoniously dropped. It was replaced by another regime of monetary control, the so-called new 'new approach'. This marked a total abandonment of the principles of the new approach. In particular, ceilings were reintroduced. The major ceiling was on bank liabilities, not assets as in the 1960s, with limits placed on the growth of private sector interest-bearing deposits (IBELs). However, de facto ceilings were also placed on bank lending to the personal sector. In addition to the IBELs ceiling the other principal weapons of the new regime were an aggressive gilt-edged marketing strategy, the Duke of York method, and a new-found willingness to alter the PSBR for monetary purposes. In 1976 the authorities adopted money supply targets, a crucial step in monetary policy. On the whole monetary policy was used wisely in the period 1974-9. Monetary growth was quickly brought under control in 1974. The resultant low rate of monetary growth, reinforced by incomes policy, enabled the rate of inflation to fall from nearly 30 per cent to less than 10 per cent. The major mistakes of policy were the very costly mishandling of overseas flows in 1976 and a disastrous period of over-complacency around the beginning of 1978.

In MPCC I argued that this regime was unlikely to work in the long run. By 1979, it was clear that this view was correct. Evasion of the IBELs ceiling grew ever-larger and the problems of monetary control grew ever greater. In 1980 the ceiling was abolished and the authorities launched a fundamental reappraisal of the techniques. In the interim they adopted a plethora of policies, relying in particular on the effect of interest rates on bank lending. The authorities were unable to prevent the growth of the money supply approaching 20 per cent p.a. between June 1979 and September 1980.

1.9 Issues in Monetary Policy

Monetary policy has become increasingly controversial over the last decade. In this section, the principal topics of controversy are collected and some of the major arguments presented. All are discussed in full in the main body of the work.

1.9.1 Rules and Discretion

In recent years there has been a rising tide of academic opinion in favour of policy rules. These would be designed to deny policy-makers any discretion in the conduct of macroeconomic policy. The earliest proponent of such rules was Friedman who argued in favour of a monetary rule whereby the growth of the money supply would be constant, at either 5 per cent or 2 per cent p.a.[20] Other authors have argued in favour of rules concerning exchange rates (e.g. the gold standard) or the budget. A number of points seem relevant.

(a) The argument for a rule assumes so high a degree of incompetence by the authorities that a fixed policy would be better than any discretion. It is not clear whether this is the case.

(b) If a rule is desirable, which rule? A balanced budget, a stable exchange rate and constant monetary growth are inconsistent with each other. Stability in one magnitude usually implies instability in the other two.

(c) How is a rule to be enforced? The case for 'discipline' is cogent, but how is such a rule to be enforced? A government with the authority to enact a rule has necessarily the authority to repeal the legislation. A rule matters only in so far as it influences the political constraints facing the political authorities. A rule can have perverse effects. For example, it might be that a government could observe a monetary rule by means of cosmetic devices. Hence its 'extravagance' would not be constrained. Moreover the opposition to this policy would be weakened because the rule was observed. Similar considerations are known to influence the case for and against different exchange rate regimes.[21]

They are equally relevant to monetary control, but the political economy of monetary control is not very well developed.

1.9.2 The Period of Monetary Control

A senior Treasury official recently said that he regarded the key issue in monetary policy as being over what period monetary growth should be controlled. In other words, does it matter if monetary growth lurches violently around a trend? How should the authorities react? Monetary growth in the UK has shown a very high variance and the authorities have not appeared to care very much. In fact the Wilson Committee has argued that even the present variance is too small, pointing out that money supply targets have meant that money has been unable to perform its buffer stock function adequately. Hence a leading commentator on monetary affairs could say that a deviation in monetary growth away from trend does not matter if it is corrected within six months. On the other hand, it is never clear and can never be clear *at the time* what is an erratic and what a systematic movement. If the money supply grows by 2 per cent in a month, it may be dangerous to ignore this on the grounds that it is a freak that will be reversed, since it could be the beginning of a sustained spurt in monetary growth. A 'stitch in time saves nine' might be a better motto for the authorities than their present Coolidge-like belief that nine out of ten troubles will disappear if you ignore them. This might be right but the tenth may be of catastrophic proportions before you respond to it. Erratic movements may influence the exchange rate and/or expectations. Hence they may matter more than orthodox wisdom suggests. Following on from this, the more faith markets have that official targets will be observed the less a deviation matters. However, given the UK's record in missing targets, this is scarcely an argument for ignoring short-term variations. Monetary stability might involve greater variations in interest rates. I think that greater monetary stability and more frequent (but smaller) changes in interest rates would be an improvement over recent experience.

1.9.3 Medium-term Policy

In MPCC, I suggested that longer-run targets for monetary growth might be set.[22] Independently but later, other authors notably Congdon suggested a similar idea. Partly in response to Congdon, the UK authorities have now adopted a 'medium-term financial plan'.[23] The case for this is really only an extension of the case for monetary targets. In particular, their effect is largely dependent on changing expectations.

It seems hard to argue that their effect is harmful and so they are likely to be benign or, at worst, ineffective.

1.9.4 Crowding-out

A major issue of monetary policy in both the US and UK between 1975 and 1977 was the crowding-out debate. Briefly, crowding-out occurs when government spending or borrowing leads to an undesired fall in private spending or borrowing.[24] Those who attach importance to this concept fear that government policy may be rendered futile, especially when attempts are made to expand the economy by expenditure increases or tax cuts. There is very little evidence either way in what has proved to be a very confused and confusing debate. The possibility of crowding-out is a real danger but one cannot conclude that it occurred at any particular period. It is important to stress how vital the role of the exchange rate was in the government's initial strategy. The crucial transmission mechanism in the Bank of England model is via the exchange rate.[25] A higher exchange rate reduces cost inflation and inflationary expectations as well as being a crucial weapon to squeeze corporate liquidity.

1.9.5 Indexation

It has always seemed to me that the case for indexation (of government debt) was unanswerable.[26] On grounds of both justice and efficiency (the double uncertainty argument), indexation is necessary. As it is now impossible to make a long-term loan on terms that are not onerous to the borrower and confiscatory to the lender, there would be a clear gain to both parties from indexation. The long-term industrial bond market has been killed off by inflation, and its resuscitation, agreed on all sides to be desirable, can only be achieved by indexation. It now seems that the PSBR cannot be financed simultaneously with an acceptable rate of monetary growth unless more indexed securities are sold. The reader is invited to consider whether the experience of the 1970s is sufficient to provide evidence to justify my enthusiasm.

1.9.6 Exchange Control

There seems to be a strong case for *inward* exchange control, perhaps on the lines of the Bardepot.[27] The need to control inward flows so as to keep monetary growth in check is self-evident. The problem is would inward exchange control work? The House of Commons Select Committee on the Treasury recently endorsed its use.

1.9.7 'Tender' Gilts

The UK authorities have always favoured selling gilt-edged stock by the 'tap' method, rather than a tender method. This means that they fix a price and let the market determine the quantity. Under a pure tender system the authorities determine the quantity of bonds they wish to sell. The market then bids and the price is determined, i.e. the market-clearing level. The proponents of tenders argue that it necessarily leads to greater stability of monetary growth, albeit at the cost of greater variations in bond prices. The 'Economist' used to argue that interest rates would be lower with a tender system, but this is clearly false and the argument is no longer advanced. In fact, so long as the Duke of York method works, interest rates on government debt are on average lower with the present method. Nevertheless on some occasions tenders would be a good idea. They would be useful, as in October 1976 or September 1980, when it is not clear how high interest rates need to be to set off the virtuous circle of the 'Duke of York'. If the 'Duke of York' technique ever ceases to work, a tender system would be necessary. The Bank has recently experimented with modified tenders and from these it is clear that a tender system could work.

1.9.8 Direct Controls

The rival arguments are as follows.

(a) A direct control of some sort is necessary to enable the authorities to correct errors of monetary policy. If used infrequently for short periods then it would not be worth finding evasive devices. Thus there is a limited but vital role for direct controls.

(b) Direct controls can never work, especially in the absence of exchange control. They will be inequitable, inefficient and ineffective. They will so distort money statistics that a rational policy will be impossible.

The saddest but probably most accurate view is that direct controls are necessary for a successful monetary policy but could never work. There are other problems concerning direct controls. There is an unfashionable but cogent paternalist argument against credit being too readily available. Myopic preferences are often cited elsewhere in economics to justify intervention, and excessive indebtedness often causes major social problems. Moreover, an excessive credit to income ratio may lead to an unstable economy. It might be that freely available credit enables consumers to smooth consumption over time, especially when unemployed. This would make the economy less vulnerable to stocks. It is at least equally likely that high credit repayments mean that current consumers' expenditure varies much more in response to transitory changes in income when the credit to income ratio is higher.

1.9.9 Lender of Last Resort

In 1980 there had been a lot of controversy about the Bank of England's role as lender of last resort. Some of this was sparked off by Professor Griffiths' brilliant sally that the Bank acted as a lender of first resort, instead of last resort.[28] It is clear that on some occasions a Central Bank must mount rescue operations and that then they would not really be acting as a 'lender of last resort'. This is the only agreed point. Orthodox analysis argues that the authorities rely on the impact of interest rates. These can be manipulated by various tools including open-market operations. Occasionally the Central Bank must squeeze the banks of funds and leave the banking system as a whole unable to meet its obligations to the authorities. The authorities then provide enough funds to permit the banks to meet their obligations but at a penal rate; in consequence, the banks will raise their interest rates. This enables the authorities to fix short-term rates. In the US the Federal Funds market has been used, in the UK the discount market, in Germany, the Lombard market. This orthodox analysis suggests that the authorities fix rates and allow quantities to adjust to these rates. Clearly the authorities can choose a level of interest rates or a quantity but not both. Hence orthodox criticism of the Bank as a lender of last resort has centred on the Bank's penchant for interest rates that are too low or too stable. The newer criticism goes further. It is argued that the availability of over-generous lender of last resort facilities influences the supply of credit available at a given interest rate. This argument is basically the case for non-mandatory monetary base control discussed in section 3.5. It is, however, not clear whether the change would mean lower monetary growth for a given set of rates or a once-and-for-all lower money supply.

References

1. Butler and Pinto-Duschinsky (1971).
2. Beckerman (1972).
3. MPCC, p. 9.
4. Beenstock in IEA (1980).
5. See *Bulletin*, vol. 20, no. 3 (September 1980), p. 281 and p. 195 below.
6. D. Weyer, Competition and Credit Control in *Bankers' Magazine* (March

1974), pp. 14-17.
    7. See Goodhart (1976), Ch. 1.
    8. Tobin (1969).
    9. See e.g. Minty (n.d.).
   10. See MPCC, p. 159 and pp. 153ff below.
   11. See Gowland (1979), Ch. 3.
   12. See MPCC, p. 154.
   13. Gresham (1949).
   14. Bagehot (1965).
   15. Goodhart (1972); Ford (1962).
   16. Macmillan (1931).
   17. Radcliffe (1959).
   18. Bank (1971), p. 8.
   19. Bank (1980), p. 7, see also Annex A.
   20. Friedman (1956) and (1968a).
   21. E.g. Gowland (1979), Ch. 2.
   22. MPCC, p. 161.
   23. For the medium-term financial strategy, see 'Financial Statement 1980/1' (HMSO) and subsequent year.
   24. See pp. 176-9 below.
   25. Bank (1979) for the Bank Model.
   26. See MPCC, Ch. 9.
   27. See Gowland (1979), Ch. 3.
   28. See e.g. IEA (1980).

2 TECHNIQUES OF MONETARY CONTROL

2.1 Introduction

The problem of *how* to control the money supply has been virtually ignored in the voluminous academic literature dealing with monetary theory and policy.[1] This neglect is especially unfortunate when studying UK monetary policy since there have been three major reappraisals of monetary techniques in the last decade, in 1971, 1973-4 and 1980-1.[2] In the UK more attention has been paid to *how* the money supply should be controlled, and for what purpose, than to *whether* it should be controlled. Until 1981, the latter problem seemed to have almost been solved by default as there was a slow drift, with relatively little controversy, from the Barber-Heath view, that monetary growth in itself did not matter, to a view that money supply targets were necessary.[3] This is in marked contrast to the US where the most debated question in both academic and media circles is whether there should be interest rate or money supply targets. There is an equally marked contrast in that all US (and nearly all academic) analysis of alternative techniques of monetary control has been within the context of a reserve base system, e.g. Ascheim's and Friedman's work.[4] In contrast, the UK has never had a reserve base system in the textbook sense. In fact it was not even a live issue whether or not to have such a system until the late 1970s.[5] In 1980, the Consultation Document *Monetary Control* produced by the authorities was principally devoted to explaining why such a system was undesirable.[6]

The problem of which technique to use is important in its own right as a neglected area of economic analysis and is crucial to analysis of UK monetary policy. It is also related to the other major issues of monetary economics. In particular, the issues of what is the transmission mechanism of monetary policy and what is the appropriate definition of the money supply are critically interdependent with this problem (see Chapter 4). It is necessary to study the interrelationships between ends and means in monetary policy. The money supply is only an intermediate target, which is controlled so as to influence inflation, output and other goal variables. It is possible to select methods of controlling the money supply which have adverse consequences for the ultimate objectives of monetary policy, or methods which complement the authorities' objectives.

20

In Chapters 2-4 all the methods of controlling the money supply are set out with explanations of how they influence monetary aggregates, and the advantages and disadvantages of the different methods are discussed. Finally, the criteria by which the authorities should select their regime of monetary control are analysed.

The problem of how to control the money supply is part of the general problem of regulation and control.[7] The most systematic studies of alternative modus operandi of regulation have been the 'tariffs versus quotas' debate in international trade theory and the arguments about how to control pollution.[8] Basically there are three alternative methods of restricting the production or consumption of a good. The first is to increase its price. The second is to ration it (i.e. impose a quantity control). The third is to reduce the efficiency of those who produce it. This last method includes an enormous range of methods from shooting the producer to licensing. Outside the monetary field, the principal analysis of such instruments has been of non-tariff barriers to trade. However, the basic analysis of the application of such restrictions to banks in the form of reserve requirements is well developed. All three methods of control can be and have been applied to the problem of monetary control. Thus one could increase the cost of holding money, ration it or reduce the efficiency of those who produce it (banks).

Money is both an asset (to the holder) and a liability (of a bank or government). It is possible to analyse control by regarding money as either an asset or a liability; hence the multiplicity of techniques. All techniques are identical in a general equilibrium framework with highly restrictive assumptions (perfect competition, perfect certainty, all markets clearing). In this case a higher price will lead to a lower quantity demanded with exactly the same price-quantity mapping as that produced by rationing, when a lower available quantity leads to a higher price. However, this result does not hold when these assumptions are relaxed. Even if the comparative static equilibria were identical, the theory of control involves analysis of how the objective is achieved.

2.2 The Creation of Money

Any method of control of the money supply necessarily involves interference with the process of money creation. The authorities seek to change the behaviour of actors in the process of money creation so as to either induce or coerce them to create more or less money than they would otherwise do. Thus an understanding of the process of money creation is necessary for the analysis of the techniques of monetary control.

The simplest case of money creation is that in an economy where currency issued by the monetary authorities, the government, is the only form of money. In this case the crucial point is that money is created, i.e. the money supply changes when and only when currency is put into circulation. The printing of money in itself does not and cannot influence the money supply; the government could fill every office in Whitehall with bank notes and the money supply would not change an iota. In a simple economy the analysis of money creation is the analysis of how currency is put into circulation; in a famous article Friedman solved this problem with his notorious helicopter.[9]

In this simple economy, the most obvious way for the government to put the money into circulation would be to spend it. Clearly, in this case, the money supply would rise, i.e. the act of spending by the government would create money. In the widest sense of 'spending', this is the only way in which money can be put into circulation. However, some forms of 'spending' are not included in the official definition of government spending. For example, the government could pay off some of its debts, which would include repurchasing bonds and other securities it had previously sold. This form of spending is called an 'open-market operation'. To summarise, in this simple economy any government spending (including the purchase of assets) would necessarily create money, i.e. increase the money supply, as would any repurchase of government obligations (bonds etc.).

Similarly, any action by the government which led private individuals to incur and settle a debt to the government would destroy money, and thereby reduce the money supply. This could be by taxation, by the sale of assets or by the sale of government securities. So by netting out these transactions we can see that money is created by the Public Sector Borrowing Requirement (PSBR), i.e. government spending and purchase of assets less taxation and sales of assets, and that money can be destroyed by government sales of securities, i.e. by private sector lending to the public sector. (A negative PSBR will reduce the money supply and net repayments by the government to the private sector will increase the money supply.) These transactions are the only ways by which money can be created in this simple economy; even the largesse scattered by Friedman's helicopter is government spending.

The process described above is applicable in any economy but needs to be expanded to include a description of the creation of bank deposits, the other form of money in most communities. Bank deposits are an asset to their holders but are also, by definition, a liability of the banks. Thus the creation of a bank liability must involve the creation of a bank asset. This proposition can be justified in two ways: first, that it follows from the balance sheet convention, i.e. from the nature of double-entry bookkeeping; and, second, that a bank is a profit-seeking body and will not incur liabilities without some compensation. Thus the process of bank deposit creation involves the simultaneous creation of a bank liability and a bank asset. The analysis of this creation, i.e. of an increase in that part of the money supply held as bank deposits, must therefore be an analysis of both bank liability and bank asset creation.

There are two forms of bank asset which need to be included in this analysis: bank lending to the (non-bank) private sector and bank lending to the public sector.[10] The case of bank lending to the private sector is straightforward. The bank exchanges a claim on itself for a claim on the borrower. In the simplest case, the bank credits the individual or corporate borrower's account with the amount of the loan. (This would describe US practice and a growing percentage of UK loans.) This is the act of money creation, the decision by the bank to lend money, i.e. to simultaneously increase its assets and liabilities. In a more complex case (e.g. the UK overdraft system) the bank may agree to credit a third party at the request of the borrower. Either way as the old banking chestnut puts it, 'every loan creates a deposit'.

Government borrowing from banks involves some seeming paradoxes. The government cannot borrow from the banking sector unless the transaction involves a third party. On the other hand the government can automatically borrow from banks to finance its spending without any transaction between the banks and the government. This latter is sometimes called 'residual finance' and involves the following process. The government needs to pay someone, e.g. a student grant or a teacher's salary. (It might pay them in currency as in the simple example.) It sends the individual a claim on the government for, say, £100. This usually takes the form of a cheque. The individual pays this into his/her bank account. At this point £100 of money has been created. The bank has accepted an obligation of £100 in the form of a bank deposit, thus the money supply has risen. In exchange the bank has acquired £100 claim on the government, i.e. its assets have risen by £100 in the form of lending to the public sector. Thus the public sector has borrowed £100 from the banking sector by this indirect method, i.e. it now owes the banks £100 more than it did before. It is crucial to the process of money creation that this, the direct impact of public spending on the money supply, is independent of how the banks hold their claim on the government. They might (implausibly) keep the government cheque. More probably they would pay it into their account with the Central Bank. They might later transform the claim into another form by purchasing Treasury Bills or government bonds. None of these have any direct impact on the money supply, nor has a bank purchase of government securities. The bank must pay with a claim on the public sector when it purchases, say, government bonds. This transforms its claims on the public sector but does not alter its total, so the money supply is unchanged.

It is vital to distinguish this, the primary or direct impact of public spending, from any secondary or indirect impact. A change in the total or composition of bank claims on the public sector *may* change the amount a bank wants to lend to the private sector or it *may* enable it to lend more to the private sector; in a reserve base system it will. However, this effect must be distinguished from the primary effect. Public spending, ceteris paribus, will have a direct impact on the money supply by creating money equal to the amount of the spending. It may change bank behaviour and so have a secondary impact on the money supply by affecting banks' willingness or ability to lend to the private sector. Any secondary effect must involve one of the primary causes of monetary expansion, usually bank lending.

Taxation has a negative impact on the money supply, i.e. money is destroyed, by the reverse process. Individuals' and corporate holdings of bank deposits and bank lending to the public sector both fall whenever a private body pays its taxes by cheque. Similarly, government sales of assets have a negative impact on the money supply just as acquisitions have a positive impact; equally, so does non-bank private sector lending to the public sector. It does not matter *why* the public and private sectors are settling their obligations to each other, the financial transaction is identical and therefore so is the effect on the money supply.

Money can be created by the PSBR and destroyed by private sector lending to the public sector whether these transactions involve currency or bank deposits. Thus these actions necessarily create or destroy money.

To summarise, there are three methods of money creation in a closed economy:

(1) the PSBR;

(2) public sector repurchases of its own debt from the non-bank private sector, i.e. a fall in private sector lending to the public sector;

(3) bank lending to the non-bank private sector.

Money creation can occur through and only through these magnitudes.

2.3 Control of the Money Supply: A Formal Model I:
A Closed Economy

This formal analysis of the control of the money supply starts by defining the money supply:

Money (M) ≡ Bank Deposits (D) + Currency held by the
non-bank private sector (Cp)   (i)

This definition is approximately the UK M_3 or Sterling M_3 (£M_3) definition. There are considerable problems in defining the money supply and these have implications for monetary policy and for the choice of technique of control. These problems are discussed above but it is important to note that interest-bearing bank deposits are included in this definition.

Bank deposits are a form of bank liability. The other form is owners' capital but this is ignored, de minimis. (This assumption is relaxed in Appendix 2A.) Therefore

D ≡ Bank Liabilities   (ii)

However, by the balance sheet convention (see Appendix 2A) bank liabilities are equal to bank assets so

Bank Liabilities ≡ Bank Assets   (iii)

therefore

D ≡ Bank Assets

Bank assets take two basic forms, real assets (branches, computers, etc.) and financial assets. The former are ignored de minimis in this analysis but are included in the analysis in Appendix 2A. Financial assets represent claims on somebody, i.e. they are loans, so

D = Bank Loans   (iv)

Bank loans may be categorised in any way so long as the categories are exhaustive. In this case the distinction will be made between bank loans to the public sector and the non-bank private sector. As these two categories include all possible borrowers, then

D = Bank Loans to the public sector (BLG) + Bank Loans to
the non-bank private sector (BLP)   (v)

From (i) and (v)

M = Cp + BLG + BLP   (vi)

Turning to the public sector's financing equation, the PSBR, the government's new borrowing must be equal to the amount lent to the government. (This equation is written as a flow because the change in the government's obligations (National Debt) alters when the market value of marketable bonds alters.)

$$PSBR = \Delta Cp + \Delta BLG + \Delta PLG \tag{vii}$$

The government sector can borrow from banks, by the residual method outlined in 2.2, or from the non-bank private sector. However, borrowing from the non-bank private sector can be either in conventional forms (such as bonds, national savings, etc.) (PLG) or in the form of currency as a non-interest bearing loan (see 2.2). Therefore,

$$\Delta BLG = PSBR - \Delta Cp - \Delta PLG \tag{viii}$$

(viii) can also be derived by saying that bank lending to the government is equal to total lending to (or borrowing by) the government (PSBR) minus lending by non-banks (ΔCp and ΔPLG). (vi) can be written as a change

$$\Delta M = \Delta Cp + \Delta BLG + \Delta BLP \tag{ix}$$

(viii) can be substituted into (ix) so that

$$\Delta M = PSBR - \Delta PLG + \Delta BLP \tag{x}[11]$$

Equation (x) is the crux of this, the flow-of-funds approach to the analysis of the control of the money supply. This is probably the simplest model of the control of the money supply as well as the one used by the UK authorities. It should be noted that the right-hand side of this equation corresponds to the methods of money creation in 2.2. It should also be noted that ΔM is sometimes called DCE (Domestic Credit Expansion) in IMF analysis[12] and the supply side counterpart in UK official publications. It represents analysis via the asset side of bank balance sheets.

Techniques of control can operate through either the liabilities side i.e.

$$\Delta M = \Delta Cp + \Delta D \tag{i}$$

or through the asset side

$$\Delta M = PSBR - \Delta PLG + \Delta BLP \tag{x}$$

As currency holdings are never directly manipulated as a tool of monetary policy for the reasons discussed in section 2.4, there are seven basic methods of controlling the money supply:

(a) price effects on deposits (D);

(b) quantity effects on deposits (D);

(c) price effects on bank lending (BLP);

(d) quantity effects on bank lending (BLP);

(e) price effects on private lending to the public sector (PLG);

(f) quantity effects on private lending to the public sector (PLG);

(g) variation of the PSBR.

The modus operandi of these techniques together with a discussion of their major advantages and problems follow in sections 2.4.1 to 2.4.7.

2.4 The Techniques

The basic methods of controlling money involve official attempts to manipulate any of the variables on the right-hand side of equations (i) and (x). Either 'price' or 'quantity' controls can be used. However, a general caveat must be entered against this method of analysis. To change one of the five variables necessarily involves changing at least one other. Indeed it is the authorities' objective to work through either the asset or liability side so as to influence both. However, there may well be undesirable, even unpredictable effects of one variable on another. These are discussed below, but a coherent monetary policy needs to look at all the variables on both sides, not just a single variable.

The most obvious method of controlling the money supply might seem to involve control of currency, especially in view of political and media comments on 'printing money'. In fact, this method of control is never used; no government or Central Bank in the developed world seeks *directly* to control the total quantity of currency. There are a number of reasons why this is so. One is a consequence of the point developed in section 2.2; the money supply only changes when currency is put into circulation, not when it is printed. All the methods of putting currency into circulation so as to change the money supply appear on the right-hand side of equation (x), so separate analysis would be double counting, especially as these methods also influence bank deposit creation. Alternatively one may note that currency is a form of lending to the public sector as well as a form of money – this is the reason it dropped out of equation (x). To some extent these characteristics cancel each other out, and to some extent they need to be analysed separately. Finally, currency is only a small percentage of the money supply, so any effect on M of Cp would be small. More important, currency and deposits are such good substitutes for each other that any reduction (increase) in currency that the authorities induced would be offset by an increase (reduction) in deposits. A number of schemes have been developed to operate directly on currency, notably by Gessell. These schemes were brilliantly if a trifle patronisingly analysed by Keynes and Gaitskell in the 1930s.[13] Their conclusion, that such schemes are inappropriate, is even more valid in the 1980s.

Hence analysis must concentrate on the seven techniques listed at the end of section 2.3.

2.4.1 Price Effects on Deposits

This method is (implicitly or explicitly) assumed in most textbooks to be the main method of monetary control, but in fact it has never been used by the authorities in any major economy.[14]

The control would work by making bank deposits less attractive relative to all other financial assets. In the textbook model it is assumed that bank deposits do not pay interest, so this is achieved by raising interest rates. Depositors then switch funds to other assets. Bank liabilities thus fall and are matched by a fall in assets. Bank loans to the public sector automatically fall if public sector assets are purchased by the depositors; otherwise, private sector loans are called in. This argument is often stated in terms of a demand-for-money function comprising both currency and deposits, but the mechanism is the same; higher interest rates reduce the equilibrium demand-for-money, therefore funds are switched etc.

In practice, this process fails to work for a number of reasons. Some of these stem from the fact that many bank deposits pay interest. A higher interest rate may only lead to the switching of funds from demand (current) deposits to time (interest-bearing) ones. Hence a narrow definition of money, such as M_1, will be affected but a broader definition, e.g. M_3, will not change. However, there would be no reduction in credit supplied by banks so the transmission mechanism would be affected.

Indeed, there may well be a reverse effect on the money supply; bank interest rates are less sticky than others, especially building societies in the UK and savings and loans associations (SLAs) in the US. Hence bank deposits may well be more attractive as a result of a rise in interest rates, at least in the short term.

While some holders may switch from bank deposits, there may well not be a fall in total deposits, merely a change of holder. In extremis the effect on the economy might be perverse. A bank depositor might switch to a finance house deposit instead. If the latter had unsatisfied potential borrowers prepared to pay a higher interest rate, spending might rise, since the original bank deposit would in effect be transferred to the would-be purchaser of a car.

Finally, the switching may very well be to highly liquid near-money assets, in which case the effect on behaviour would be small.

2.4.2 *Quantity Effects on Bank Deposits*

A quantity control on deposits acts in a simple, almost simplistic manner. Bank deposits are rationed, hence their total is lower than it otherwise would be. The major example is the 'IBELs ceiling' or supplementary special deposit scheme used in the UK from 1974-80, sometimes inelegantly called 'the corset' in the media. This was operated by placing a ceiling on the total of each bank's interest-bearing deposits (interest-bearing eligible liabilities — IBELs), and the method of rationing was left to the banks. This scheme is discussed in detail below (8.1).

This restraint on bank activities would also restrict their lending. Thus many of the arguments in section 2.4.4 concerning ceilings on bank lending apply. The crucial problem with any 'quantity control' on financial aggregates is the classic problem that arises with any rationing in any market. As every elementary textbook demonstrates, rationing will almost inevitably lead to a 'black market'. This is certainly the principal danger with all rationing in financial markets. Transactions are altered so that they do not come within the regulations or are conducted by alternative routes. For example, instead of A lending to B by placing a deposit with a bank, which on-lends the funds, A may lend to B directly. The bank could still perform its usual function by introducing A to B and guaranteeing repayment in exchange for a commission. A would not hold a bank deposit but only a claim on B guaranteed by the bank, so the form of the control would be satisfied. Yet the intent of control would have been evaded. A discussion of how the particular form of ceiling used in the UK was evaded is included in section 6.1. The crucial point for the conceptual analysis is that quantity rationing of bank deposits can be evaded by 'black market' techniques which are perfectly legal.

Thus this technique of control may be ineffective. It is also likely to be inequitable since those officially within its ambit will be discriminated against compared to the black marketeers. For example, other institutions are likely to grow up to do the work of banks (or 'near-banks' may move closer to being 'banks') and the banks will be unfairly hampered from resisting this competition. Inefficiency is another likely cost of rationing. Rationing always produces resource misallocation. Furthermore the new method of carrying out banking can be presumed to be less efficient than the methods previously used, otherwise the new method would have been used in the first place.

Besides ineffectiveness, inequity and inefficiency there is a further problem, perhaps the most serious of all. This is that direct controls distort the statistics. 'Black market' transactions will not be included in the official statistics of money and will probably not be recorded at all by the authorities. (Evasion is legal, but no one will boast to the authorities of their success in evading controls!) Thus the authorities' ignorance of what is happening may be increased considerably. Their statistics will certainly be an underestimate of reality, but by how much they do not know. To give an example, assume the official statistics state that the money supply is £50,000m and the optimal level is £55,000m. Is policy too slack or too tough? The real level may be, say, £53,000m or £57,000m, so it is impossible to answer the question. This problem emerged in the UK in August 1980. The money supply statistics for July showed a jump of 5 per cent because of the partial reinclusion in the official statistics of some black-market transactions after the abolition of the IBELs ceiling. Official spokesmen expressed the view that all figures from August 1979 to April 1981 would be so heavily distorted by the control and its removal as to be seriously misleading. The problems for the rational conduct of monetary control are obvious.

Despite these problems, it is possible to construct a persuasive case for this form of direct control. The first plank of the counter argument is that the control is unlikely to be evaded totally, so it will have *some* effect. As with any direct control, the authorities are likely to be able to ensure lower and more stable interest rates. (This point is discussed below in section 2.4.4.)

The other arguments are more technical and derive from theoretical perspectives. The first is an analysis of black-market transactions. Clearly, the borrower is unaffected but the lender holds a different security. He may hold a claim on a large company guaranteed by a bank, he may hold a deposit with a near-bank of some sort, or an unguaranteed claim on the lender. The significance of this difference depends upon one's view of how monetary policy operates. In any version of a portfolio balance approach, such as Friedman's or Tobin's, the holder's behaviour may be affected. Some of the alternative assets may not be regarded as 'money', or they may be less liquid. Thus diverting transactions into unorthodox channels *may* have the desired effect.

Another case for a limited use of ceilings stems from the proposition that no evasive device is costless. Thus the ceiling will not be evaded so long as the cost of evasion exceeds the benefit. If the control is used infrequently and for short periods this condition will be met. Such a weapon may be useful, depending on the authorities' objectives. In particular, it may be useful if the authorities wish to correct an error in their policy. If other techniques are slow-acting, then a ceiling could be effective for a short time while the other policies take effect. The UK authorities, it could be argued, used the IBELs ceiling effectively in May 1978 for this purpose, perhaps only by accident. Finally, the control may have favourable 'cosmetic effects' (see Chapter 8 and the author's earlier analysis, p. 14). To summarise, there are considerable problems with this means of control, but the technique is not devoid of merits.

2.4.3   Control of Bank Lending to the Non-bank Private Sector by Price

This method of control is relatively straightforward. The government induces a rise (fall) in the rates of interest charged by banks on their loans to the private sector so as to induce a lower (higher) demand-for-bank-credit by the non-bank private sector. This reduction in bank assets is matched by a fall in bank liabilities (i.e. deposits) so the money supply falls. This method of control was the centrepiece of the 'new approach' to 'competition and credit control' in the UK in 1971 and was supposed to be the main technique of control from 1971-3. It has also been given considerable prominence by the Conservative government since 1979.

The basic modus operandi of this technique is the process of money creation described in section 2.2; each loan frustrated is a deposit not created. However, it is interesting to explore the details of the effects of the repayment of loans. A loan can be repaid either with a bank deposit or with cash. In the former case the banking sector's assets and liabilities fall by the same amount, and bank deposits and bank lending to the private sector are both reduced. If the individual repays the loan with cash, both bank deposits and the total of bank assets are unchanged. The composition of bank assets changes as bank lending to the private sector is reduced and bank lending to the public sector rises; currency held by a bank is a form of lending to the public sector. The money supply is reduced because non-bank private sector holdings of currency are lower. This illustrates the argument in sections 2.2 and 2.4 that money creation can be analysed in terms of PSBR, bank lending to the private sector (BLP) and private holdings of public sector debt (PLG) without direct reference to currency or bank holdings of public debt.

It is also interesting to note that this method of control requires a rise in the rate of interest charged by banks. This is likely to mean higher rates paid by banks, so long as there are any competitive pressures in banking or any conventions linking rates paid by and charged by banks. This is likely to work to frustrate any attempt to reduce bank deposit rates relative to other rates, the modus operandi discussed in section 2.4.1. Both sections 2.4.1 and 2.4.3 discuss ways in which higher interest rates can reduce the money supply. The two techniques are certainly not complementary as different interest rates are involved and the relative movements in rates necessary for one technique could frustrate the other.

This method of control puts the whole emphasis of monetary policy on the demand-for-*credit* not, as in the IS/LM approach, the demand-for-*money*. The method requires a stable, relatively elastic demand-for-credit function so that the effect of a change in interest rates on the demand-for-credit and so on the money supply is predictable and significant. Unfortunately, there is much less evidence that this is so than for the demand-for-money. A recent empirical study by the Bank of England concluded that control of the money supply by this means was unlikely to work.[15] This is by no means the only evidence. Nevertheless, all the available evidence is inconclusive.

There are two further problems about the demand-for-credit. One is that it is likely to shift in a perverse way. If the authorities mount a successful squeeze on the economy, stocks pile up and profits decline (in the short run) so the demand-for-credit function shifts; firms have almost no choice but to borrow. This is especially so if the authorities aim to influence inflation by squeezing companies until they are unable to pay wage claims. This is the transmission mechanism favoured by monetarists and accepted by many UK neo-Keynesians. The authorities relied on this mechanism in 1968/9 and 1979/80.

The other problem is that it is not clear whether the demand-for-credit should depend on real or nominal interest rates. However, there is a strong theoretical case for the proposition that real rates are the relevant ones especially if loans are used to finance holdings of real assets. Most of the evidence seems to support this proposition. In this case if inflationary expectations rise then real rates fall and the demand-for-credit rises. This may lead to a vicious circle. Inflation rises and with it inflationary expectations, unless the authorities respond decisively and quickly. The authorities then raise nominal rates but real rates are still no higher, probably lower, than before the rise in inflation. Hence, both monetary growth and inflation continue to rise, and rising nominal rates are insufficient to prevent an (inflationary) fall in real rates. This seems to have happened in the UK in 1972-3 and 1979-80. Friedman argued that similar problems occurred in the US in the 1960s and in the late 1970s, although he stated his argument in terms of lax monetary policy leading to high nominal rates.

In practice, the most serious problem arises because of the need for a significant variation in interest rates over time. Interest rates have to be varied to maintain the monetary aggregates at the desired level; even in a stable, long-run Friedman-type world interest rates have to vary to offset shocks to the system. The technique may also involve high nominal rates. It is very clear that politicians dislike both high and variable rates and many central bankers share their prejudice. This may reflect political exigencies notably the votes of mortgagees. Such political factors are relevant to monetary policy but there are also economic arguments to support this view. Business confidence, for example, may be higher if interest rates are stable.

Finally, it can be argued that use of this weapon, indeed of any interest rate weapon, throws an undue proportion of the cost of adjustment onto the construction industry. This is so for a number of reasons. The first is that the desirability of longer-lived investments is affected more by changes in interest rates than that of shorter-lived ones — an inevitable consequence of the nature of net present value calculations. All buildings have longer lives than any other investment and so are more affected. Of greater importance is that most construction is financed by bank loans. The nature of building makes a builder the ideal customer for a traditional banker — there is tangible collateral and the loan is self-liquidating, when the building is sold. Finally, buildings are usually bought on credit. All buildings provide concrete security so a supply of funds is normally available for their purchase. A demand for funds also exists because the price is usually very large relative to the income or profits of the purchasers.

In view of this catalogue of problems it may seem strange that anyone advocates this procedure. In fact no method of controlling the money supply is without cost. There are gains from this method. Administratively it is the simplest method. It avoids all the problems caused by having to define money or banks. It avoids inequity or misallocation of resources (except perhaps in its effects on the building industry). Finally, it will work. A sufficiently high interest rate will cut the demand-for-bank-credit and thus the money supply. Unfortunately no one ever knows how high 'sufficiently high' is or whether the necessary level is either politically feasible or economically disruptive.

2.4.4 *Quantity Controls on Bank Lending to the Non-bank Private Sector*

Bank lending can be controlled by quantity methods. These usually involve the placing of a ceiling on lending by each bank; sometimes the ceiling is only applied to some category of customer, e.g. personal borrowers. Ceilings can be expressed in terms of levels or changes but the difference is purely cosmetic; if a bank's loans are £100m a ceiling of 105 per cent, a ceiling of £105m and a limit on growth of 5 per cent are identical. Ceilings are nearly always designed to restrict bank lending, but occasionally minima have been set — in France, for instance, banks have been compelled to lend at least xm. francs to various categories of borrower.[16] In the UK, banks have agreed to similar schemes for export finance. Normally, however, such ceilings are designed to restrict lending as part of a deflationary policy. They were a normal weapon of control in the UK from 1952-71, and in France in various forms from 1946 onwards. They were used for the first time in the US in 1979 but were dropped in 1980. Some of these controls were designed to be part of a credit rather than a monetary policy, e.g. in the UK in 1965-7 and in France. There are thin lines between an extreme Keynesian wishing to restrict credit to affect investment and saving, a moderate monetarist who believes the major transmission mechanism is via credit availability, and a monetarist who restricts bank credit so as to limit the growth of the money supply. Whatever the motives or objectives of a restriction on bank lending, to be effective it must reduce the money supply below the level it would otherwise have been, for the reasons discussed above (2.2 and 2.4.3). Any loan frustrated or repaid will mean that the money supply is lower than it otherwise would be.

The arguments discussed in section 2.4.2 are all relevant here. 'Black markets' are likely to develop to circumvent controls, as they did in the UK in the late 1960s (Chapter 3). Thus direct controls on credit might be ineffective, inequitable and inefficient. Inequity is especially likely to arise with this technique of control because credit is granted by such a wide range of bodies ranging from shops to banks through the whole gamut of financial institutions and intermediaries. To control the whole range has proved beyond the power or inclination of all but the French authorities. In any case the range of institutions is so wide that discrimination is inevitable either by treating 'likes in an unlike fashion' or 'unlikes in a like fashion'; the classic legal definitions of inequity. Inefficiency is almost equally inevitable. The structure of financial institutions is likely to be made more rigid and competition inhibited. Both allocative and X-inefficiency are likely to result.

It is usually argued that the use of quantity controls will lead to a higher level of investment than the use of interest rates. This argument is sometimes linked to the planning argument since the bias towards investment fits in with the 'steel-eating' pro-investment inclinations of most advocates of planning. Alternatively, it is argued that the use of interest rates leads to a misallocation of resources, by reducing the level of investment relative to consumption. In either form the argument is quite widely used. The rationale for the proposition can be either theoretical or econometric. In the latter form, empirical work normally shows that the demand-for-credit by individuals, i.e. consumers, is less sensitive to interest rates than the demand by industrial companies. From this it is deduced that a rise in interest rates would lead to a fall in fixed investment and stockbuilding, although this is not necessarily true. The alternative theoretical argument is that a rise in interest rates will necessarily reduce the optimal level of investment. However, the effect of interest rates on consumers' expenditure is two-edged since the 'substitution effect' towards more saving is likely to partially or totally be offset by the 'income effect'.

Another argument concerning the misallocation of resources is that credit ceilings are biased against small firms. The argument rests on the assumption that it is either legally impossible or impracticable or undesirable to adjust absolute and relative interest rates charged to different borrowers by enough to clear the market. Therefore, banks have discretion about who to lend to, either through necessity or choice. In this case they are likely to reduce the riskiness of their loans portfolio by engaging in equilibrium rationing, as this is in both managerial and shareholders' interests. It is normally believed that loans to small companies are riskier and so their borrowing suffers disproportionately. Moreover, both managers and shareholders stand to gain by reducing the banks' transactions costs since this either increases managerial leisure or profits. The smaller the number of loans made for a given quantity of lending, the smaller the costs, both financial and in terms of managerial time. Thus one would predict discrimination in favour of large borrowers. However, it is worth noting that there is a counter argument. If smaller companies pay higher interest rates, then a bank may respond to the ceiling, which reduces profit opportunities by increasing the proportion of high-risk, high-yielding loans. Indeed any microeconomic analysis would suggest that this would be the case.[17]

The most controversial and interesting form of 'inefficiency' is the 'conscious' resource misallocation which the authorities seek to bring about by sectoral controls. As every economic textbook proves, allocation by price is efficient and pareto optimal in the absence of externalities or other forms of market failure. One of the advantages of direct controls is that they permit sectoral allocation of credit, that is the authorities can compel banks to lend to, say, exporters and not to, say, property companies even if the latter offer a higher rate of interest and greater security. If social costs and benefits differ from private ones this sectoral allocation might improve resource allocation. Any dedicated Paretian (if such exist!) would argue that privileged access to credit is inefficient compared to a straight subsidy. Incontrovertibly, allocation within each sector is likely to be worsened (since highly profitable exporters willing to pay more deserve priority over less profitable ones). The basic question can only be posed not answered. Dirigistes would argue that sectoral allocation of credit was a highly desirable weapon of beneficient intervention and cite the use of this weapon in the French 'Plans' to support their case. Believers in laissez-faire would indignantly deny their case.

A more practical problem with sectoral controls is that they are very easy to evade and impossible to police. Some discussion of the evasion of such controls in the UK is included in Chapter 3, but the general principle is usually called the displacement effect in textbooks. To take an example outside financial markets, imagine an aunt who wishes to give her student nephew a Christmas present of £10 but does not want him to spend it on alcohol. She may fondly believe that by giving him a book token she achieves her object, but this is not so. Her nephew can use the token to buy a book he would have bought anyway and increase his expenditure on alcohol by £10. Similar manoeuvres are likely in the financial case. A government may allow individuals to raise bank loans to repair roofs but not to buy a new car. Imagine an individual who wishes to both repair his roof and buy a car, but with funds of his own for only one. If no loan were available he would use his own funds to repair the roof and not buy the car. He is not allowed to borrow to buy a car but he can borrow to repair his roof and use his own funds to buy the car. Thus while the form of the control − individuals can borrow only for house repairs − is satisfied the effect is the reverse of the government's intention. The loan, whatever its notional purpose, has enabled the borrower to buy a car he otherwise would have been unable to buy. Thus the purpose of the control has been negated.

Companies can similarly use funds to enable them to do something other than the nominal purpose of the loan. Complex chains of credit are possible. For example, governments frequently try to discriminate in favour of export and against retail credit. An exporter might react to privileged access to credit by making less use of trade credit from his suppliers. These suppliers can then expand credit to their other customers who are thereby enabled to grant better credit terms to retailers, who then increase consumer credit. Even longer chains were very evident in the UK in the late 1960s when qualitative credit controls were in force.

None of the above are the really decisive issues in the argument for and against direct credit controls. The first crucial argument is that they distort official statistics and so make the rational conduct of monetary policy impossible. (For the analagous argument, see section 2.4.2.) This is unanswerable, but its importance depends on the amount of evasion. The second argument which sways many politicians is that direct controls hit the consumer durable industry very hard and make it bear an excessively high share of the burden of monetary policy. In practice, whilst this argument is relevant, such industries are bound to suffer (or gain?) most from cycles. It is not clear whether the cyclical nature of this industry is caused by direct controls, or their misuse, or even macro policy generally. A stable monetary policy should have meant stability in the demand for consumer durables.

The single most convincing argument against this method of control is that it is ineffective. It has been argued, e.g. by the Bank of England,[18] that quantity restrictions on credit are ineffective because they are so easily evaded by black-market devices. Credit transactions can take place through alternative channels. These may not involve a bank if the lender lends directly to the borrower without a bank acting as an intermediary by taking a deposit and making the loan sometimes called 'disintermediation'. Alternatively some institution outside the regulations may act as a bank in all but name. Finally, banking services may be provided in substance but not in form; e.g. if a bank charges a commission for introducing a borrower and lender, and guarantees the repayment of a loan. The last two are often called 'parallel markets'.

Such devices can be used on an extensive scale, as they were in the UK in the 1960s. However this leaves a number of interesting questions unanswered. If one believes that the transmission mechanism of monetary policy is by credit availability, evasion of these techniques makes monetary policy ineffective. If a portfolio balance approach is used such evasion may be regarded as facilitating the workings of monetary policy. Comparing the situation with this control to one without it, the lender holds an alternative security instead of a bank deposit. The alternative may not be regarded as money (Friedmanite analysis) or may be regarded as less liquid (Tobinite analysis), but either way both monetarists and neo-Keynesians would expect a substantial impact on behaviour. Thus the nature of the alternative security has to be analysed. If an individual held a claim on Shell or held a bank-guaranteed security he might well view these as money. If the claim were less marketable (e.g. issued by a small company or private individual) he would be less liquid or in monetarist parlance he would hold less money.

The great appeal of direct controls on credit compared to price methods has usually been that they appear to enable monetary control to be achieved with a lower level of interest rates, and with greater long-term stability of rates. The initial argument is simple and obvious. As with any other form of rationing, price is lower if markets do not clear by price because a lower price is fixed by administrative fiat and the resulting excess demand dealt with by official decree. Elementary demand theory argues that the authorities need to fix price to prevent the borrowers bidding up the price of the restricted quantity available. Thus if the controls were never evaded rates *could* be lower. However, if the controls are evaded, one must examine the price in the alternative market. As with rent control, the price in this market will necessarily be higher than where the entire market allocation is by price. One cannot say whether average rates will be higher or lower.[19]

In summary, direct controls on credit raise all the standard problems of any direct control; equity, efficiency and effectiveness. They also distort official statistics with the resulting dire consequences. On the other hand they offer an opportunity to the authorities to keep interest rates lower and more stable than they otherwise would be, and to intervene in the sectoral allocation of credit to achieve other objectives of policy. The controls spare the construction industry the consequences of interest rate policy but hit consumer durable manufacturers and retailers instead. One can argue that with sufficient political will any control can be enforced so long as the authorities are prepared to pay the necessary cost in terms of political freedom, efficiency of resource allocation and direct enforcement costs. In the French context the necessary costs have seemed acceptable. In a different environment and with different traditions rigid enforcement has been regarded as excessively costly in the UK and US. As a matter of political reality, credit controls would always be evaded to some extent in Britain and the USA.

2.4.5 Non-bank Private Sector Lending to the Public Sector by Price

This technique comprises any method of inducing the non-bank private sector to purchase public sector debt by making the securities more attractive. The most obvious method of doing this is to offer a higher rate of interest. In all but name, two other methods are identical: either offering the security at a discount or granting tax concessions, since both offer a higher effective rate of return. Other devices would include making the stock more marketable. This technique is often called open-market operations, but the term is also used to describe methods used to change the composition of bank portfolios so as to induce them to reduce bank lending without any direct impact on the money supply (see Chapter 3). The form of open-market operation discussed here has a direct, one-for-one impact on the money supply, unless the purchase is financed by borrowing from banks, in which case the borrowing exactly offsets the direct impact. As described in section 2.4.2, a private (corporate or personal) purchase of government securities reduces both bank lending to the public sector and bank deposits when the security is purchased. If the security is purchased with currency, the switch from money to non-monetary public debt also reduces the money supply as described above.

This technique has been used in the UK since 1974 as an active element of monetary policy. Clearly any purchase of bonds, savings certificates, etc. has the same effect but one should distinguish deliberate attempts to vary this total from passive acceptance of private sector actions. There are some problems associated with this technique. The first is a danger that it might crowd-out private sector investment by making it impossible for private companies to borrow. Any reduction of monetary growth aims to cut private spending, at least in money terms. However it may curb the 'wrong' sort of private expenditure, because the authorities have preferences about which expenditure is curbed. This may mean that more of any deflation is reflected in output than in price – this argument is especially common in the US.[20] Finally, it could affect the long-run stability of the private bond market, and so cause structural rather than immediate problems. Personally, I believe this argument is grossly overrated, but it is hard to refute.[21] The next problem concerns the type of security used. If short-dated securities are sold it might be argued that these are so liquid that there is no effect on private sector behaviour, or that the securities should be counted as part of the money supply. Samuelson has argued this about sales of Treasury Bills in the US and the authorities in the UK have had similar worries about local authority borrowing.[22]

Finally, it has been argued that this technique cannot be used as a short-term weapon since the authorities cannot sell bonds at the time of their choosing; the UK authorities argued this in 1971 and there has been a long debate about the issue of how to sell bonds in the UK (see pp. 89 and 148). The most extreme form of this argument was put by Hicks who claimed it would be hardest to sell bonds at the time when one most wanted to sell them.[23] Basically his argument was that bonds were most attractive in depressions and least attractive when the authorities wished to deflate. This is considered below in the context of the UK gilt-edged market in which it was originally conceived.

In summary, this technique is very attractive to most monetary authorities although it obviously makes the maintenance of low, stable rates impossible. However, its effects might be cosmetic and might have longer-term costs. More seriously, it may be difficult to sell securities when the authorities wish to, at least in sufficient volume.

2.4.6 Quantity Controls on Non-bank Private Sector Lending to the Public Sector

It is possible to use direct controls on non-bank private sector lending to the public sector in order to influence monetary growth. These controls compel individuals or institutions to purchase public sector debt, at least on occasion. This action affects the public/private sector cash flows and so has the same effect on the money supply as the other methods of influencing the flow of private sector payments to the public sector. In the Anglo-Saxon world these 'forced loans' are usually deprecated. They are probably unconstitutional in the US. In England forced loans have had a bad press since Magna Carta and are normally thought to have been a significant factor in Richard II, Richard III and Charles I all losing their thrones and their lives. Given how thoroughly forced loans are regarded as a 'bad thing' in the language of *1066 And All That*, it is surprising how frequently they have been resorted to in the UK. Post-war credits are the best-known example, being invented by Keynes for their *monetary* effects. Until 1961, Trustee legislation had something of the same effect and building societies are still restricted in their choice between public sector and bank debt. The largest 'forced loan', however, was the import deficits scheme of 1968 whereby importers had to lend, interest free, for six months a sum equal to 50 per cent of the value of their imports. Many of these devices acted as forced loans only by accident, but they had monetary effects none the less. In Europe the conscious use of forced loans is more common, especially in Germany, Belgium and to a lesser extent Italy. The principal arguments for and against this scheme are political in that they are concerned with basic civil rights and the problem of how easy it should be for a government to finance its deficit. There is a small economic point, however. If non-bank financial institutions, e.g. insurance companies, are forced to lend to the public sector, perhaps as a percentage of assets, it *may* reduce the advantages of being a 'non-bank' and so help with some of the problems of monetary control discussed elsewhere in Chapters 2-4. Otherwise, all the problems of direct controls apply, with probably greater force than elsewhere.

To summarise, this device raises most of the problems of other direct controls. Even if these are avoided, some argue that it is a form of taxation. It is not a serious candidate for widespread use in the UK, although some left-wing Labour groups have advocated it.

In one form, however, it has considerable attractions, i.e. as 'import deposits'. These are normally advocated as a form of import control which is legal under GATT (and EEC) rules, but the 'forced loan' aspect is important. At the least it reduces the inflationary impact of import controls. This was a major weapon, albeit an accidental one, in the 'Jenkins squeeze' in the UK in 1968-9.

2.4.7 Variation of the PSBR

Varying the size of the PSBR has a major impact on monetary growth so long as the public sector is sufficiently large. In 'mixed' and 'social market' economies the public sector's deficit is one of the major causes of monetary growth; this is especially true of Britain and Germany but is increasingly true in the US. Hence attention has increasingly been paid to the possibility of altering the PSBR as a means of controlling the money supply. Indeed government spending and taxation are now often thought of as monetary rather than fiscal weapons by policy-makers. This reflects in part and in part is reflected in the academic proposition that the two cannot be regarded as independent weapons. The analysis in section 2.4.2 explained why government spending, taxation and acquisition or sale of assets directly influence the money supply. Varying the size of the PSBR has been a major weapon of monetary policy in the UK since 1974. Indeed, the major determinant of official policy towards the PSBR has been its monetary effects.

The PSBR can be altered by

(a) raising (lowering) taxation.

(b) reducing (increasing) expenditure on current goods and services.

(c) reducing (increasing) expenditure on transfer payments.

(d) selling (buying) assets. In the UK, these have included BP shares (1977 and 1979), a whole host of securities in 1980-1 (for the 'sale of the century', see Chapter 10) and council houses.

(e) cutting public sector lending to the private sector. Notably in the UK, this applies to local authority mortgages in 1975-8.

A hard-line monetarist would argue that all reductions in the PSBR would have identical deflationary effects, and vice versa for increase. A Keynesian would agree about the direction of the effects of policies designed to reduce the PSBR but would not agree that the extent of their impact was proportionate to the change in the PSBR or the money supply. The major argument in favour of this method of control is that its effects neither depend on the correct definition of money nor on predicting the response of banks and the public to the change in interest rates. There are neither dangers of evasion nor of lack of knowledge of the relevant elasticity. If pursued 'à outrance', the policy cannot fail to work. Certainly, *if* the government can control its deficit, this method will succeed in reducing or stimulating monetary growth.

However, there are a number of problems with this technique of control. The first is that the reduction in the PSBR will be offset by an unpredictable (?) amount. Part of the reduction in private sector cash flows caused by the lower PSBR will be offset by reduced purchases of public debt and part of it by increased borrowing from banks. This is especially so with some methods of reducing the PSBR. BP shares, for example, may well be a substitute for public sector securities for some purchasers. Reduced loans to the private sector may be offset by increased borrowing from banks; to cite another UK example, this occurred when export credits were reduced. (This problem is discussed in section 10.2.)

The next problem is that the authorities may not find it easy to control the PSBR. This partly reflects lack of sufficiently strong control of some elements of expenditure but much more the nature of taxation and expenditure. The government can set tax *rates* and levels of welfare benefits but the amount raised and spent is hard to predict as it depends inter alia on income, unemployment, inflation, the pattern of expenditure, etc. These magnitudes may be affected by monetary policy; e.g. a tighter monetary policy will almost certainly increase unemployment at least in the short term. It is also difficult to vary expenditure and taxation especially in the short term. For example, income tax rates and the number of teachers employed cannot be varied as easily as interest rates for both legal and practical reasons. The costs of varying the PSBR are large for both the private and public sectors. The cost of disruption and compliance costs are not inconsiderable. Finally, nearly all public expenditure is desirable in that it increases social welfare, and similarly virtually all taxation is undesirable and unpopular.

If is often necessary to reduce the PSBR but it is not a costless option. Given its efficiency, this technique has to be a major element of monetary policy, but it should probably be a strategic not a short-term tactical weapon.

2.5 The Open Economy

2.5.1 The Overseas Dimension

Overseas factors are of relevance to monetary policy for several reasons. The first is the obvious one that the balance of payments may be either a target or a constraint of government economic policy. This may have implications for the government's preferred level of monetary growth. The authorities may wish to or be forced to pursue a strict monetary policy to reduce a balance of payments deficit. Moreover, there is a link between domestic credit expansion and the exchange rate (see Appendix 2B). This link does not depend on accepting the monetary theory of the balance of payments. This may mean that the government seeks to influence monetary growth to defend the exchange rate, or to reduce the exchange rate. Germany and Switzerland on occasions have had money *targets* in excess of 20 per cent p.a. to attempt to hold down their exchange rate.[24]

This is not strictly relevant to the choice of techniques of monetary control. The impact of various transactions on the money supply is relevant. This is discussed in detail below (2.5.2), but basically a balance of payments surplus increases (and a deficit reduces) the money supply. This may lead to conflicts of objectives in official policy. It also adds a number of additional techniques of control, discussed below in section 2.5.4.

Another problem arises in that the existence of an overseas sector makes some techniques of control much harder to operate or less likely to be successful. For example, direct controls may be frustrated by transactions involving overseas agents (see Chapters 8 and 9). It can be argued that the growth of the Eurocurrency markets has rendered any autonomous monetary policy impossible. Italy, in particular, has suffered from this, but German experience seems to suggest that autonomy is still possible — at a price. Any method of control which involves the use of interest rates may be rendered less effective if a higher (lower) rate induces a capital inflow (outflow) with the opposite effect on the money supply to that desired. Keynes argued that such effects should be countered by variations in forward rates and that monetary policy should be conducted as if the economy were closed.[25] This is related to one of the propositions held in common by Friedman and Keynes.[26] They have both argued that governments should set monetary policy targets for domestic reasons. The overseas dimension is relevant only in so far as transactions with foreigners threaten to move money supply and interest rates from the target levels; as a matter of prescription governments should offset these by suitable policies ('sterilisation operations'). As a matter of analysis, overseas factors are exogenous shocks which may lead to unfortunate consequences especially when the authorities react in a stupid and perverse fashion. This was how both Friedman and Keynes explained the spread of the slump in the 1930s.[27]

The Keynes-Friedman analysis is the orthodox approach to the analysis of the interaction of domestic and overseas forces. Their approach is the one adopted here. Overseas and domestic forces are not independent of each other but the two together determine the money supply. Extreme advocates of the monetary theory of the balance of payments would deny the validity of this approach. They would reject the possibility of controlling the money supply and would say that the analysis in section 2.4 is an analysis of how the exchange rate and/or official reserves are determined. Their views are set out in Appendix 2B together with an explanation of why the orthodox view is adopted here.

2.5.2 The Overseas Impact on the Money Supply

It is important to consider the two ways in which the existence of an overseas sector can change the money supply. The first stems from the fact that governments normally purchase and sell foreign currency in order to manage the foreign exchange rate, and to provide their citizens with foreign currency to purchase goods, take holidays abroad etc. Any such acquisition (or sale) will have exactly the same impact on the money supply as when the government buys or sells any other asset. Thus the sale of foreign currency to a domestic resident (to enable him to go on a foreign holiday) will have exactly the same direct impact on the money supply as the payment of taxes or the sale of government bonds. It would be logical to include all acquisitions of assets as part of the PSBR and treat sales of foreign currency as a reduction in the PSBR, but by an anomaly of official statistics, they are not so treated. If the PSBR is amended to include the net purchase of foreign currency, the adjusted total is usually called the domestic borrowing requirement (DBR). The crucial point of the analysis is that an acquisition of a foreign asset must be financed. The question posed is 'Has the government acquired or supplied any of the native currency (in the UK sterling)?' If the answer is 'yes', there is an overseas impact. This is positive if the government has supplied sterling and negative if it has acquired it. For many transactions the answer is no, hence there is no impact. These include government borrowing in foreign currency from any source including the Eurocurrency market and the IMF. Another form of government borrowing which does not affect the money supply is foreign purchases of government securities (effectively these are bought with foreign currency). If the government uses the foreign currency acquired by these means to support the pound, then there will be an impact on the money supply. However it will be the *intervention* which has an impact – in reducing the money supply – not the borrowing.

This analysis confirms for an open economy the crucial result derived above in section 2.4.2. Only if the government borrows from a private non-bank domestic source does official borrowing reduce the money supply. A fortiori, this is the only way in which the PSBR can be financed without increasing the money supply. No borrowing in foreign currency can have any direct impact on the money supply.

There is also an overseas impact which works through the banking system. Foreigners may hold deposits with or borrow from native (UK) banks. One might choose to treat the foreigners as part of the non-bank private sector and so include their deposits in the money supply, as the US authorities do. One need not take note of the difference between a loan to a resident and to a non-resident; the impact of both on the money supply is identical. This simple internationalist viewpoint is not normally adopted, however, because it ignores the political reality that transactions with foreigners are regarded as different; if only because balance of payments statistics are relevant to macroeconomic policy. The UK, for example, includes only resident deposits in the money supply. Hence if a deposit is transferred from a non-resident to a resident this will increase the money supply, and the transfer of a deposit from a UK citizen to a foreigner will reduce the money supply. Such transactions are likely to occur in the course of international trade; one transfers a deposit to a foreigner by writing a cheque in his favour to pay for an import. Thus transactions between residents and foreigners which are settled by means of cheques drawn on UK banks will affect the money supply.

The other aspect of money creation involving the overseas sector is that a loan to a foreigner will create a deposit, as described in section 2.2. This deposit may be held by a resident or by a non-resident. Hence loans to non-residents *may* increase the money supply but need not necessarily do so. This uncertainty can be resolved and the impact of deposit transfers incorporated by looking at *net* bank claims on foreigners (loans to foreigners less foreign-held deposits). If these rise, the money supply increases, e.g. if a foreigner borrows from a UK bank. If net claims fall, the money supply is reduced. If a bank deposit previously held by a UK citizen is now held by an Australian, the liabilities of UK banks to foreigners are higher, and so net claims are reduced and the transfer reduces the money supply.

To summarise, the impact of the overseas sector may increase the money supply in two ways, so there are two more primary causes of monetary expansion:

(a) if the public sector acquires foreign assets and purchases them with the native currency;

(b) if a bank increases its net claims on foreigners.

2.5.3 A Formal Model II: An Open Economy

This section extends the analysis of section 2.3 to incorporate an open economy. The money supply is redefined as bank deposits *held by residents* (Dr) plus currency held by the private sector (Cp).

$$M \equiv Dr + Cp \tag{ia}$$

Bank deposits held by non-residents (D_F) are also a bank liability, so equation (ii) becomes

$$D_F + Dr \equiv \text{Bank Liabilities} \tag{iia}$$

Bank liabilities are still equal to bank assets, i.e. to bank loans, so equation (iii) and (iv) are unaffected.

$$\text{Bank Liabilities} \equiv \text{Bank Assets} \tag{iii}$$

$$D_F + Dr \equiv \text{Bank Loans} \tag{iva}$$

However, a new category of bank loans has to be incorporated, bank loans to the overseas sector (BLF). As the non-bank private sector is the *resident* non-bank private sector, equation (v) becomes

$$Dr + D_F = \text{Bank Loans to the Public Sector (BLG)}$$
$$+ \text{Bank Loans to the non-bank private sector (BLP)}$$
$$+ \text{Bank Loans to the overseas sector (BLF)} \tag{va}$$

This can be rewritten as

$$Dr = BLG + BLP + BLF - D_F \tag{vb}$$

$BLF - D_F$ represents bank's net claims on foreigners (BCF).

The advantages of using this variable were stated in section 2.5.2, so

$$Dr = BLG + BLP + BCF \tag{vc}$$

(ia) and (vc) give (via), exactly as (i) and (v) gave (vi).

$$M = Cp + BLG + BLP + BCF \tag{via}$$

The public sector's financing equation needs to be amended by replacing the PSBR with the DBR so (viia) and (viiia).

$$DBR = \triangle Cp + \triangle BLG + \triangle PLG \tag{viia}$$

$$\triangle BLG = DBR - \triangle Cp - \triangle PLG \tag{viiia}$$

It is useful to rewrite (viiia), to include the PSBR. As the DBR is the sum of the PSBR and public sector acquisition of foreign currency (PAF)

$$DBR = PSBR + PAF \tag{viiib}$$

so from (viiia) and (viiib)

$$\triangle BLG = PSBR - \triangle Cp - \triangle PLG + PAF \tag{viiic}$$

(ixa) is merely (ix) written in changes instead of levels, as (vi) and (via) were.

$$\triangle M = \triangle Cp + \triangle BLG + \triangle BLP + \triangle BCF \tag{ixa}$$

(viiic) can be substituted into (ixa).

$$\triangle M = PSBR - \triangle PLG + \triangle BLP + \triangle BCF + PAF \tag{xa}$$

The first three terms on the right-hand side are the same as in equation (x) and are equal to DCE, given the assumptions made here. The final two terms represent the overseas impact on the money supply (O) and (xa) is sometimes written as

$$\triangle M = DCE + O \tag{xb}$$

Both elements of O can be negative and so the overseas impact may be to increase or to reduce monetary growth.

This analysis suggests two further methods of control of the money supply:

(h) price effects on O;

(j) quantity effects on O.

These are analysed in section 2.5.4.

2.5.4 The Techniques II: An Open Economy

Price Effects on the Overseas Impact. This method of monetary control is used to induce transactions by foreigners which will cause the money supply to fall. As explained in section 2.5.2 such transactions nearly all appear on the debit side of the balance of payments. Thus this technique is to deliberately 'worsen' the balance of payments by some means or other so as to reduce monetary growth or vice versa. A capital outflow in some form or other is the likeliest way of achieving this in the short run. If a UK citizen buys a villa in the South of France, or a German car, then either a sterling deposit will be held by a foreigner instead of by him, or the UK government will have supplied him with foreign currency and acquired sterling from him. This payment by the citizen will have exactly the same impact on the money supply as if he had made a tax payment or purchased government bonds.

This deficit could be induced by a higher exchange rate, lower interest rates, a smaller forward discount or lower tariffs (vice versa for an expansionary policy). Most governments have rejected this technique as either unworkable, counterproductive or simply absurd. Normally, one objective of a tighter monetary policy is to *improve* the balance of payments, so the means would make the end impossible. Moreover, some of the methods of inducing an outflow — especially lower interest rates — would increase domestic credit expansion; hence until recently this policy was a non-starter. Nevertheless, in recent years in the UK, notably in November 1977 and 1979-80, the government has used this device. It has allowed exchange rates to rise to a higher level than the government would have otherwise wanted so as to avoid a positive impact (i.e. an inflow). The device has mainly been used in a passive fashion in the sense that the government has allowed a high rate to avoid an inflow rather than force up the rate to cause an outflow. However, there have been some indications that the authorities were forcing the rate up in 1980 by various means to promote a more deflationary overseas impact.

This device fits in quite well with one transmission mechanism of monetary policy: curbing corporate liquidity so that firms spend less, especially on wages. As the whole issue is so central to UK policy in 1979-81 it is discussed in more depth in Chapter 10. At a conceptual level it can work but at what cost? This depends on the response of firms, the nature of the economy etc., and cannot be answered in general terms. One would expect it to be more useful in circumstances where governments wish to pursue expansionary policies. Higher tariffs and an artificially low exchange rate would fit very well into a traditional expansionist mould.

Quantity Effects on the Overseas Impact. 'Quantity Effects' here means some form of exchange control designed to prevent an inflow or an outflow. As described above (2.5.2), any flow will influence the money supply. Conventional exchange controls that prevent outflows mean that the money supply is higher than it otherwise would be. Exchange controls which inhibit inflows have been used by the Germans and the Swiss to try to restrict their rate of monetary growth. On the whole the German controls seem to have been successful and the Swiss unsuccessful. The UK adopted a variant of this policy by relaxing outward exchange controls in November 1979 (see Chapter 10).

Exchange controls have to be enforceable to be of any use, and many commentators have been sceptical of their possible efficiency. This issue is discussed in the Introduction (p. 13) in the context of the UK, with the conclusion that inward exchange control is highly desirable *if it can be enforced*. This qualification is important, but otherwise inward exchange control imposes few costs, except on banking profits, and can be of substantial value in avoiding inflows. Outward exchange control is much more dubious.

Appendix 2A: Accounting Conventions and Banking Sector Models

As the terms are conventionally used, the difference between assets and liabilities is called 'net worth'. In microeconomic theory, net worth constraints are conventionally imposed. These state that an individual's increased holdings of assets plus his purchases of goods cannot exceed his income (including capital gains) plus any borrowing. The accounting convention is essentially a rearrangement of this constraint. 'Net worth' is defined as a liability so that assets equal liabilities. In the case of companies, this is further justified by the fact that the net worth of a company is the property of its equity shareholders. Thus net worth is equal to the claim the shareholders would have on it if it were wound up. A claim is a liability so one may regard corporate net worth as a liability to the owners, i.e. equity shareholders. This is especially clear if the American style of accounting presentation is used; this is increasingly used in UK accounting.

The economists' approach is

Net worth = Assets − Liabilities
    500   1200 −   700

The US accounting convention is:

Assets	1200
represented by Liabilities to third parties	700
(Difference) Liabilities to shareholders	500

In the case of a bank its assets can be categorised as:

(a) real assets (buildings, computers, etc.) (R);

(b) financial assets (Loans) (BLG + BLP).

Its liabilities are:

(a) deposits (D);

(b) other liabilities to third parties (T);

(c) liabilities to shareholders (S).

Necessarily (as $S = R + BLG + BLP - D - T$; economists' analysis)

$R + BLP + BLG = D + T + S$ (balance sheet convention)

In the text (p. 25) it was assumed that $R = T + S$, so equation (v) was derived. In the version of the model used in the presentation of UK official statistics, $T + S - R$ is called (net) non-deposit liabilities (N). This extra term should appear in equations (iv), (v), (vi), (ix) and (x), i.e.

$$D = \text{Bank Loans} - N \tag{ivα}$$

$$D = BLP + BLG - N \tag{vα}$$

$$M = Cp + BLP + BLG - N \tag{viα}$$

$$\Delta M = \Delta Cp + \Delta BLP + \Delta BLG - \Delta N \tag{ixα}$$

$$\Delta M = PSBR - \Delta PLG + \Delta BLP - \Delta N \tag{xα}$$

However, N is both fairly small and rarely varies significantly so the omission in the text is not significant.

Appendix 2B: Monetary Theory of the Balance of Payments

This theory argues that the authorities determine the domestic supply of money, i.e. DCE. The actual money stock is determined by the demand for it which may be regarded as exogenous. The overseas impact on the money supply (O) (the difference between these two aggregates) adjusts to satisfy the relationship that the supply and demand for money are equal, i.e. $DCE + O = \Delta M$. Thus DCE and the demand for money determine O, i.e. the balance of payments. If DCE exceeds the exogenous change in the demand for money, the private sector then holds more money than it wishes to and will use the excess to purchase foreign assets or goods. If the domestic money supply is less than demand, then assets and goods will be sold to foreigners to procure the extra money needed to equate supply and demand. In either case, the balance of payments adjusts to the level determined by DCE and the demand-for-money.

The crucial distinction between this approach and the orthodox one is the assumption that the demand-for-money is exogenous. Both theories agree that the demand for money depends on real income prices, interest rates and wealth. The monetary theory, however, holds all of these constant. The orthodox theory, on the contrary, assumes that nominal income is the variable which adjusts. Thus when DCE rises the money supply rises. This leads to an increase in the level of nominal income, probably in the price level. In consequence, the demand for money rises and so the supply of and demand for money are again in equilibrium. Classical monetarism argues that only prices adjust. The monetary theory of the balance of payments argues that only O adjusts. Both seem too extreme and dogmatic since prices, output and the balance of payments may all adjust. Hence a modified version of the orthodox theory seems best. Some of the pioneers of the monetary theory — e.g. Dornbusch — accept such results, so the orthodox approach is not incompatible with many of the valuable insights offered by the alternative theory.

References

1. The major exceptions are Ascheim (1961) and various ephemera by Friedman, some of which are reprinted in Friedman (1968).

2. See Bank (1971) and (1980).

3. Note the changing tone of official statements on monetary policy, p. 198.

4. Ascheim (1961); Friedman (1968).

5. The issue was raised by the author in Gowland (1977a). Gordon Pepper started to give it prominence in Greenwell's *Monetary Bulletin* in 1978. See Foot (1979).

6. See Bank (1980).

7. See Dosser, Gowland and Hartley (1982), Ch. 2 (by Hartley).

8. See e.g. Burrows (1980).

9. See Friedman (1969).

10. See Appendix 2A for other assets. There are also some trivial cases, e.g. the creation of money to pay staff salaries.

11. Rearranged this would give the budget constraint equation in its original form. If PSBR is split into interest payments and other, the modern equation is derived.

12. See Polak (1951).

13. See Gaitskell (1933); Keynes (1936).

14. This method involves altering the rate of return on bank deposits *relative to all other assets*. See 2.4.5 for the effect of charging the rate of return on public sector debt *relative to all other assets*. The two must not be confused even though in a two-asset world, they would collapse into one.

15. See Moore and Threadgold (1980).

16. See OECD (1975).

17. For a consideration of the microeconomic impact of monetary policy see Miller (1980).

18. See Bank (1971). Argument occurs in *Bulletin* from 1969, see p. 199.

19. Proof available from author.

20. Especially in various articles in *Time* and *Fortune* in 1978-81.

21. See Gowland (1979), Ch. 4.

22. In his *Newsweek* column.

23. See Hicks (1952).

24. See Gowland (1979), Ch. 3.

25. See Keynes (1971), originally published in 1925.

26. See Friedman (1969); Keynes (1971).

27. See Friedman and Schwartz (1963); Keynes (1972), originally published in 1932.

3 TECHNIQUES OF CONTROL II: PORTFOLIO CONSTRAINTS AND THE RESERVE BASE SYSTEM

In many textbooks the reserve base system of control is implicitly or explicitly assumed to be the only technique used other than price effects on deposits (2.4.1). In the UK this system has never been used, and the authorities believe that it could not work (p. 11). There have been ratios of various kinds in the UK, but they have neither been intended to nor have they operated as a reserve ratio in the textbook sense. On the other hand, the reserve base system in one form or another *is* used in the USA, Germany, Venezuela, Australia, New Zealand and South Africa.

The reserve base system is a special form of the general group of controls known as portfolio constraints. These operate by restricting the efficiency of banks so as to restrict their output (formally analogous to shooting bankers!). The mechanism of the control is to insist that banks hold in some specified subset of assets either a minimum percentage of their total assets or a quantity equal to a specified fraction of their deposits. This may make banks less willing to authorise loans or take deposits if the assets specified are unattractive. Alternatively, it may make it impossible for banks to lend or accept deposits if the quantity of the asset is strictly controlled, that is the constraint may be binding. A special form of reserve base control is called money base control. In this case reserve assets are defined as cash (either currency, or central bank deposits or both). Such a scheme was widely discussed in the UK in 1980.[1] It is worth emphasising that it has been denied that reserve base control is a separate means of control. The Bank has argued that it is only a method of influencing interest rates (para 4.2 of the Green Paper). In contrast Friedman regards

> Direct control of the money base as an alternative to interest rates as a means of controlling monetary growth. Of course, direct control of the monetary base will affect interest rates, but that is a very different thing from controlling monetary growth through interest rates.

This point is discussed below, in section 3.5.

3.1 The Reserve Base System: The Formal Model

The formal model of the reserve base system can be used with any definition of the money supply so long as it comprises all or some subset of currency held by the private sector plus bank deposits. 'Bank' can be defined to include any institution, as it is in Germany. Here the definition adopted will be a broad one; all non-bank private sector holdings of currency (Cp) plus all bank deposits (D) (if a subset of D is to be excluded D is redefined appropriately).

$$M = D + Cp \tag{i}$$

A behavioural assumption is added. This is that private sector demand for Cp is such that Cp is a constant proportion (e) of M; without this assumption the system can be used as a device for controlling deposits.

$$Cp = e M \tag{ii}$$

Next it is assumed that the authorities compel banks to hold a quantity of certain specified reserve assets (R) at least equal to a specified minimum fraction of their deposits; the minimum reserve ratio (Z). (If the reserve ratio is 20 per cent, $Z = 1/5$.)

$$R \geqslant Z D \tag{iii}$$

Alternatively, one may believe that there is some asset which banks will always want to hold as a reserve — 'the Swiss system'.[2] It has been argued that this described the eighteenth- and nineteenth-century gold standard, but it is clear that there were never any fixed minima for the banks.

If one assumes

(a) that banks are *short-run* profit maximisers,

(b) that reserves yield no profit to banks,

(c) that banks are perfectly competitive,

then banks will hold no excess reserves and the inequality (iii) may be replaced by the equality (iv)

$$R = Z D \tag{iv}$$

that is by

$$D = \frac{R}{Z} \tag{iva}$$

Now, (iva) and (ii) can be substituted into (i):

$$M = \frac{R}{Z} + e M \tag{v}$$

and by rearrangement

$$M = \frac{R}{Z (1 - e)} \tag{vi}$$

This is the crucial equation of the reserve base system, known as the ratios equation. There are special cases of the equation, when either gold or currency is assumed to be the reserve base. If X = total currency, whether held by banks or individuals, and $1/Z = y$

$$M = \frac{Xy}{(1 - e + ye)} \qquad \text{(vii)}$$

This equation is also critical in that Friedman and Schwartz and Cagan used it to try to prove the exogeneity of the US money stock over the period 1867-1960. They argued that this equation explained the growth of money and that Z, R and e were exogenous and independent of income.[3]

There are two further techniques of control within this framework:

(k) varying the size of the reserve base (R);

(l) variations in the reserve ratio (Z).

3.2 The Operation of the Reserve Base System

3.2.1 *The Reserve Base*

To operate a reserve base/minimum reserve ratio system, the authorities must be able to control the quantity of reserve assets in existence. To do this, three rules must be observed.

(a) The reserve base must be defined carefully and precisely.

(b) The authorities must be the sole source of issue. Strictly, the authorities only need to be the sole source of issue at the margin; a fixed quantity of private-sector-created reserve assets could be permitted. It must not be possible for the banks to obtain privately created reserve assets to offset a squeeze on their reserve holdings.

(c) The authorities need to police the system carefully. The authorities must know how many reserve assets the banks currently hold. They must also know how many potential reserve assets are available to the banks. These potential reserve assets can be a 'privilege' entitling banks to purchase reserve assets at a non-penal rate, as in Germany. Alternatively, some assets which would be acceptable as reserve assets may be in private sector hands; this is inevitable if currency is a reserve asset.

Both the US and German authorities have followed these rules. In the US the Federal Reserve System defines reserve assets as currency held by a bank plus its deposits with the Federal Reserve System; these do not pay interest. In Germany the reserve base consists only of deposits with the Bundesbank.

If reserves do not pay interest, they impose an additional burden on banks almost akin to the tax on banking discussed below (4.2.7). If a bank is compelled to hold, say, 15 per cent of its assets in a non-interest-bearing form when interest rates average 10 per cent, this is the equivalent of a 1½ per cent tax on its assets. Conventional analyses of reserve base models tend to ignore this phenomenon. In fact reserve assets are assumed to be costlessly available to banks up to a certain point, and then unavailable (or available at infinite cost so that banks face a reversed L-shaped supply curve). This assumption is relaxed and the implications explored in section 3.5.

There are many possible reserve bases; the broadest possible definition is to include the whole of bank lending to the public sector as a reserve asset. This was advocated by Sir John Hicks and revived by Courakis in 1970.[4] One objective of this scheme is to encourage bank purchases of bonds to 'support' the market. It is argued that this would alleviate the problems discussed in section 2.4.5 in selling public sector debt. (See also the discussion below about gilt-edged marketing in the UK, pp. 89 and 148.) This is related to one of the traditional arguments about reserve base schemes, which is that they have little effect in themselves but may help or hinder debt management policy.

A more conventional definition of the reserve base is much narrower. It is normal practice to define the reserve base to include only central bank deposits and one or two other assets, especially currency. There are also problems about how to specify the minimum. German practice is to make it a criminal offence if the reserve holdings ever fall below the prescribed level. US practice is to require the percentage to be met only on a moving average basis. These variations have little effect on the workings of the system over a longer period, and will be ignored from here on; both the conceptual nature of the scheme discussed here and the case for and against it (3.5) are independent of such variations. However, the variability of interest rates may increase if a very rigid system is used.

3.2.2 High-powered Money

Reserve assets in a reserve base scheme are normally a subset of public sector debt. Borrowing by the public sector can be divided into categories by type of asset as well as by type of lender (2.3). The PSBR is equal to the sum of the changes in

    (a) private sector holdings of currency;
    (b) private sector holdings of reserve assets (other than currency if currency is a reserve asset);
    (c) private sector holdings of non-reserve assets (other than currency

if currency is not a reserve asset);

(d) bank holdings of reserve assets;

(e) bank holdings of non-reserve assets.

The direct impact on the money supply resulting from a change in the PSBR is the sum of (a) + (d) + (e). Friedman, however, wished to analyse the possible indirect impact through changes in reserve assets. Assuming currency to be a reserve asset, the change in reserve assets is the sum of (a) + (b) + (d). He called (a) + (d), i.e. those items common to both lists, high-powered money. Central bankers have argued that this analysis is confusing and useless to policy whereas Friedman thinks high-powered money should be the target of monetary policy.

3.2.3 The Central Bank's Role and Problems

In a reserve base system a central bank has to face two major operational problems.[5]

(a) Banks may hold excess reserves; that is reserves in excess of the legal minimum. The assumption in 2.6.1 that deposits equal the reserve base times the inverse of the reserve ratio may not be valid. It is worth emphasising that excess reserves are held by profit-maximising banks. The existence of excess reserves means that it may not be sufficient for a central bank to alter the total of reserves. There may be no effect on the money supply if banks reduce or increase excess reserves by an equal and offsetting amount. Even if a change in the reserve base has some impact on the money supply there will not be a predictable or systematic relationship between the change in the reserve base and the subsequent change in the money supply.

(b) The Central Bank is compelled as 'lender of last resort' to supply reserve assets in unlimited quantities if banks request them. The Central Bank can fix the price at which these are supplied and influence the reserve base through this mechanism. It usually lends the reserve assets it supplies in this way, that is the bank is obliged to hand them back at a later date in exchange for non-reserve assets. In practice, the loan is usually renewed. These assets are called 'borrowed reserves'. The authorities usually like to maintain a substantial total of borrowed reserves so that variations in this magnitude may be used to influence bank behaviour.

Two definitions that have been mentioned above are crucial to analysis in a reserve base system:

Total Reserves   = Required Reserves + Excess Reserves.

or Excess Reserves = Total Reserves − Required Reserves.

and Total Reserves = Borrowed Reserves + Non-borrowed Reserves.

Both excess reserves and non-borrowed reserves have often been targets of day-to-day operations of monetary policy. Excess reserves represent the potential for credit and money creation open to banks. Non-borrowed reserves represent that part of the monetary base beyond the immediate control of the authorities. However, the usual target variable has been 'free reserves', defined as

Free Reserves = Excess Reserves − Borrowed Reserves.

Free Reserves have always been the major operational target in Germany and frequently also in the US (especially before 1971), because they represent the extent to which the money supply could be expanded by the banking sector even if all the borrowed reserves were called in by the authorities.

3.2.4 The Federal Funds Market

In a reserve base system a market in base assets is likely to develop. It is interesting to observe how the US authorities use such a market, the 'inter-bank market for Federal Reserve funds', to facilitate the workings of monetary policy.[6] This market is usually called the Federal Funds market. In this market, effectively, banks borrow reserves from each other and from the Fed. Strictly speaking, the participants trade assets by exchanging cheques drawn on the Federal Reserve for one day against those drawn on the following day, but clearly this is a loan in all but name. All transactions are on an overnight basis. A large but declining percentage are arranged by a single broker, Gavin Bante.

The market performs several crucial functions. Its principal one, from the Fed.'s point of view, is to minimise excess reserves. Any individual bank can hold excess reserves, but these will normally be lent to a bank with inadequate reserves. Individual banks will hold excess reserves but these are minimised for the system as a whole. Secondly, the Federal Reserve supplies reserve assets (borrowed reserves) to the market at a price which it fixes. In the very short term, the Fed. allows the quantity of reserves to adjust to this price. However, the price (the Federal Funds rate) is varied so as to maintain the desired quantity of borrowed reserves. (Friedman has argued that the rate has often become an end in itself.[7]) Since November 1979 the rate has been allowed to vary much more. Finally, the market acts as a transmission mechanism for the effects of a monetary squeeze. Only the New York banks normally deal in this market directly. They are traditionally net borrowers. The major banks elsewhere have a correspondent relationship with a New York bank and either lend to or borrow from the correspondent such funds as they need. Their needs in turn depend in part upon smaller banks in their locality, who obtain their reserve assets from the regional bank. For example the Calhoun Bank in Fulton, Georgia, places its excess reserves, if any, with the National Bank of Georgia (NBG), and NBG lends Calhoun any reserve assets it may need. NBG lends any surplus reserve assets to (or obtains them from) Manufacturer's Hanover Trust. If the Federal Open Market Committee raises the Federal Funds rate or cuts borrowed reserves by any other means, initially only 'Manny Hanny' is affected. However, this New York bank then transmits the effect to NBG, by offering/charging a higher rate on/for excess reserves. In turn, Calhoun is affected as NBG changes its rates.

3.3 The Reserve Base System: The Tools

The authorities can seek to manipulate a reserve base system by

(a) changing the reserve ratio. The principal merit of this approach is that it can be used to affect a specific definition of the money supply. It can even be used to affect different definitions of the money supply in different ways. For example, if M_1 is growing too quickly and a broader definition (US M_2) too slowly, the Fed. can raise the reserve requirements on demand deposits and reduce them on time deposits. It seems to be agreed that, in the US, changing the reserve ratio is a rather clumsy and slow-acting weapon.

(b) 'open-market operations' to change the composition of banking sector portfolios. The authorities can seek to persuade banks to buy assets such as Treasury Bills, so as to transform their claims on the public sector such that they hold less reserve assets. The problem is that the efficacy of the policy depends on how banks respond. On the whole, the change will be least effective when it is most needed. To take the extreme examples: in the middle of the speculative boom of 1929, a marginal increase in Treasury Bill rates did not persuade banks to reduce reserve assets and lending; nor did reducing Treasury Bill rates have much impact in the mid-1930s in the US.

(c) changing the total of bank lending to the public sector. This can be done via any of the methods discussed in sections 2.4 and 2.5. The measures discussed there would have an indirect as well as a direct impact on the money supply in this case. It avoids most of the problems associated with (b). Nevertheless, it is unsatisfactory to many who want a reserve base system precisely because they wish to avoid relying on the tools analysed above.

(d) reducing the quantity of potential reserve assets. This policy aims to reduce reserve assets held by non-banks, so as to reduce the supply available to banks. This can be done by various means of which buying the assets concerned is the simplest. This policy — changing the composition of private sector claims on the public sector — imposes further constraints on both debt management and open-market operations. It would be simpler to avoid the problem by a suitable definition of reserve asset to include only central bank deposits as in Germany.

(e) changing the price or availability of reserve assets (reducing borrowed reserves). It is worthy of note that in essence this transaction consists of simultaneously increasing (or reducing) government claims on and obligations to banks. As Table 3.1 illustrates this has an expansionary (contractionary) effect on the money supply.

Table 3.1

A. Bank's balance sheet

Reserve base	10	Private deposits	100
Lending to private sector	90		
Liabilities	100		

B. The government borrows 10 from the banks, increasing their reserve base, and redeposits it.

Reserve base	20	Private deposits	100
Private lending	90	Government deposits	10
	110		110

C. Now, however, the banks can lend more (as their reserve ratio is 18 per cent) and (by the operation of the credit multiplier) money creation continues until the ratio is once more 10 per cent.

Reserve base	20	Private deposits	190
Private lending	180	Government deposits	10
	200		200

The case for and against these measures has been thoroughly canvassed.[8] To summarise the conclusions, it is clear that all these tools have to be used. All have a role to play in any integrated monetary policy based on a reserve base mechanism of control.

3.4 The Reserve Base System: The Behavioural Underpinnings

The analysis in sections 3.1 and 3.2 is subject to criticism on the grounds that no behavioural explanation is offered as to *why* changing the reserve base should change the money supply. The traditional answer to this criticism has been 'credit multiplier' analysis.[9] This argues that a bank responds to an increase in reserve assets by increasing its lending. The loan is redeposited and a fraction lent out and so on ad infinitum. For example, suppose the reserve ratio is 20 per cent. Government spending increases both the deposits and the reserve assets (central bank deposits) of one bank by 10. This bank can, therefore, increase its lending by 8 and still hold 2 of extra reserve assets to satisfy the law. The bank can, if necessary, use the other 8 to satisfy the liability on itself created by its loan. It is assumed that the borrower transfers this claim to someone else (i.e. spends the money). Thus the bank's balance sheet shows a rise of deposits of 10 balanced by 8 of lending to an individual and 2 of reserve assets. This increase in deposits of 10 is the primary creation of money caused by the spending. The bank's loan has also created a deposit of 8 in another bank. The second bank faced with an increase of 8 in deposits and 8 in reserve assets can increase its lending by 80 per cent of 8 (6.4) and so on. In addition to the primary creation of 10, the government spending has generated a chain of bank lending of 10 (0.8), 10 $(0.8)^2$, 10 $(0.8)^3$ and so on. The sum of this geometric series, including the initial 10, is 50, i.e. deposits have risen by 5 x the change in the reserve base, or in general by the reciprocal of the reserve ratio x the change in the reserve base. This seems to offer a behavioural justification for equation (iv), p. 53.

This conventional analysis is unsatisfactory in two ways. One is that there is no reason why every loan should be spent and the recipient choose to hold the proceeds as a bank deposit. Instead he might choose to hold cash. For example the initial borrower above might have taken his newly acquired loan in cash and the cash might never have been paid into a bank either by him or those to whom he paid it. In this case the increase in the money supply would be 18. The monetary consequences of a change in the reserve base would seem to be unpredictable. The primary effect (in this case 10) is clear but the induced lending may create money of 8 or 40, or any amount in between. The assumption of a fixed proportion of holdings of currency to money has to be made to rescue credit multiplier analysis. If the fixed ratio is 30 per cent, then of the 8 lent out, 2.4 will be held as cash and 5.6 paid into banks to generate further second-round effects. For an increase in government spending of 10, there will be a first-round effect of a rise of 3 in currency and 7 $(10 \times (1-0.3))$ in deposits. The second-round effect will be 10 $(1-0.3)$ 0.8, the subsequent rounds will be 10 $(0.7)^2$, $(0.8)^2$ etc. The resultant formula is the same as equation (vii), p. 54. This 'leakage analysis' can be expanded to take account of almost any possible behaviour; the resulting multiplier formula often being several lines long.[10]

No simple extension of the model can deal with the second objection. This is that there is no reason to assume that banks can lend in unlimited quantities at will, which the credit multiplier story assumes. Accordingly, it is conventional to treat reserve base analysis as an explanation of the *supply* of credit. The demand-for-credit is then added and the model is complete.[11] The most simple, indeed simplistic, way to resolve the problem is to assume that banks always reduce the interest rate they charge on loans so as to ensure that someone is willing to borrow. In this case one is postulating a perfectly inelastic supply of credit which is equal to

$(\frac{1}{Z} - 1)$. reserve base, where the minimum reserve ratio is Z.

This formula can be rewritten as

$$\frac{1-Z}{Z} . R$$

Thus, if the reserve base is 10 and the reserve ratio 20 per cent (0.2), the supply of credit is

$$10 (\frac{1}{0.2} - 1), \text{ i.e. } 10.4 - 40 \text{ (or } \frac{0.8}{0.2} . 10).$$

In this case the model of the credit market is as in Figure 3.1(a). An increase in the reserve base shifts this curve to the right as in Figure 3.1(b). Rates fall and credit extended rises.

It is obvious that this assumption is absurd. Thus it is conventional to treat this figure as the maximum of loans, and to assume that the supply curve is elastic but asymptotically approaches this limit, as in Figure 3.2. There are many ways in which this result can be derived. An elegant and simple one is as follows. Assume that banks are utility-maximising firms, with profits and the avoidance of risk as the arguments in their utility function. For the sake of simplicity, the rate of interest is defined as the expected rate of return on a loan, that is it is a pure rate of interest, and borrowers pay a risk premium in addition. If the rate of interest is zero, then there is no return from a loan but some risk, so no loans will be made. As interest rates rise, the amount of expected profit rises for each unit of loan granted. However, there is no increase in risk per unit of loan. Hence the quantity the bank wishes to lend will rise, i.e. there is an upward-sloping supply curve for credit. When the reserve base changes, the curve shifts and interest rates and credit move (Figure 3.2), as they did in the simple case. *There is no*

Figure 3.1: The Simple Model

(a)   (b)

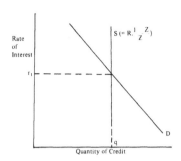
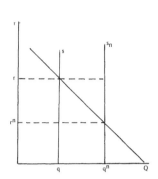

N.B. In 3.1(b), the reserve base rises from r to r^n, and the supply of credit shifts from s to s_n.

Figure 3.2: A More Realistic Model

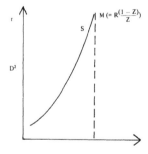

reason why the shift should be parallel or even predictable.

Those who, like the author, follow Tobin in believing in the 'new view of money' regard most of the above analysis as unnecessary. No elaborate justification is necessary for an upward-sloping supply curve because it is a reasonable a priori assumption in any market. If one treats the reserve base requirement as a constraint on bank behaviour, the shift in the supply curve can be derived without any fuss. It can also be argued that an increase in short-term, liquid, non-interest-bearing public sector assets (that is, in reserve assets) will lead to an increased desire to hold less liquid, higher-yielding private sector assets so as to achieve a better portfolio balance. Such analysis can be extended to a non-mandatory base. A desire of a bank to maintain, ceteris paribus, some sort of balance of different types of asset is rational. At the least, it may be the only possible approach to the problem of profit maximising under uncertainty for an oligopolist and oligopsonist. At best, it may be fully optimal when transactions costs are taken into account. This 'new view' also incorporates the impact of a change in lending to the public sector in non-reserve asset form.

This will also have some impact on bank behaviour. Hence, the 'new view' is that there is an elastic supply curve for credit (to the private sector). This shifts according to both the total and composition of bank holdings of public extra assets, including any legal distinctions. Thus the result can be derived without any need for credit multiplier analysis. (See Coghlan, however, for the contrary view of this argument.[12])

There is a minor problem concerning whether the change in reserve assets involves an increase in total bank lending to the public sector. This is related to the question of how credit is defined in this model. There are two more serious problems. The first is that the supply curve may be backward (downward) sloping. This problem has never been recognised in the literature. However, it can be derived in various ways.[13] The simplest is to assume that some managerial theory of the firm explains bank behaviour. If one follows Baumol's model, there is a binding minimum-profit constraint on a firm. Simon's 'profit-satisficing' model is similar in effect but not in origin. In this case a higher rate of interest will enable the profit constraint to be satisfied at a lower level of loans. For this reason, the curve could slope backwards. A general model of managerial behaviour would put both the bank's size and 'managerial slack', including managerial leisure, into the bank management's utility function. Making extra loans involves all sorts of costs for the management including time, effort and the risk of being seen to make a mistake. On the other hand, a larger total of loans increases the size of a bank and so the prestige of its management. If these considerations fail to offset the benefits of leisure, the extra profits that accrue from higher rates will lead to a smaller loan portfolio.

Another problem is implicit in the work of Jaffee.[14] His ideas are most easily analysed in terms of the response of a bank to an increase in its lending to the public sector, whether this is in the form of reserve assets or not. The standard analysis is that the response is an increase in lending to the private sector, as derived above. The alternative is that there is a *reduced* desire to lend. Banks might have a target level of total assets. An increase in public sector assets may lead to a pari passu reduction in private sector assets. More plausibly, both size and the avoidance of risk must be included in a bank's utility function. The increase in public sector assets will lead to a reduction in private sector assets so as to leave the bank with a larger, less risky portfolio. This response is consistent with the 'new view' of money.

3.5 Reserve Base Systems: The Case For and Against

It is very hard to find systematic, thorough and rigorous statements of the case for a reserve base system.[15] There is a tendency to assume that such a system must work. In one sense this is true, but the crucial questions are under what conditions and what is meant by 'work'? A reserve base/minimum reserve ratio system does put a maximum value upon the size of various financial aggregates, principally various categories of bank deposit. As every definition of the money supply is the sum of some of these plus currency, then each definition of money can be controlled.

A very strong counter argument can be mounted, as has been shown by the British authorities.[16] This Bank of England argument is in two parts.

(a) A reserve base system cannot be more effective than an increase in interest rates and to be effective will raise interest rates by precisely the same amount as if interest rate techniques had been used without a reserve base system. Hence, at best, the textbook reserve base system is redundant, but see 3.6 for possible uses of non-textbook uses of reserve ratios. By Occam's Razor it should not be introduced.

(b) There are a number of problems with a reserve base system that make it undesirable.

In brief, it would be redundant if the definition of 'bank' and 'money' were both precisely known and fixed. As neither of these assumptions is valid, any reserve base scheme will be ineffective and distortionary. The second of these arguments will be considered first. The argument has some affinity to that used in the case of direct (quantity) controls. However, there is a crucial difference. Direct controls have to be applied to each bank. The reserve base system applies to *the banking system as a whole*. While there are dangers of evasion and the distortion of official statistics, some of the problems of direct controls do not apply. There are no inhibitions on banking competition; banks can compete freely with each other for business. They will also compete for reserve assets so the cost of reserve assets will rise as banking efficiency rises. This means that the margin between the interest rate on borrowed reserves and on bank loans will fall compared to a regime of ceilings. There is *less* danger of inducing structural rigidity, although some is inherent in any system of regulation, other than by price. Resource allocation is unlikely to be *as adversely* affected both within financial markets and in terms of the effect on real markets. There are very substantial dangers that a reserve base system will be evaded and will produce distortions in statistics, and so make a coherent and rational monetary policy impossible. These are inevitable unless the assumptions above are met, i.e. it must be certain what a bank is, what money is and that these definitions will never change.

The first point may seem trivial, since it ought to be clear what a 'bank' is. However, the problem of to whom the regulations should apply is a major one. In the US Federal Reserve, reserve requirements apply to 'member banks', i.e. to those banks who are under the supervision of the Federal Reserve system. Any bank may be a member but it is only compulsory if a bank either has deposits in excess of $400m or has an office in one of the 12 reserve cities, i.e. those in which there is a Federal Reserve bank. Otherwise, a bank may operate under a state charter and be subject to the laws of the state concerned. Over the last 30 years, the share of 'member bank' deposits in total deposits has fallen from nearly 90 per cent to about 70 per cent of total deposits. In recent years the increasing share of deposits outside the control of the Fed. has led to money growth of about 1½-2 per cent p.a., so to achieve actual growth of 5 per cent, the Fed. has had to keep the growth of currency plus member bank deposits down to 3 per cent. This led one Vice-President of the New York Fed. to say that it made control of the money supply 'as poor as that of a fisherman trying to reel in a tuna on a line that was alternately as unyielding as an anchor chain and as elastic as a rubber band'. The existence of Federal Reserve reserve requirements puts a burden on banks equal to a tax of about 1 per cent of deposits p.a. This makes them less able to compete with banks outside the system. Furthermore, some banks have switched from member to non-member status, e.g. the Farmers' Glory bank of Texas.[17]

This could happen in any system because deposits will be switched to institutions not subject to the requirements since they can offer a higher rate of interest. They can offer a higher rate of interest *because* they are not subject to the burdens of the reserve requirement. This problem has not arisen in Germany, because the Bundesbank has adopted a very wide definition of a bank and because the financial structure is much less complex than in the US or the UK. One might also add that they have shown much greater political will in enforcing their policy. For example, Federal Reserve requests for legislation to reduce their problem were rejected by Congress for over ten years until some of their requests were implemented in 1980. There are about 90 directors of SLAs and 15-20 directors of state-chartered banks in Congress. Both SLAs and state-chartered banks would lose by the changes. The two facts may be related.

This switching of deposits is likely to lead to a less efficient financial system. The financial institutions outside the system are unlikely to be as efficient as those within it, otherwise they would have taken the deposits in the first place. In the US the incentive to an efficient small bank not to grow is enormous. The cost of growing beyond $390m is virtually prohibitive. There will be further resource costs as not all banks are alike. Thus reserve requirements will place differential burdens on different banks according to their type of business – wholesale or retail, category of borrower etc. This will artificially favour some banks at the expense of others, and so be unfair and distortionary. There is a serious problem of defining whom the controls should apply to, especially as whatever is excluded will grow faster. Indeed, previously unknown types of institution may come into existence only to evade the rules – without the Federal Reserve rules, would any Massachussets bank not have a branch in Boston? This problem will produce inefficiency and inequity, and will make the conduct of monetary policy much less effective both directly and by distorting measures of monetary growth.

The other problem – what the controls should apply to – is about equally serious. Broadly speaking, the proposition (sometimes called Goodhart's law) applies (see 1.2). If, say, the money supply includes 60-day deposits but excludes longer-term ones, there will be an incentive to create 61-day deposits. In principle, a sufficiently varied and extensive set of reserve requirements could avoid this, e.g. if 60-70-day deposits are within the controls but with a lower ratio, and 71-80 days with one lower still and so on. In practice this is impossibly complex. Again evasion, inefficiency, inequity and distortions will arise.

Nevertheless, one must conclude by emphasising that these costs will be lower in the case of a reserve base system than with direct controls. Hence, to prove its case against a reserve base system, the Bank of England needs to prove that it is redundant compared \o interest rate controls.

3.5.1 Reserve Bases and Interest Rates

The Bank of England case for the redundancy of a reserve base follows from the behavioural analysis in 3.4. If an alteration of the reserve base/ratio is to influence the money supply, it must do so by shifting the supply curve for *credit*. As in Figure 3.3(a), if the reserve base system works as it is intended to it can reduce the money supply by shifting the supply curve from S1 to S2. The quantity of credit falls and so does the money supply, by $Q1-Q2$ (plus possibly the fall in the reserve base, depending on how the fall was achieved).[18] However, if markets clear by price, then interest rates will rise from r_1 to r_2. The same increase in rates, from r_1 to r_2, would reduce credit by the same amount, Q_1-Q_2, because it would cut the demand for credit. Therefore, in equilibrium there would be no difference between the effects of changing interest rates or the reserve base. In Figure 3.3(b) a similar result is obtained when the supply curve is elastic.

Furthermore, any direct impact of a fall in the reserve base, which arises if private lending to the public sector has risen, can also be accounted for by the change in interest rates necessary to induce this increase. It might even be argued that a reserve base system will reduce the impact of changes in interest rates on the money supply, because of the impact on relative rates. For example, if Treasury Bill rates were increased to induce banks to buy bills and so reduce their holdings of reserve assets, then the margin between long and short rates would fall. Hence the long-dated securities bought by the non-bank private sector would be relatively less attractive, so less would be bought and the money supply would be higher. This is perhaps an extreme case which also ignores the effect of higher overdraft rates on short-term rates. Nevertheless, the need to control the reserve base adds an extra dimension to the problem of managing *relative* interest rates. As argued above (1.5), relative interest rates are at least as important as absolute ones in controlling the money supply, so the extra constraint could have

Figure 3.3: A Reduction in the Reserve Base

(a)   (b)

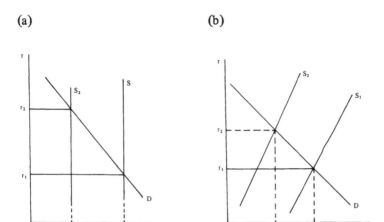

Figure 3.4: A Reserve System Reduces the Deviation of Money from Target

(a)   (b)

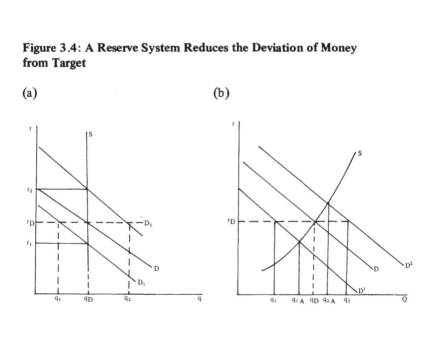

adverse effects.

The basic Bank of England proposition is simple but it implicitly assumes certainty and explicitly assumes that markets clear by price. The first assumption is invalid and the second is highly dubious, so the two will be examined in turn. Uncertainty can take many forms but the crucial uncertainty in this case concerns the demand for credit and the elasticity of supply. The impact of uncertainty on the demand for credit can be analysed in many ways. The simplest is to assume that the authorities know the *expected* demand curve but the *actual* demand curve shifts around this expectation (i.e. there is a stochastic term in the demand function). This can be represented diagramatically by assuming that there are two equally possible states of the world and that there will be a different demand curve in each. (See Figures 3.4(a) and 3.4(b)) D_1 in the first state and D_2 in the second. The authorities have to act on the basis of the mean expectation of the demand curve (D). For this case, the analysis is shown in Figure 3.4(a) for the inelastic supply curve. The authorities wish the money supply to be such that the optimal quantity of credit is Qd. If they rely on interest rate controls the best that they can do is fix rates at rd. In this case in state 1 the quantity of credit will be q1 and in state 2, q2. If instead a reserve base system were used, then the quantity would be qD in each case, at interest rates of r_1 and r_2 respectively. The case for the elastic supply curve is shown in Figure 3.4(b). In this case, the authorities cannot be certain of obtaining Qd, but are closer to it (at q1a and q2a respectively) with the reserve base system than without it. In this case, uncertainty does create a case for a reserve base system. This will be valid unless the supply curve is perfectly elastic which is impossible in a reserve base system (or demand perfectly inelastic in which case there is no equilibrium and the interest rate policy is ineffective anyway). Similar results can be derived for the case where the authorities are uncertain about demand elasticity and about supply elasticity.[19] Thus in the face of uncertainty, there is a case for a reserve base system to control the money supply.

3.5.2 Reserve Bases and the Variability of Interest Rates

One caveat that might be entered against the argument in section 3.5.1 is that greater certainty about the level of monetary growth will be purchased at the cost of greater variability in interest rates. Friedman and many others would not think that this was a significant cost relative to the benefit. However, many others, including most central bankers, would see it as important to consider the impact of a reserve base system on the variability of interest rates. It cannot be disputed that in the model analysed in section 3.4.1 there is a trade-off between variability in interest rates and certainty of control of money (and monetary variability). It is important to decide which interest rate matters. In the UK, the authorities have aimed at stability in bank base rates and in three-month rates at the expense of massive variability in the overnight inter-bank market. Rates of 100 per cent and 2 per cent in the same month are common. A range of 10 per cent in one day between transactions made early in the day and at 2.45 p.m. is not unknown. The peak in this market was 1,256 per cent, in 1967; 750 per cent was reached in 1980. Gilt-edged rates have also had a higher variance than in Germany and the US. It is also vital to decide how variability is to be defined. Under a reserve base system there would undoubtedly be more changes in bank base rates but each change would be smaller. Is the market more or less variable? Is the variance an adequate measure of variability? Moreover, it is difficult to answer the question about variability in general. The exact form of the system would influence the outcome. Even more important, so would the manner in which the Central Bank operated the system. The Bank devised a system in 1979 to act as straw man and had little difficulty in showing that, if operated in a particular way to achieve specified objectives, variability would be greater.[20] On the other hand, the Federal Reserve system operated a reserve base system in the 1940s so as to achieve no variability in rates. Neither seems very relevant.

It can be argued that a reserve base system would reduce variability in rates. The author has argued in various places that a reserve base system could lead to less variability in rates. On the other hand, the Bank of England has argued that it would lead to greater variability.[21] These contrasting propositions need to be analysed. A heuristic argument for my view is that the variance of rates in the Federal Funds market is much less than in the UK overnight inter-bank market. This, I argued, is a consequence of the reserve base system. The importance of how the system is operated is revealed by the much greater variance in US prime (base) rates since Volcker became Chairman and decided to try to achieve greater day-to-day control over the size of the base. His problems have been considerable.[22] One point that must be emphasised is that my argument is that there would be less variability in rates for a given path of growth of the quantity of money or credit. It was not clear whether the Bank of England view was the converse or that more variability in rates would be the price of less variability in monetary growth.

The case for less variability rests on the assumption that quantities do not fully or instantaneously adjust by price. This is a likely response to uncertainty. If a bank faces an increase in the demand for credit, it does not know whether this is permanent or temporary, nor does it know what demand its rivals face. Hence, it would be rash to raise interest rates sufficiently to eliminate the excess demand. Temporary quantity rationing is a much more rational response especially in view of the administrative, psychic and goodwill costs of changing interest rates — particularly in the case of first increasing and then reducing them. Hence it is reasonable to assume that markets are not fully cleared by price. Such disequilibrium models were developed initially by Fair and Jaffee for financial markets and have been widely adopted in microeconomic literature. This type of model is used in the Treasury's financial model so it is certainly not anathema to the authorities.[23]

The full argument is somewhat complex, so the presentation here is heuristic. Assume that there is an optimal path of monetary growth. For the sake of simplicity, let it be further assumed that this could be attained with stable interest rates if the world were not subject to exogenous shocks. If the authorities left interest rates at their long-run optimal level the shocks would mean that the money supply's growth varied in a random fashion around this path. It might in fact be desirable to let this happen; almost certainly the Bank of England believes so. However, in the real world such variations would produce both direct effects on the economy and have an impact on expectations that might be undesirable. Furthermore, such problem events can be distinguished from events which should lead to variations in monetary policy. Thus it is not unreasonable to examine what would happen if the authorities sought to eliminate these variations. If they did so by any quantity control, including reserve base control, the impact on rates would be small. (My model assumes that rates change by a fraction α of the amount necessary to clear the markets, the lower α, the smaller the variation.) If, instead, the authorities chose to try to maintain the optimal growth path by varying interest rates they would be at worst the same as in the simple equilibrium case (when $\alpha = 1$). They would otherwise be larger than this especially if the response depends on low short-run rather than higher long-run elasticities. Furthermore, a quantity control may act as a signal to the market in a world of uncertainty and so avoid the 'overkill' otherwise necessary.[24]

3.5.3 Bank Behaviour and the Efficiency of the Financial System

It was argued above that a reserve base system would lead to some inefficiency because of its affinity to a direct control. More importantly, it would lead to significant changes in banking practice. Such would be the inevitable result of so radical a change in the operation of monetary policy. It is not clear whether the changes would improve the efficiency of the system or not. Whereas in section 2.6.5 it was clear that disintermediation, evasion and the growth of non-banks would lead to resource misallocation, the structural change could operate for either good or ill. It might be argued that such a system would encourage banks to relate their changes more to marginal social cost and so improve efficiency. There is little restraint and no penalty currently attached to a bank suddenly increasing its lending. This means it can provide at very low cost the service of offering its customers extra liquidity by allowing them to overdraw at will. If this facility is used, interest is paid but the *right* to overdraw is often free. This will lead to sudden surges in monetary growth when the facilities are used. There may or may not be a high cost in terms of macroeconomic management to sudden surges in monetary growth. Thus it is neither clear what the social cost of liquidity is nor whether overdraft facilities which are free to both bank and customer are desirable. In a reserve base system the bank would have to hold excess reserves so it would bear the cost of providing the service. It might or might not pass this on. In fact some bankers have argued that a reserve base system would kill the overdraft system. Others argue that it is on the way out anyway, e.g. local authorities no longer have free facilities. Still others think the consequence would be a system of commitment fees. Finally, sceptics, including other bankers, believe the result would be no change at all. There might, however, be an increase in term loans held as precautionary balances in place of overdraft facilities. This would lead to a structural increase in the demand-for-money and probably reduce the observed relationship between money and spending. (See the analogous point in section 2.4.3 above.)

In summary, the impact of a reserve base system would probably be large but unpredictable. This is a powerful Conservative argument for the status quo.

3.6 Reserve Base: Some Extensions

3.6.1 Reserve Base as a Predictor: The Bank of England Proposal

In the Consultation Document, the UK authorities proposed an interesting variant on a non-mandatory reserve base system.[25] Their argument was that movements in the reserve base, defined in terms of bank behaviour, should be good predictors of their future lending. In other words, if there were going to be either an increase in the demand for bank lending or a structural (outward) shift in supply it would be reflected in movements in the reserve base before the extra lending occurred. The proposal was that interest rates should be raised when the base increased. Indeed, an automatic linking of rates to movements in the base was suggested as a possible policy. This proposal was in many ways more Friedmanite than the monetary base ideas discussed elsewhere in the document. It is clear that this idea will not be adopted as it has almost no supporters. The principal merit of the scheme was that it offered a possible way round the 'too little, too late' dangers of relying on interest rate techniques revealed in 1972-3, and the alleged 'too much, too late' reaction in 1976-7 and 1979-80. However, there were two major problems with the proposal. One was that bank behaviour is not so predictable as to justify an automatic link. This is especially so given the problems discussed in section 3.4. Furthermore, the temptation to 'massage the figures' in order to break the link would undoubtedly be felt by politicians.

A more fundamental problem is that a rise in the reserve ratio can reflect either a fall in bank lending below expectations or an anticipated rise. In a stationary state, there would be no change in the absolute level in the former case and a rise in the latter. However, when both variables are stated relative to a trend the problem of distinguishing them can be considerable. Certainly it is too large to justify an *automatic* link. Presumably, one of the arts of central banking is to predict future movements of bank lending on the basis of present trends in bank portfolios, and to act accordingly in a discretionary fashion.

3.6.2 An Interest-elastic Demand for Currency

Most bank deposits pay interest, hence it is reasonable to assume that the rate of interest paid on deposits influences the demand for currency. In other words, currency holdings are not a fixed percentage of money holdings, as assumed in the simple ratios model, but are determined by a demand function with a negative interest elasticity. This phenomenon has to be analysed within a full model of the financial system beyond the scope of the present work.[26] However, the principal result of this extension is to reduce the efficiency of the working of the reserve base system.

3.6.3 The Cost of Reserve Assets

The obligation to hold reserve assets imposes a burden on the banking sector, depending on whether or not reserve assets pay interest, but this is not the same as the cost of acquisition. In the textbook model it is usually assumed that this is infinity, i.e. banks can never obtain more than the amount predetermined by the authorities. This is never true because in practice reserve assets can always be obtained at a price: the question, then, is what price will the authorities impose as lender of last resort. This in turn depends on the rise in interest rates that they will be prepared to accept to restrict the growth of money base above its optimal level. At one extreme, the UK reserve assets system in force since 1971 can be characterised as one in which reserve assets can be obtained at negligible cost. It is possible to reinterpret the whole of the reserve asset mechanism in terms of the cost of reserve assets. In this case the whole mechanism is less clear-cut, and the difference between reserve base and other methods of control is reduced.

3.7 The Reserve Base: Some Conclusions

It seems clear that sole reliance on a non-mandatory reserve or monetary base system would lead to disaster. No one knows the minimum cash ratio that a bank needs. Some bankers are sure that it is well below 1 per cent, even without any incentive to minimise its use. One would expect the ratio to fall to 0.3 or 0.4 per cent over a period of a few months as the ingenuity of bankers was applied to the problem. Moreover, the ratio would fall every time an attempt was made to squeeze the base. The idea of an unstable credit multiplier of about 300 is a nightmare that no central banker could be expected to manage. The case for monitoring the cash base and even for its occasional manipulation is strong. To use it as a major tool of policy would be foolhardy with present knowledge and under current circumstances.

It is clear that any detailed analysis of the reserve base system reveals that it is not as clear-cut or simple as the textbook presentation. It is also clear that a reserve base system has some of the characteristics of direct controls − with the crucial distinction that they apply to the banking system as a whole, not to individual banks. It is also clear that their impact depends in part on their effect on the level and structure of interest rates.

The control will also have an impact on rates. Nevertheless one cannot go so far as to say that the effect will be identical to that of interest rate changes. A reserve base system is more effective than a pure system of direct controls, but involves higher rates. It can control money at a lower level of rates than reliance purely on the price mechanism but at a cost in terms of evasion and efficiency.

It is probably true that the greatest single form of evasion would be by means of overseas transactions. Hence the case for a reserve base system would be much greater if there were exchange control. Or vice versa, a whole-hog advocate of a reserve base should probably support exchange control. It must again be stressed that the impact of any reserve base system depends on how it is used. The authorities could set the 'rules of the game' so as to produce virtually *any* result.

References

1. See Bank (1980).
2. See Bank (1980), p. 9.
3. See Friedman and Schwartz (1963); Cagan (1965).
4. See Hicks (1952); Courakis (1973).
5. See Boston (1976).
6. See Boughton (1972).
7. E.g. in Friedman (1968).
8. E.g. Ascheim (1961).
9. See e.g. Culbertson (1972).
10. E.g. in Coghlan (1980).
11. See Culbertson (1972).
12. See Coghlan (1980).
13. See Culbertson (1972) for an alternative derivation.
14. See Jaffee (1975).
15. As Bank (1980) puts it 'only a limited discussion'. Of some value are Rose in IEA (1980), Lewis (1980), Turner (1979), Ascheim (1961) and various ephemeral pieces by Johnson of Lloyds.
16. See Foot et al. (1979); Bank (1980).
17. See MPCC, p. 112.
18. See Gowland (1981).
19. Ibid.
20. See Foot et al. (1979); Bank (1980).
21. See Bank (1980); MPCC; Gowland (1977a).
22. See e.g. Davenport (1980).
23. The results of the relevant research (by Spencer) can be seen in Treasury (1980).
24. For a more extended account, see Gowland (1981).
25. See Bank (1980), p. 12.
26. See Gowland (1981).

4 TECHNIQUES OF CONTROL III

In this chapter I propose to set out those forms of control not considered earlier and then present some possible criteria of choice between all the possible modus operandi of control.

4.1 Other Techniques of Control

There are various other forms of control which have not yet been considered.

(m) 'Regulation Q'.

(n) A tax on banking.

(p) Licensing.

(q) '100 per cent' reserve ratio 'banking'.

(r) Restricting bank competition.

Some of these are included for the sake of completeness or intellectual interest. Only (m) can be considered at all likely to be introduced by any authority.

4.1.1 'Regulation Q'

This technique takes its name from the (US) Federal Reserve Regulation which bears this name. It consists of restricting the rate of interest paid by banks on deposits (usually only on small deposits). It has had a long and chequered career in the US, normally being used by Democratic administrations and abolished (or not used) by Republican ones. The forbidding in the US of the payment of interest on current accounts is similar to Regulation Q in effect. It was an 'escape clause' of 'competition and credit control' in the UK and was used in 1973. It has survived in the US despite both academic criticism and official condemnation by the Hunt Commission, but is now due to be phased out in 1986.[1]

The policy is a combination of a price effect (2.4.1) and a quantity control (2.4.2) on deposits. It is normally imposed to protect building societies and SLAs so as to keep mortgage rates down by inhibiting bank competition. It is impossible to defend the control. On ethical grounds state-imposed price discrimination in favour of the wealthy is outrageous. On both ethical and Paretian grounds it is clear that if governments wish to subsidise mortgages they should do so overtly and not at the expense of small savers. The restriction on competition encourages inefficiency. Finally, the control is very easy to evade. This can be done by parcelling small deposits into large ones or booking the deposits abroad: for example, a transaction where it is agreed in Pittsburg that X will be credited with a deposit in the London branch of the same bank. Parcelling small deposits has produced the money market fund in the US. Evasion by foreign deposits contributed to the growth of the Eurocurrency market.[2] In both cases the result has been to make US monetary policy much harder to operate. Of all controls, this one is the most unfair, least effective and most disastrous in its effects.

4.1.2 A Tax on Banking

A classic method of reducing the output of an industry is to tax it. A tax could be placed on banking so as to reduce its output, money. The modus operandi would be to force deposit and loan interest rates further apart so as to reduce the supply of deposits to and demand for loans from banks. The idea is interesting in principle.[3] However, it would (rightly) seem to be very unfair to banks and in addition could work only if the authorities were able to define the term 'bank'. The dangers of evasion, inefficiency and the distortion of official statistics would be considerable.

Moreover, a direct tax on banks has many disadvantages compared to the effective tax of the reserve base system. The UK government introduced a tax on banks in 1981 but this was retrospective, calculated on past deposits, and so invariant at the margin.

4.1.3 Licensing

Licensing has a very proper role to play in the prudential control of banks. In principle, one could use it for monetary control. Restricting the number of banks would presumably reduce the quantity of deposits, but evasion would be massive, both by licensed banks doing more business and by new institutions and new payments mechanisms. A variation of licensing is some sort of 'negotiable entitlement' system of the sort analysed by the Bank of England.[4] In practice, this sort of scheme is a special case of a reserve base system.[5]

4.1.4 '100 per cent Reserve Ratio Banking'

This is a traditional 'Chicago School' proposal, mainly associated with (the Chicago-born) Simon. It was at one time espoused by Friedman,[6] and is a proposal to abolish banking as it is conventionally practised since no institution could both accept deposits and make loans to the private sector. Thus money creation by banks would become impossible. This and the closely related social-credit doctrines of Douglas are mainly historical curiosities. It is impossible to assess the effect of the policy because the change in institutional structure would be so great that any predictions would be impossible.

4.1.5 Monopoly Banking

A monopolist restricts output to increase profit as every elementary textbook proves. Therefore monopoly banks would restrict output (money). This argument is almost faultless although it relates to the level of the money supply not its growth. There are other arguments against banking competition, notably that they make bank failure more likely and direct controls harder to enforce.[7] However, it is virtually impossible to prevent any competition; direct controls to do so would be evaded. Cagan has pointed out that monopoly banks could profitably *cause* inflation by expansion of the money supply.[8] This 'technique' is mainly of importance in emphasising the importance of structural factors for monetary policy-makers.

4.2 The Criteria of Choice

Altogether, 15 methods of controlling the money supply have now been analysed, and there are many variants of each so the total number of methods is very large. As the authorities can combine any number of techniques of control into regimes of monetary policy, there are an almost infinite number of possible regimes of control. As nearly all the techniques have some merits and some demerits, the range of regimes which have some merit is considerable. (More technically, only a small proportion of the set of possible regimes is dominated by one or more other regimes.) The number of possible criteria for selecting a regime is also considerable. Nevertheless some (partially overlapping) criteria stand out. These are discussed below, as a series of questions.

4.2.1 Why is Money to be Controlled?

It is a standard feature of economics that the answer to any question is 'it depends on the objectives'. Indeed it is so common as to be a joke. Nevertheless it can be a useful answer. In some cases the method of control may negate the principal or a secondary objective of monetary policy. For example, the purpose of monetary control may be to maintain a 'healthy' balance of payments, to quote one statement of the objectives of monetary policy.[9] In this case, any reliance on manipulating the overseas impact on the money supply would be counterproductive. Similarly, some governments have switched to monetary policy to avoid frequent changes of fiscal policy, or because spending and taxation cannot easily be changed, as in Italy and the USA. Here, varying the PSBR would not be a feasible or desirable technique. In general the means must be consistent with the end. Moreover, the techniques should not interfere with whatever other objectives governments may have, such as efficiency and income distribution.

4.2.2 What is the Transmission Mechanism of Monetary Policy?

Hume said that it did not matter how monetary factors worked, because, like underground streams, they might have effects through any of 100 channels but the final result would be the same. Naive, black-box monetarists have argued that transmission mechanisms are irrelevant. In general this view is unacceptable; even in Hume's metaphor it matters where the water reaches the surface. In particular, the technique chosen must not be such as to interfere with the transmission mechanism appropriate to the economy concerned. If monetary policy influences behaviour through credit availability, then the implications are clear — similarly if the mechanism is through interest rates. The means must not be self-contradictory.

4.2.3 Over What Period is Money to be Controlled?

Friedmanite monetarists wish to maintain a stable rate of monetary growth. Pragmatic monetarists wish to vary it from year to year, like Volcker, Chairman of the US Federal Reserve system. Some authorities do not mind about large fluctuations away from targets over the short run; others do. There are thus four possible approaches that may be adopted. Each one would require a different package of techniques of monetary control; for example, the PSBR is most suited to long-run targets when month-to-month variations do not matter.

4.2.4 What is the Definition of Money?

Some techniques are much more appropriate to some definitions than others. In particular the asset-side techniques are more appropriate to broader definitions of money. In addition, the technique must not make the target variable meaningless (see Introduction, p. 4).

4.2.5 What is the Institutional Structure of the Economy?

The effectiveness of different techniques depends considerably upon the structure of the economy. For example, the wider the range of financial institutions, the harder it is to make direct controls operate, and the less effective a reserve base system is. It is also true that political tradition is interrelated with this factor, so that in Germany, for example, it is easier to make controls work because it is more clear what a bank is and because punishment is more acceptable for breach of regulations.

4.2.6 What is the Government's Ideology?

In the choice of technique, ideological preference is likely to be decisive. For example, a laissez-faire government which believes in a market economy will dislike direct controls and like the idea of selling off public sector assets as ways of reducing monetary growth.

In brief, techniques should be chosen so as to be effective both in maintaining monetary control and in helping to achieve all the objectives of economic policy.

References

1. For the academic analysis, see Tobin (1970).
2. See Gowland (1979), Ch. 3.
3. See Gowland (1981).
4. See Bank (1980), p. 28.
5. See Turner (1979) and Gowland (1981).
6. See Friedman (1956).
7. See MPCC, Ch. 6.
8. See Cagan (1972).
9. See 1976 Budget Speech.

5 THE NEW APPROACH

5.1 The Road to the 'New Approach': Monetary Policy in the UK 1952-71

The 'new approach' to 'competition and credit control', introduced in 1971, was an attempt to apply the lessons of history so as to produce a scheme of monetary control which was both operationally feasible and as immune to criticism as possible. Failure to appreciate this point in 1971 led to much misunderstanding of the 'new approach', especially by the press. The scheme was wrongly presented as representing the conversion of the Bank to monetarism. Equally inaccurately, it was presented as another application of the market principles of the newly elected (1970) Heath government then in its 'Selsdon man' phase, when, for example, it introduced museum charges.

The experience to which 'competition and credit control' was a response had been acquired over a period of 20 years. The relevant starting point of this history is the late 1940s, when informed commentators on both sides of the Atlantic gave an ever-increasing role to monetary and financial policy in their analysis of economic developments – the first 'new monetarism'. Criticism focused on Dalton's cheap money policy and, in the US, on the 'Fed.-Treasury Accord'. Both these policies consisted of (largely successful) attempts to peg interest rates at an artificially low level by unlimited support operations. A likely consequence of such operations was massive monetary expansion, since the authorities were, in effect, committed to carrying out expansionary open-market operations regardless of their monetary consequences. In any case the policies meant that the whole of the public sector debt was a very liquid asset (irrespective of its notional maturity structure) since holders knew they could always sell at a price equivalent to that then prevailing. For these reasons it was argued that this policy was inflationary and a prime cause of the then unprecedented 'great inflation'.[1]

In 1951 these criticisms were heeded: in the US the 'Accord' was brought to an end, and in the UK Bank Rate was raised for the first time since 1932 (except for a quickly reversed increase on the outbreak of war). This was part of the incoming Conservative government's policy of 'setting the people free' by replacing rationing and other direct controls by a less dirigiste system of demand management.

This raising of Bank Rate was of both symbolic and practical significance. It was symbolic of a new active financial policy, although the direct impact of higher interest rates is harder to judge. The change in interest rates was quickly followed by the imposition of hire purchase controls, on 29 January 1952.[2] These introduced a minimum deposit and a maximum repayment period. Such controls were to be one of the major weapons of financial policy for the next 20 years. HP controls were usually accompanied by other direct controls on credit, especially on bank advances. The other wing of the new policy was frequent variations in Bank Rate. With a half exception in 1957, interest rates were normally raised for overseas rather than domestic reasons – the idea being to induce a capital inflow by the higher interest rate; this policy was theoretically justified by Mundell and has been analysed by Hutton, whose results cast doubt on its effectiveness.[3] It was regarded as a 'credit policy' rather than a 'monetary policy', though it obviously had effects on the money supply.

In 1955 this policy was put to its first serious test, when at the height of a boom the authorities pursued a bizarre combination of an easy fiscal policy (notably by cutting income tax by 6d in April) and a tight credit policy (directives to banks to restrict lending and HP controls). The credit restraint was intended to offset the effects of the easy fiscal policy. As one commentator put it, 'Having only recently rediscovered monetary policy, the Bank of England and Treasury officials overestimated the extent to which this could cancel out the effects of a budget handout.'[4] In addition, the cynic could not fail to observe the juxtaposition of the tax cuts (19 April) and the general election (26 May). Brittan attributes about half of the responsibility to electioneering and the rest to a miscalculation of the impact of monetary policy. Predictably the official policy led to massive overheating of the economy and so in the autumn the authorities were forced to reverse their April Budget, taking comfort no doubt from their newly tripled majority in the House of Commons. Whatever the official motives, their policy had, and was seen to have, failed. The effect was to damage the image of 'the resources of a flexible monetary policy' (to quote Butler's Budget speech of April 1955). It is remarkable how long-lasting was the impact of these events. The image of monetary policy was seriously damaged and it became conventional wisdom that it was ineffective.

Distaste for and dislike of 'monetary policy' was reinforced by the unpopularity of the 1956-8 credit squeeze, especially in business circles. This led the authorities to set up the 'Committee on the Workings of the Monetary System', whose report (known after its Chairman as the

Radcliffe Report) appeared in 1959.[5] The Radcliffe Report was regarded as putting the capstone on the view that monetary policy was ineffective. This is not the only possible interpretation of the report, which took a generally 'Tobinesque' approach to monetary policy, stressing a very chimerical concept called 'liquidity'. In so far as this was defined it was a weighted average of all assets in the economy with weights declining as assets became less liquid. However, this aggregate should in turn be multiplied by a variable representing market sentiment. This variable was the real money supply, the 'M' of the quantity theory. The Radcliffe argument against the use of monetary policy was the impossibility of measuring money by this method as much as its ineffectiveness. Indeed some followers of Radcliffe argued that monetary policy should not be used because it was *too* powerful — and unpredictable. The propositions on portfolio movements in the report are very Tobinesque.

The Radcliffe Report endorsed a limited but significant role for financial policy. The means of control advocated were interest rates and — *so long as capital markets remained imperfect* — direct controls on bank lending and hire purchase. The authorities could exploit the imperfections so as to have small but significant impacts on the economy. More important, direct controls would be fast-acting, whereas fiscal policy was rather ponderous. Special deposits were also recommended. Introduced in 1961, these were deposits lodged — at Treasury Bill rate — with the Bank of England by the banks and calculated as a percentage of eligible liabilities. Although bearing some superficial similarity to a variable reserve ratio, they were intended to increase the speed of the movement of assets in response to official policy and/or to restrict 'liquidity' rather than to operate as a reserve ratio scheme. This last objective was in fact ruled out in the report.[6] All three themes of the Radcliffe Report were to re-emerge in the 'new approach'.

The authorities continued to follow the general lines of the policies developed in the early 1950s. Hire purchase finance companies were asked to exercise restraint in December 1964, and the familiar controls on repayment periods and minimum deposits were actively used in 1965 as the government slithered towards the deflationary policy stance, ultimately reached in the July 1966 measures. There was a new development in the control over bank credit — explicit ceilings were imposed rather than guidance or moral persuasion. Nevertheless, it was very much the same mixture as before, even after the adoption of a DCE target in 1968 and a gesture towards monetarism with the IMF 'Letter of Intent'.[7] Thus the late 1960s saw a battery of 'ceilings', 'requests' and similar restrictions placed on bank lending. In 1971, this policy was abandoned because the authorities believed it could no longer work, if indeed it ever had, and it was replaced by the 'new approach' to competition and credit control. The authorities had become 'increasingly unhappy about the effects of operating monetary policy in this way over a prolonged period of time', as the Governor of the Bank of England expressed it in May 1971.[8]

5.2 The Effects and Effectiveness of the 'Old Approach'

The arguments which convinced the authorities to abandon the 'old approach' are those stated in section 2.4 above. The control of bank lending by quantity means, like any other direct control, may produce inefficiency and the misallocation of resources, it may be inequitable, it may be ineffective and it may prevent the optimal use of other instruments. Rightly or wrongly, the authorities believed that it had done all of these things.

The Governor very concisely summarised the argument about efficiency in 1971: 'I do not need to labour the ill effects. It is obvious that physical rationing of this kind can lead to a serious misallocation of resources, both in the economy and in the financial system and that inhibiting competition between banks can do much damage to the vigour and vitality of the entire banking system.'[9]

The inequity of the controls arose in part from their ineffectiveness and in part from their form. They discriminated very harshly against the clearing banks, who bore the brunt of the impact of the controls. The clearers found some ways of evading some parts of the controls but in general lost business to new institutions which grew up to evade the controls and to existing uncontrolled financial intermediaries.

The classic reason for the ineffectiveness of controls is the 'black-market' proposition. The Bank of England called this the problem of 'squeezing the balloon', i.e. any attempt to squeeze it merely pushed air into a different part of the balloon, as new financial markets and mechanisms arose to replace those which were controlled. There was the successive growth of 'parallel markets', which duplicated banking transactions outside the controls. These included money brokers, the inter-corporate loan market and various near-banks and banks in the secondary, tertiary and fringe banking sectors.

The controls were of two kinds: 'qualitative' and 'quantitative'. The authorities sought to control both the allocation and total of credit flows. This attempt to influence sectoral allocation led to a special problem. Assets could be 'reshuffled' so as to satisfy the form of the control without having any economic impact (as in the example below). In the implementation of these controls, the 'privileged' sector was to be allowed unlimited funds. The major forms of privileged borrowing were export credit and shipbuilding finance. The least-favoured categories of borrowing in the allocative schemes of the authorities were borrowing by the personal sector and, usually, property developers. This category was called the 'restricted' or 'non-privileged' category. Industrial borrowing was sometimes privileged, sometimes restricted and sometimes in a middle category that was neither. In the stylised example below, only two categories are shown, and the purpose of this example is to show how the form but not the substance of the control could be satisfied. Let us say that the authorities order the bank to cut non-privileged lending to 20 (in reality they restricted its growth, but the point of the example remains). The bank then exchanges 30 of non-privileged lending for 30 of the other financial institution's privileged lending. The result is shown in Table 5.1. All economically relevant magnitudes are unchanged − total of borrowing by the privileged sector (90), of borrowing by the non-privileged sector (60), of bank liabilities (100), and of the other financial institution's liabilities (50). Yet the form of the control is satisfied. The result could − and probably did − happen as a result of normal market response rather than collusion, as the bank sought alternative assets and the displaced lenders sought alternative sources of funds. The insurance companies, for example, found property companies an ever-more attractive home for funds and the banks increased their holdings of government securities.

Table 5.1: Evasion of Controls by Rearrangement of Portfolios

	Assets	Bank Liabilities	Uncontrolled financial intermediary Assets	Liabilities
Privileged lending	50		40	
Non-privileged lending	50		10	
	100	100	50	50
Privileged lending	80		10	
Non-privileged lending	20		40	
	100	100	50	50

It should be stressed that there was nothing illegal in any evasive techniques. Indeed it can be argued that duty to clients and shareholders demanded such action. The evasive devices designed to evade the quantitative controls were often known as 'disintermediation' as a bank ceased to act as an intermediary between borrower and lender. Strictly 'parallel market' implies that a new intermediary has replaced the original one and 'disintermediation' that the transaction now occurs without a middleman. However the terms tended to be used interchangeably, so the terms 'parallel market' and 'disintermediation' were used to describe the inter-corporate money market and the general use of trade credit whereby companies lent money to each other so as to evade the controls. Furthermore − and this worried the authorities still more − as new institutions continually sprang up to perform the functions of controlled ones so the range of controls, and the number of institutions covered, had to grow continually. This problem was perhaps exaggerated by the authorities, but a desire to control the whole balloon (to use their metaphor) grew as the experience of operating controls became more and more frustrating.

This experience, of course, is a classic example of how black markets develop when non-price rationing is used without adequate powers of enforcement, as analysed in Chapter 2 above. The attempts to allocate credit between sectors were, or seemed to be, as ineffective as simple microeconomic theory would suggest. The authorities had very clear ideas about who should get credit and who should not, but the general evasion blurred the distinction.

In brief, the authorities felt their tools were ineffective, and, more crucially, that the effect of the controls had so distorted the statistics that the authorities were unable to pursue a rational policy. Hence the search for an alternative, which led to 'competition and credit control'.

Whether the authorities were in fact so hamstrung is a moot point, in both senses. The impact of hire purchase controls has been analysed by Allard,[10] who found that they had a significant, if small, impact on spending. The only serious study of the impact of inter-corporate flows on monetary policy found that in the 1950s about 60 per cent of the impact of squeezes was offset by movements in trade credit.[11]

If one believes that the evasive devices were both more widely used and better developed in the 1960s, as commonsense would suggest, then indeed the controls were close to useless. The huge explosion in credit after the removal of controls in 1971 led many observers to conclude that they must have been effective − not a totally logical view.[12] It is difficult to form any conclusive views on the subject of how effective the controls were. What is important is that the authorities believed they were ineffective.

5.3 The New Approach: The Theoretical Background

In 1971 the authorities had to find a new means of controlling the
money supply, as they believed they lacked both a method of controlling credit flows and a means of measuring them. Not surprisingly, they
responded in textbook fashion. They resolved to control credit and
money by market means, that is by price, which in financial markets
meant by interest rates and by interest rates alone. As the Governor
put it:

> Basically what we have in mind is a system under which *the
> allocation of credit is primarily determined by its cost* [and in
> which] we expect to achieve our objectives through market means
> [italics in original]. [The authorities would change interest rates]
> and the resulting change in relative rates of return will then induce
> shifts in the asset portfolios of both the public and the banks.[13]

They resolved to rely on only one out of the host of available
techniques. In part this decision reflected the fact that different people
saw it as a means of achieving different objectives (5.6). In part it
reflected a conscious elimination of all the alternatives. The authorities
obviously could not use any quantity controls. They, unsurprisingly,
ruled out a reserve base system. They ruled out any direct impact on
bank deposits and decided to control money through bank assets, i.e.
the supply side. This largely reflected a view of the transmission
mechanism of monetary policy and, in part, a belief that the problems
discussed in section 2.4.1 render impossible any attempt to *directly*
influence bank liabilities by interest rates. Thus they restricted themselves to a consideration of the impact of price factors on bank assets.
The possibility of using the PSBR to influence the money supply was
rejected because the PSBR was regarded as a tool of fiscal policy and
the authorities believed the two should be independent. It then seemed
impossible that any UK government would deliberately worsen the
balance of payments. So no consideration was given to the overseas
impact as an instrument of policy, indeed it was an objective of policy.
Thus the PSBR and the overseas impact were regarded as exogenous to
monetary *policy*. They were to have a major impact on the monetary
aggregates and in creating the environment in which the authorities had
to manoeuvre, but they could not be altered to facilitate monetary
policy.

Thus there were only two techniques of control which were not rejected by the authorities — price effects on bank lending and on private sector purchases of public sector debt (2.4.3 and 2.4.5). The authorities completed their intellectual striptease by ruling out the latter (5.4). Thus, in a sentence, the 'new approach' was to control money (and credit) by means of the impact of interest rates on bank lending to the non-bank private sector.

In general, private borrowing from banks was to be controlled by interest rates and by interest rates alone (although there was an escape clause reserving the power to issue guidelines, discussed below). The modus operandi was to push up the marginal cost of banks' funds (wholesale money rates) and assume that this would compel them (as profit maximisers) to raise the cost of overdrafts (so that marginal cost still equalled marginal revenue). Banks would go on bidding for funds so long as but only as long as it was profitable to do so.

It is essential for this system that there be an elastic and stable demand for credit. So one might expect the authorities to have firm econometric or other evidence to substantiate this. It is surprising that the authorities' faith in economic theory was such that they adopted the new policy without any such evidence. Obviously, the imposition of ceilings and their effect in driving credit markets 'underground' had made estimation difficult.[14] Nevertheless, the consequence was clear. No one knew what the effect of any given change in interest rates would be on bank lending. No one knew by how much demand exceeded supply.

An increase in bank lending might be the result of

(a) an increase in demand;

(b) the satisfaction of previously frustrated demand;

(c) the re-entry into the official statistics of 'black-market' transactions.

The authorities knew neither the impact of interest rates on (a) nor the possible size of (b) and (c). Thus their problems were enormous. It must be stressed that when a previously frustrated demand for credit was satisfied this represented a genuine increase in the money supply, official comments notwithstanding.

In brief, the authorities declared their faith in the potential of changes in interest rates to influence bank lending so as to reduce the money supply. They further avowed their willingness to accept however much variability in interest rates (and whatever level) was necessary to make the policy work.

5.4 Debt Management I: The Background

There are a number of different forms of non-bank private sector lending to the public sector in the UK; Table 5.2 gives the total of each for 1971 and 1979. However, only one of these forms has been of major importance for monetary policy – gilt-edged securities, i.e. marketable government bonds. 'National Savings' are the largest of the remainder. These comprise various non-marketable securities, such as (tax-exempt) National Savings Certificates, and the National Savings Bank. During the period of the 'new approach' the Page Report termed these a social service to savers rather than a tool of monetary policy.[15] Later on, Healey used them as a minor tool of policy. Nevertheless, the variations in National Savings flows were always too small and unpredictable to be an instrument of policy. Furthermore, any attempt to market these securities aggressively would draw funds from the building societies, whom the authorities wanted to protect at all times (e.g. by 'Regulation Q'), especially during the period of the 'new approach'. Thus they did not wish to use sales of National Savings as a tool of policy and could not even if they had wanted to.

Table 5.2: Non-bank Private Sector Holdings of Public Sector Debt (£m)[a]

	1971	1980
Gilt-edged	12,264[b]	41,908[c]
National Savings	3,574	7,902
Tax Reserve Certs, Certs of Tax Dept etc.	326	821
Treasury Bills	67	126
Local Authority Debt	n.a.	13,281

Notes: a. All foreign currency loans ignored; figures to the end of March.
b. At market value.
c. At nominal value.

The next largest category comprises various forms of local authority security. These have always induced a schizophrenic attitude in the authorities. On the one hand they are a form of non-bank private sector lending to the public sector so any sale of local authority securities will reduce the money supply. Thus in the early 1950s, after 1962 (until about 1966) and in the late 1970s the local authorities were encouraged to borrow as much as they could directly. In the post-Radcliffe era, and in the period immediately before and during the 'new approach', the reverse was the case. The local authorities were encouraged to borrow from the government, via the Public Works Loan Board, and not to issue marketable or non-marketable securities. There were various reasons for this. One was that overall central control of local authorities was strengthened. The other two were reasons of monetary policy. On the one hand, local authority bond issues often caused problems for Bank of England management of the government bond market, as the two were close substitutes. This was the case even though the Bank controlled the timing of local authority issues. The other was that local authority securities were normally very short-dated so only a hard-line monetarist could regard their issue as being contractionary. Even some monetarists disagreed and felt that local authority short-term deposits should be part of the money supply. In summary, it was not clear that local authority debt sales were desirable and in any case manipulation of them for policy purposes was difficult to achieve. As with National Savings, the reappraisal in the later 1970s found a useful supportive role in monetary policy for local authority debt sales.

Non-bank purchases of Treasury Bills raised a similar issue as they were very liquid but not money. Were sales desirable to reduce the money supply or undesirable as they had no effect on private sector liquidity (and vice versa for expansionary policies)? It could even be argued that Treasury Bills were more liquid than a bank deposit of equal maturity — governments cannot go bankrupt and banks can. Thus Treasury Bill *sales* might be expansionary (at least in a Tobinesque framework)! This debate over non-bank purchases of Treasury Bills has probably been the major area where the pure monetarist-Keynesian debate has been of relevance to official policy. In any case the amount involved was too small to matter very much. The same is true of the various forms of tax reserve certificate that have been in existence over the years.

Hence debt-management policies in the UK have had to and continue to operate in the gilt-edged market.[16] There are two alternative theories of debt management. The first is the classical theory of debt management. This states that the objectives of debt management are to maximise the maturity of the debt and to minimise interest costs. If the two are in conflict the normal apparatus of microeconomic choice theory is applied to generate the optimal structure. This theory can be applied to individuals and companies without any problem. However, the implication for a government is that all debt should be money, since this is interest-free and of infinite maturity. This gives rise to the alternative theory that the objective of debt management is to secure the optimal structure of private sector portfolios, especially of money holdings, irrespective of the resultant service cost of the debt. In the UK it is clear that the second motive has predominated since the Second World War.

The authorities have sought to sell varying quantities of gilt-edged securities to the non-bank private sector to achieve the goals of financial policy. The success of this policy clearly depends on the nature of the non-bank private sector's demand function for these securities. There were two conflicting theories about this demand function. One was the 'economists' theory'. This was based on the assumption that demand curves slope downwards. The demand for bonds would be a negative function of price, i.e. a positive function of interest rates since the price of a bond is negatively related to the yield, the rate of interest. Thus the economists' theory argued that the higher the rate of interest the greater would be sales.

In contrast to the economists' theory that sales by the authorities would be a *positive* function of the *level* of interest rates, the 'cashiers' theory' argued that sales would be a *negative* function of the *change* in rates (The two theories were eventually reconciled in the 'Duke of York' theory in 1973; see section 8.2). In other words, the cashiers' theory stated that the way to increase sales was to reduce interest rates. There was a perfectly logical rationale for this (to an economist) paradoxical theory expressed by the Bank.

The Bank's first proposition was that the market is dominated by short-period maximising holders. This is certainly valid. The average turnover rate for long-term government bonds in the UK in the late 1970s exceeded 100 per cent p.a.; in other words, these bonds were held on average for about 10 months.[17] As there are some very long-term holders of gilts (the proverbial widows and orphans), by the same token there are obviously many very short-term holders, and it was, and is, quite reasonable for the Bank of England to be primarily concerned with these large (institutional) holders. If anyone is investing on a short-term basis, the bulk of his return will come from capital gains, not income. In other words, holders of gilts are more concerned about possible changes in bond price, i.e. interest rate, than about the level of interest rates. So it is reasonable to say that someone will buy bonds if and only if he expects the price to rise, i.e. rates to fall.[18]

The Bank of England theory next postulated that expectations in the bond market were extrapolative. (It is interesting to note that Keynes thought they were regressive; this was the basis of his 'normal rate of interest'.) Hence the cashiers' theory was that if rates fell (prices rose) this generated expectations of a further fall in interest rates, i.e.

of capital gains. Hence a fall in rates would generate an increase in demand, and the authorities could sell gilts in large quantities. The extra demand would also generate a fall in rates and so increase demand still more. It is clear that the authorities were right in believing that there were extrapolative expectations present in the market, although they may have been induced by the authorities' own behaviour. These expectations, it seems, would have yielded profits, at least on a daily basis,[19] but not perhaps on a monthly basis.[20]

There was one logical flaw in this theory. A rise in price would be self-perpetuating and so ultimately the authorities would have been able to sell an infinite quantity of bonds at an infinitely high price. The cashiers' theory was the classic boom psychology. However, a slight modification rescued the theory. The rise in prices would stop when there was a sterling crisis − a safe bet in the 1950s and 1960s. At this point expectations changed and the bubble was burst. It is impossible to reconcile extrapolative expectations with a rational, efficient market. However, one can argue that the authorities' behaviour was such as to violate the assumptions of a rational and efficient market. Hence the problems discussed below (8.2) in the period 1974-80 are not relevant. Extrapolative expectations were consistent with profit maximising because of the authorities' policy of 'leaning into the wind'. Leaning into the wind meant that the Bank intervened to smooth out variations in price.

This was justified on two grounds; one being the maximisation of long-run demand for bonds,[21] the other being the cashiers' theory. The authorities bought to generate the initial rise in prices. This set off a 'selling season' which continued until the sterling crisis. Then the Bank intervened and bought to slow down the fall in prices. Thus it was argued that it was only possible to sell bonds by managing the market in this fashion. This had various disadvantages; one of them being that it 'gave rise to very large speculative transactions and made the speculative management of portfolios altogether too easy'.[22] Less discretely, the Bank guaranteed large profits to anyone who wanted them, since, by smoothing, the Bank ensured that once a price movement in a given direction had started it would continue for a long period, and that the movement in the opposite direction would be equally well signalled. Thus one had ample opportunity to buy at the bottom of a bull market and sell just after the peak: profitable management of portfolios was indeed 'altogether too easy', although whether there was anything speculative about it was questionable.

Even more seriously, 'leaning into the wind' was making the whole of the public sector debt a very liquid asset. A 30-year bond is a highly liquid asset if the holder knows he can always sell it at close to the current market price.[23] Thus in 1971 the Bank felt that the only method of selling bonds to the non-bank private sector was to 'lean into the wind'. This was undesirable in that:

(a) it was self-defeating;

(b) it put the timing of gilts' sales beyond official control;

(c) it guaranteed profits — at the bank's expense — to anyone who wanted them.

5.5 Debt Management II: The 'New Approach'

The change in the gilt-edged market under the 'new approach' was if anything even more dramatic than in the credit market. 'The Bank were no longer prepared to respond to requests to buy stock outright, except in the case of stocks with less than one year to run to maturity'.[24] This exception was to permit smoothing of the effect of the maturing of a large issue.

> But any modifications to existing arrangements to be complete had to provide for the implementation of an easy monetary policy under which it might come to be appropriate for expansionary open market operations to be engaged in. For this reason, the Bank reserve the right to make outright purchases of stock at their discretion and initiative.[25]

It should perhaps be noted that the authorities retained the 'tap system' of gilt-edged sales. The authorities would fix a price at which they were prepared to sell (more or less) unlimited quantities of the 'short-tap' stock (say about four years) and of the 'long tap' stock (usually about 20 years).[26] These stocks were issued in large quantities, most of which remained with the authorities and were gradually sold later. By varying the terms of the 'tap stocks', the authorities sought both to control the volume of sales and to indicate their policy stance. Statistical research has proved unable to discover any such systematic relationships between sales and these indicators.[27] The alternative would be a 'tender' method (as used sometimes in the US, and for Treasury Bills in the UK) where the market determines the price for a quantity fixed by the authorities (p. 13).

The Bank retained their traditional method of selling Treasury Bills by tender. This system had always had one peculiar feature. This was that the Bank acted as a perfectly discriminating monopolist and creamed-off 'consumers' surplus'. All bidders were compelled to pay the price they bid, not the market-clearing price. The other major characteristic of the system was that the discount houses had agreed to 'cover the tender'. This meant that the London Discount Market Association (LDMA), acting as a cartel, had agreed to enter a syndicated bid for any volume of Treasury Bills the authorities chose to sell at each Friday's auction. 'Outside bidders' were allowed to participate. If they bid at a price higher than the LDMA syndicate, they received the quantity they had bid for at the price at which they tendered. (Lower bids received no Bills.) The percentage of the tender allocated to the LDMA varied depending on the volume of outside bidding.

This arrangement was varied by 'competition and credit control'. Under the new arrangement, the LDMA continued to 'cover the tender' by bidding for the whole amount of bills on offer but not at a common price. Thus, the percentage of bills obtained by each house would vary with its bid. There was a danger that individual members of the LDMA would receive either no bills or their full allocation. In practice, they avoided this by entering a range of bids, at various prices. They could thus guarantee that some bills would be allocated to them, but paid a higher price to do so; i.e. the yield on their Treasury Bills would be lower. Judgement became necessary to run a discount house.

In general, one can say that this ended an era for discount houses, and they had to become competitive animals to survive. They appear to have done so with great success.

Thus, to summarise, the authorities abandoned both their policy of supporting the gilt-edged market and any idea of using it as an active part of monetary policy. They also abandoned the cartel arrangement for the Treasury Bill tender.

5.6 Escape Clauses and Ambiguities

There were two escape clauses written into the 'new approach'. One was that 'the authorities would continue to provide the banks with such *qualitative* guidance as may be appropriate'. Although the authorities did not reserve the power to reintroduce quantitative guidance, this escape clause amounted to reserving the power to drop the entire system and was inconsistent with such avowals as:

> We have in fact been operating a system of bank lending ceilings
> with declared official priorities almost continuously since 1965.
> We have, however, been increasingly unhappy about the effects of
> operating monetary policy in this way over a prolonged period. In
> this audience I do not need to labour the ill effects. It is obvious
> that physical rationing of this kind can lead to serious misallocation
> of resources, both in the economy and in the financial system.[28]

The most obvious reason for this inconsistency is that the authorities
were not unanimous and that this represented a sop to those, especially
in the Treasury, who wished to see direct controls on personal lending
retained. Moreover, it was viewed as being a necessary transitional step,
while hire purchase controls remained, to maintain equity between
finance houses and banks. In addition, the Radcliffean view that direct
controls should be used so long as markets were imperfect enough to
make them effective implied in the context of the 1970s that direct
controls could be used in an emergency because they would still have a
short-term impact, even a quickly reversed one.

The other escape clause (paragraph 15) was that the Bank reserved
the right to impose limits on the interest rate paid on retail deposits to
protect building societies 'because the impact of such competition on
savings banks and building societies would need careful consideration'.[29]
This is usually known as Regulation Q, after its US equivalent, and it is
ironic that the Hunt Commission were recommending its abolition in
the US at about this time.[30]

One would not be excessively cynical in believing that this was
essentially included for political reasons and stemmed from a need to
keep mortgage rates down; the four million mortgagees are probably
the most carefully cultivated political lobby in the UK. One economic
justification is offered by the slow speed of adjustment of building
societies' rates (like those of SLAs in the USA).

It does, however, seem iniquitous by any standards to make the
holders of small bank deposits pay for the government's desire to
subsidise those buying homes while allowing larger holders to receive
the market rate. To the Bank's credit, this piece of outrageous political
expediency would, they hoped, be temporary and never used: 'the need
for such limits would be open to reconsideration in the light of changed
circumstances' — which means to those who specialise in Bankology,
'We hope to drop it.'[31]

There were ambiguities about the 'new approach', since the
authorities never made it clear whether they wished to control M_3 for

its own sake or because it entailed controlling other variables, i.e. whether it was a target or an indicator, or what it indicated. It was never clear whether the authorities thought they were running a credit or a monetary policy. This intellectual confusion was probably a major political bonus in rallying support for the 'new approach'.

There were at least five different reasons why those involved were attracted by the scheme. It appealed to those who sought to control

(1) nothing. It was very unpleasant to have had to administer discriminatory controls in the late 1960s, especially as they penalised the clearing banks so much. Thus, many in the Bank wanted to get rid of controls at almost any price.

(2) money. Some neo-monetarists were happy in that M_3 was a definition of the money supply.

(3) credit. As someone put it, M_3 was 'the whole balloon'. In the USA M_3 is called the credit proxy and is regarded as a measure of credit not money.

(4) liquidity. It was thought that at last a measure of Radcliffean liquidity had been found. M_3, so long as it was controlled by market means, would accurately measure this rather chimerical concept.

(5) DCE. The only important difference between DCE and the change in M_3 is the overseas impact on the money supply (2.5). DCE had become part of the UK scene after Jenkins' two letters of intent in the 1960s. Those who wanted to control DCE were happy to control its first cousin.[32]

Thus everyone was happy with M_3 as target (or indicator), for a variety of reasons.

5.7 Special Deposits and Reserve Ratios

No mention has been made so far in this chapter of the 'reserve ratios' that were introduced as a part of the 'new approach'. They have deliberately been left until last because they were only a very minor part of the 'new approach'. Despite a superficial resemblance to a variable reserve ratio on the US model, the ratios did not and were not intended to operate as a reserve base/minimum reserve ratio system like the textbook model discussed above (2.6). This point was made above but it cannot be emphasised too strongly. The UK has never had a reserve ratio of the textbook variety. In particular, there was never any intention of operating the *competition and credit control* ratios in this way. Instead, the ratios were designed to strengthen the authorities' control over interest rates and to speed up the asset movements caused by interest rate changes. Special Deposits had a similar role. The Governor of the Bank was very explicit on this point in 1971.

> It is not to be expected that the mechanism of minimum reserve ratio and Special Deposits can be used to achieve some precise multiple contraction or expansion of bank assets. Rather the intention is to use our control over liquidity, which these instruments will reinforce, to influence the structure of interest rates. The resulting change in relative rates of returns will then induce shifts in the current portfolios of both the public and the banks.[33]

In 1980, the point was made again by the authorities in the Consultation Document.[34]

There were originally two ratios: a 12½ per cent uniform minimum reserve ratio for banks and a 50 per cent public sector lending ratio for discount houses. Given their objectives, the authorities consciously ignored the basic rules of a textbook system:

(a) define the reserve asset tightly;

(b) be the sole source of issue;

(c) police it carefully.

They defined reserve assets as a ragbag collection. (See Chapter 3 for a comparison with the US or West German system.) Many of the assets were liabilities of the private sector, not of the authorities. Enormous loopholes were left such that the banks could create an extra £10,000m of reserve assets in 1972 (i.e. enough to expand M_3 by 320 per cent if the textbook 8:1 ratio held). These loopholes are discussed below. No figures were available of the size of potential reserve assets. Furthermore, and very crucially, the ratios were set as near to average levels in the past as possible; they were not designed to be a 'portfolio constraint', as are the textbook ratios.

The banks were asked to maintain a sum equal to 12½ per cent of their eligible liabilities in 'eligible reserve assets'. Eligible liabilities were deposits in sterling, net of inter-bank items, with initially less than two years to maturity. Reserve assets – described above as a 'ragbag' – comprised

> balances with the Bank of England (other than Special Deposits), British government and Northern Ireland government Treasury Bills, company tax reserve certificates, money at call with the London

money market, British government stocks with one year or less to final maturity, local authority bills eligible for rediscount at the Bank of England and (up to a maximum of 2 per cent of eligible liabilities) commercial bills eligible for rediscount at the Bank of England.

Eligible money at call with the London money market will comprise funds placed with members of the London Discount Market Association, with certain other firms carrying on an essentially similar type of business (the discount brokers and the money trading departments of certain banks traditionally undertaking such business) and with certain firms through whom the banks finance the gilt-edged market, namely the money brokers and jobbers. In order to constitute an eligible reserve asset, funds placed with these firms must be at call (or callable, if not explicitly at call) and must be secured (in the case of the jobbers, on gilt-edged securities).[35]

Later the definition was changed marginally.[36] It should be noted that cash was never a reserve asset. It should also be noted that the definition was ambiguous in some respects. This did not matter, given the authorities' objectives, but makes any attempt to apply 'multiplier analysis' impossible.[37]

The discount houses were asked to keep 50 per cent of their borrowed funds in 'specified categories of public sector debt' – there were some minor categories of public sector debt that did not qualify, notably local authority bonds with more than five years to maturity. In 1973, this ratio was abandoned. Instead, discount houses were required to maintain two new ratios. One imposed a maximum on gross assets to own capital, the other on 'unidentified' (private sector) assets to own capital. These were mainly imposed for prudential reasons. The differential treatment of banks and discount houses was responsible for some of the 'loopholes' in the reserve assets scheme. The discount houses had a 50 per cent public sector lending ratio to total liabilities in which call and callable money were included. So if a bank exchanged £100 of Treasury Bills and £100 of its liabilities (say a Certificate of Deposit) for £200 of call money, the discount houses' reserve ratio was satisfied while the Bank's reserve ratio rose. As shown in Table 5.3, the reserve ratio of both parties could increase. The transaction was, of course, only possible so long as the discount house trusted the bank not to 'call' the call money. In Table 5.3 neither party satisfies the ratio. If the next day is a banking Wednesday, the minima must be observed, so the bank exchanges £5m Treasury Bills and £3m of its CDs for £8m call money. Now the position in Table 5.3 ensues and the regulations are satisfied.

Table 5.3

Bank Assets		Liabilities	(£m)
Reserve Assets	10	Eligible liabilities	100
(of which Treasury Bills 5)			
Non-reserve assets	95	Non-eligible liabilities	5
	105		105
		Reserve Asset Ratio 10 per cent	
Discount House Assets		Liabilities	
Public lending	24	Own capital	5
Private lending	26	Call money	45
	50		50
		PSLR = 48 per cent	
Bank			(£m)
Reserve assets	13	Eligible liabilities	103
(+ 8 call money − 5 Treasury Bills)			
Non-reserve assets	95	Non-eligible liabilities	5
	108		108
		Reserve Asset Ratio 12.62 per cent	
Discount House			
Public lending	29	Own capital	5
(+ 5 TB)			
Private lending	29	Call money	53
(+ 3 CDs)	58		58
		PSLR = 50 per cent	

The Bank had recognised the danger of 'transactions' designed to substitute 'window-dressing' arrangements for genuine observance of the minimum reserve ratio,[38] but in the technical sense these transactions are not window-dressing since they represent a legitimate commercial transaction for both sides.

Later,[39] after the discount houses' ratio was replaced by the two gross asset ratios, a CD/call money swap was all that was necessary to create reserve assets.

Other loopholes were even simpler. A bank could exchange 1-5-year gilts for a discount house's gilts with less than one year to maturity, or exchange local authority bonds for bills with the relevant local authority. Local authority loopholes became of increasing importance later. Local authority overdrafts could also be replaced by bills. A very small reduction in the interest rates they paid was sufficient to induce local authority finance directors to acquiesce in the manufacture of reserve assets. (Indeed one can argue that the District Auditors' Act 1906 compels them to acquiesce.)

At this stage, the reader may be tempted to ask, 'Why did the authorities bother with reserve ratios?' After all, he or she might legitimately argue that the authorities have other tools to control short-term interest rates. The answer is that the functions of the ratios were minor but not insignificant. If the speed of response were increased, this was, obviously, of major assistance to the operation of monetary policy. It is not clear how much Special Deposit calls did achieve this. Casual empiricism, like economic theory, suggests that it was not much, while whenever the ratios threatened to be effective the authorities, as in June 1972, had to intervene. In 1980 the authorities expressed similar scepticism in the Green Paper.

The ratios did, however, provide some support for the market in public sector debt — banks were less likely to dump gilt-edged stock to try to meet an unexpected call for funds. This actually slowed down the movement of interest rates, i.e. worked against the authorities' wishes. Nevertheless, by always inducing banks to respond to short-term or unexpected cash-flow problems by borrowing in the overnight inter-bank market — a major operating area of policy — the authorities made their task easier.

5.8 The New Approach: A Summary

The 'new approach' to 'competition and credit control' was a decision to rely solely on one means of controlling financial aggregates. The new modus operandi was to induce a change in the interest rate charged by banks on their loans to the non-bank private sector. A higher interest rate would reduce the demand for bank credit. Thus the growth of M_3 would be restrained. M_3, the principal monetary aggregate in the authorities' view, was regarded by them as a measure of credit and liquidity as much as a measure of monetary growth. In fact the Bank was very careful to avoid the term money supply altogether. Supply had very unwelcome overtones; it implied a supplier. The Bank was very anxious not to be regarded as a supplier of money. They were even more anxious to deny that it was their sole or even major function.[40]

As part of the 'new approach', the Bank abandoned several of its traditional policies. These included 'leaning into the wind', the support of gilts' prices and the cartel arrangement for the Treasury Bill tender. Less ancient policies were also dropped, in particular ceilings on bank lending. Hence there was quite a lot that was new about the 'new approach'. Further changes were to follow, e.g. the replacement of Bank Rate by MLR in 1972.

Nevertheless, the authorities had not abandoned their adherence to the Keynesian fine-tuning basic approach to economic management, pace Barber's Budget speeches. Nor had they abandoned their belief that monetary and fiscal policy were independent of each other.

Appendix: Principal Events and Data 1952-71

Principal Events[41]

1951 R.A. Butler becomes Chancellor. Re-emergence of monetary policy.

1955 (19 April) R.A. Butler reduces taxes and relies 'on the resources of a flexible monetary policy to counter an over expansion of demand'.

(27 October) Taxes raised.

1957 (April) Radcliffe Committee established.

1958 (19 June) Special Deposits announced.

1959 (20 August) Final Report of Radcliffe Committee.

1960 (28 April) 1st Call for Special Deposits.

1965 (5 May) Reimposition of ceilings on bank lending — the control remains in force until 1971.

1967 (23 November) 1st Letter of Intent with IMF following devaluation of 17 November 1967.

1969 (22 May) 2nd Letter of Intent, including DCE Target.

1971 (14 April) Publication of 'Competition and Credit Control' following de facto abolition of ceilings in budget.

Data 1964-70

	Inflation (% p.a.)	Balance of payments (current account)	Real GDP (% growth p.a.)	Unemployment (%)	M_1[a] (% growth)	M_3[a]
1964	3.3	−355	5.9	1.7	6.8	7.3
1965	4.8	−27	2.8	1.4	3.1	5.9
1966	3.9	100	1.8	1.5	5.8	9.3
1967	2.5	−301	2.7	2.3	0.6	3.6
1968	4.7	−275	3.7	2.4	6.5	9.3
1969	5.4	+462	1.7	2.4	2.4	7.6
1970	6.4	735	2.2	2.6	1.7	2.4

Note: a. Financial year 1963/4 etc.

References

1. E.g. in Schwartz (1959), a collection of reports from the *Sunday Times* originally published in the late 1940s and early 1950s; and Brown (1955).

2. See MPCC, p. 22 n6 for details of the controls.

3. See Hutton (1977); Mundell (1968).

4. From Brittan (1965).

5. See Radcliffe (1959).

6. E.g. para. 508 of Radcliffe (1959).

7. There were two Letters of Intent, 23 November 1967 and 22 May 1969. They are most easily accessible in Wadsworth (1972).

8. From Key Issues in Monetary and Credit Policy: Text of an Address by the Governor to the International Banking Conference on 25 May 1971 in Bank (1971), p. 7. (Hereafter the speech is abbreviated to Key Issues.)

9. Ibid., p. 8.

10. See Allard (1974).

11. See Brechling and Lipsey (1974).

12. E.g. Deputy Governor's Speech, Does the Money Supply Really Matter? (11 April 1973) in *Bulletin*, vol. 13, no. 2 (June).

13. Key Issues in Bank (1971), pp. 8-9.

14. See Moore and Threadgold (1980).

15. See Page (1973).

16. On debt management see Johnson (1974), especially article by Goodhart; Gowland (1977b); and Courakis (1973).

17. See Gowland (1977b).

18. See Goodhart's and Norton's papers in Johnson (1974).

19. See Gowland (1975a).

20. Goodhart and Gowland (1977) and (1978).

21. See Section VI of Johnson (1974), especially heading 23; and Courakis (1973).

22. Chief Cashier's Sykes Lecture in Bank (1971).

23. Liquidity being defined in terms of (a) how quickly, (b) at what cost and (c) with what degree of certainty about the price an asset can be converted into purchasing power. Money is by definition perfectly liquid. Given the low transaction costs and same-day settlement, gilts were highly liquid on all three counts.

24. *Bulletin*, vol. 11, no. 2 (June 1971), p. 151.

25. From Competition and Credit Control reprinted in Bank (1971).

26. For the tap system see *Bulletin*, vol. 19, no. 2 (June 1979), p. 132.

27. See Goodhart and Gowland (1978).

28. From Key Issues in Bank (1971), p. 9.

29. See Bank (1971), p. 3.

30. For a summary and critique of the report see the documentation prepared for the Home Ways and Means Committee, US government official publication, 6263.

31. See Bank (1971), p. 5.

32. Letters of Intent, see n7 above. Until 1970, the difference between DCE and the growth in M_3 was usually much smaller than since 1971.

33. Key Issues in Bank (1971), p. 10.

34. See Bank (1980), especially Appendix 2.

35. See Reserve Ratio and Special Deposits in Bank (1971), p. 13.

36. Competition and Credit Control: Further Developments in *Bulletin*, vol. 13, no. 1 (March 1973), p. 53.

37. For analyses of the Discount market see Parkin (1970) and Alford (1968).

38. From Competition and Credit Control reprinted in Bank (1971), p. 17.

39. Competition and Credit Control: Modified Arrangements for the Discount Market in *Bulletin*, vol. 13, no. 3 (September 1973), p. 300.

40. See the declarations of policy, p. 199.

41. A full chronology appears in MPCC, pp. 177-85.

6 THE HISTORY OF COMPETITION AND CREDIT CONTROL

One can divide the period of the operation of the new approach into four distinct phases, although precise dating is not possible. In the first phase, from May 1971, the accent was on easy credit in order to try to reduce unemployment. This lasted until the sterling crisis of June 1972. From June 1972 until October 1972 there was an interim phase while the authorities reviewed the position. From October 1972 onwards, they 'willed the end but feared the means', and tried to control credit and money without increasing interest rates. In July 1973 the authorities accepted the consequences of their own system and raised Minimum Lending Rate (MLR) by 4 per cent in two weeks, to an unprecedented 11½ per cent. From July to December 1973 the competition and credit control regime was operated in something like its intended fashion, but in December the new approach was replaced by a new 'new approach'. This new regime and its workings are discussed in Chapter 8. In this chapter the four phases are examined in turn.

6.1 The Era of Easy Credit, May 1971-June 1972

In May 1971 the authorities produced their first draft of the new scheme,[1] and on 17 May introduced one of its key elements by ceasing to support the market in gilt-edged securities, except for stocks with less than a year to maturity. 'Purchases of longer-dated stocks will in future be made only at the Bank's discretion and initiative.'[2] On 28 May the Governor's address laid down the main features of and philosophy underlying the new system, so it seems reasonable to date the new regime from May rather than its formal implementation in September, even though both general and specific guidelines on credit remained in force. Growth of 2½ per cent in restricted lending was permitted in the quarter ending in June so the guidelines had little impact in this period.

The Chancellor of the Exchequer had explained in his Budget speech that his overriding policy aim was to reduce unemployment, and that consequently he would cut taxes further and make no effort to reduce 'the rate of increase in the stock of money . . . until inflation abated'.[3] (Or less discretely, the government would adopt a passive monetary policy in so far as this was necessary to accommodate inflation and an actively expansionary one to reduce unemployment.) In the first half of the year, the money stock (M_3) rose by over 5 per cent, partly the result of a large capital inflow (or the authorities' failure to 'sterilise' this) and partly of large borrowing by local authorities. The private sector increased its borrowing by over £100m or about 13 per cent.

On 19 July, the Chancellor introduced a new package designed to stimulate demand, including heavy cuts in indirect taxation and the end of credit controls. The indirect tax cuts and an associated nationalised industry price restraint policy were designed to complement the CBI's policy of restricting price increases in private industry to 5 per cent p.a. for the year to July 1972, i.e. for *one* year only. The aim was to reduce inflation directly — to be mischievous — 'at a stroke' and to persuade unions to moderate their wage claims and so, indirectly, reduce the inflation rate. The consequences were to be disastrous for the size of the public sector borrowing requirement and for monetary policy. It seems that on this point the monetarist analysis is incontrovertible. The monetary expansion caused by buying down the retail price index exceeded any cost-deflationary gain.

In the third quarter, the money supply (M_3) rose by 2.4 per cent. Large borrowing by the private sector (£604m) and a growing public sector borrowing requirement (£355m) were partly offset by large sales of gilt-edged securities to the non-bank private sector, amounting to £513m.[4] In September, the Bank repaid £395m of Special Deposits and in exchange forced the London clearing banks to subscribe £750m of three new government stocks (5¼ per cent Treasury stock in 1973, 5½ per cent in 1974 and 6¼ per cent in 1977) as envisaged in May.[5] This closely followed the parallel of 1952 when the authorities had repaid a precursor of Special Deposits, known as Treasury deposit receipts. It is difficult to know whether this was intended to be a purely technical operation to slow down the impact of the repayment of Special Deposits. However, this was all it was in practice, as the banks only held the stock until the second quarter of 1972, when the banks sold large quantities to permit extra lending to the private sector. At least this was the effect from each bank's point of view. At an aggregate level, of course, the total of bank assets rose by the full amount of the extra lending (assuming that whoever bought gilts from the banks would have otherwise purchased them from the Bank).

During this period interest rates fell steadily. The Treasury Bill allotment rate was 6.77 per cent at the beginning of the year, 5.68 per cent on 30 April and 5.54 per cent on 16 July. The rate then rose for technical reasons in August but fell to 4.92 per cent on 3 September, after Bank Rate had been reduced to 5 per cent on 2 September from 6 per cent (its level since 30 April). This was one of the last agreed tenders by the discount houses acting as a cartel. Under the new arrangement (see Chapter 5) the rate fell to 4.72 per cent by the end of September and 4.28 per cent by the end of November, but then rose slightly and finished the year at 4.41 per cent.

In the fourth quarter there was a sharp acceleration in the growth of the money supply (to 4.4 per cent). The figure originally published showed an even larger acceleration − to 5¾ per cent. The initial published figure is relevant as well as the later revised figure, as the authorities' actions should be judged in the light of the information then available. This consideration reinforces the argument that the authorities should have acted. Similarly the original figures showed bank lending to the private sector rising to nearly £800m, but later revisions reduced this to £588m. Very large sales of gilts to the non-bank private sector (£410m), and total purchases of public sector securities of £576m, still left a substantial proportion of the PSBR to be financed by the banks (£891m).

The authorities' reaction to this development would obviously be crucial. It is difficult not to believe that this was the period when the authorities lost control of the situation. The authorities were so worried about unemployment that they decided not to act, in fact to encourage the monetary trends. This was partly a reflection of the attitude (which might not unfairly be termed panic) towards unemployment. However, it must be stressed that there was general support in the City and the media for the policy − one prominent gilt-brokers' circular argued that monetary conditions were too tight and further relaxations should be implemented (by large purchases of gilts from the non-bank private sector and cuts in interest rates). Furthermore, the Bank of England's demand for money equations apparently suggested that very high growth in money supply was necessary. The article which emphasised this appeared in March 1972[6] − 'an apparently rapid rate of monetary expansion might actually be restrictive in its effect when associated with a strong increase in output', as the Chancellor both hoped and forecast in his Budget speech. Later research in the Bank significantly changed the coefficients in the equations on which this conclusion rested.[7]

'Barberism' reached its apogee with the 1972 Budget.[8] Despite (or because of?) the government's defeat in the miners' strike of early 1972, the Chancellor cut taxation by £1,200m and expected to increase the PSBR by 200 per cent to £3,360 million. This swing occurred despite his forecast of high growth (5 per cent p.a.) which meant that the constant employment budget deficit rose still more (not that the UK authorities used this concept). This reflected the aim of reducing unemployment (then 3.8 per cent) at almost any price. The authorities also believed that increasing real take-home pay by tax cuts would buy off union militancy. Incomes policy was still, apparently, ruled out on ideological grounds and as contrary to election pledges.

The Budget also included a provision to allow interest on loans to be offset against tax (restoring the pre-1969 position) so long as the interest charge exceeded £35. This cut the cost of borrowing for persons by the amount of their marginal tax rate — about one third for standard ratepayers and by up to 95 per cent for very high rate tax-payers. It is not clear whether the likely effect of this on the demand for credit was considered — certainly it is not mentioned in any official statement at the time. Yet it is an incredible omission in view of the emphasis in 'Competition and Credit Control' on allocation of credit by cost.

In the first quarter of 1972, the money stock rose by 4¾ per cent, largely fuelled by an increase in bank lending to the private sector of £1,610m. Inflows from abroad ceased to increase the domestic borrowing requirement (following the Smithsonian Agreement in December 1971). Sales of gilt-edged stock to the non-bank private sector were only £109m, against £726m in the same quarter of 1971 and £420m in the previous quarter. Total purchases of public sector debt by this sector were £279m, a fall of £326m on the first quarter of 1971. The other forms of public sector debt partly offset the £617m fall in sales of gilts. The increase in other public sector debt sales reflected technical factors in local authority finance. Thus the gilts' figures reflected the underlying deterioration better than the total figures. Another potentially worrying feature was that most of the new borrowing was by property and financial companies.

In the second quarter, M_3 rose by 7¾ per cent and this was even after large capital outflows in June had reduced the growth by about 2½ per cent. DCE rose by £2,110m (after £1,223m in the first quarter). The statement in the September 'Bulletin' that 'the money supply has recently been rising very fast' was a considerable understatement.[9] 'Barberism' had also been associated with a massive deterioration in the balance of payments. Virtually any theory of the exchange rate would have predicted a 'crisis' given the monetary and balance of payments consequences of the authorities' policy. Hence the authorities should not have been surprised when there was an outflow of over £1,000m in the second half of June, triggered off by a threatened dock strike. Nor should it have surprised anyone that the UK was forced to let the pound float and leave the EEC 'snake' (wherein exchange rate movements were limited to 2¼ per cent between member countries within the Smithsonian 4½ per cent band). From 23 to 27 June foreign exchange markets were closed. When they reopened sterling fell from $2.59 to $2.41 but recovered in July to $2.44, representing a 6¾ per cent devaluation on a trade-weighted basis against its Smithsonian parity.

6.2 The Reappraisal, June-October 1972

'Floating' was part of the dash-for-growth strategy (an attempt to avoid the overseas constraint which it was felt had prevented a similar Maudling experiment from succeeding in 1963-4).[10] So it would have been illogical — but not necessarily impossible — for this to have triggered off the reappraisal. The authorities certainly allowed money market rates to rise in response to overseas forces. Rates had drifted upwards in May but were still below January's level. In the second half of June, the rate on inter-bank deposits rose from 5.69 per cent to 7.75 per cent. The Treasury Bill rate similarly rose (by over 1 per cent) and Bank Rate was increased by 1 per cent to 6 per cent on 22 June.

The fact that the clearing banks needed massive support from the Bank may have worried the authorities. A sale and repurchase agreement (involving £356m of gilts) from 23 June to 14 July was necessary to enable the banks to meet their obligations. Alternatively, the banks could have either borrowed on the overnight inter-bank market, where rates here were already 200 per cent, or sold gilts with equally dramatic effects on interest rates. By any standards, the sterling outflow had precipitated a major banking crisis.

The first sign of the reappraisal was when the Governor of the Bank sent a letter to the banking system asking the banks to make credit less readily available to the property sector.[11] It had virtually no impact. Property company borrowing had risen from £447m to £1,019m in the year to August 1972. It rose to £2,094m in the next 15 months, which illustrates the ineffectiveness of the letter. Loans to 'other financial companies', many of them engaged in lending to property companies, rose to £2,737m in November 1973 (from £643m in May 1971). Furthermore, in November 1973 the authorities reclassified £600m of advances into these categories, so the total growth of bank lending to the property sector was over £4,000m in the period after the letter.

Despite the perceived need for the letter, interest rates – the policy weapon of the new system – were not used further. In fact, inter-bank rates fell until mid-September and then levelled out at about 7½ per cent. (It must be emphasised, though, that the crisis had pushed base rates up to 7 per cent.) The authorities were anxious to see that credit continued to stimulate the economy, and yet that excessive credit and money growth were restrained. Almost harking back to the 'real bills' doctrine refuted by Ricardo, they obviously wished to distinguish between speculative froth and the needs of trade. Unfortunately, this implied a wish for sectoral controls which was inconsistent with 'a system under which the allocation of credit is primarily determined by cost'.

In the third quarter, M_3 rose by 4¼ per cent, bank lending to the private sector contributing £1,108m to this, while the offset from sales of public sector debt to the non-bank private sector, £199m, was the lowest total since 1970. This may have reflected the problems of selling gilts on a falling market (p. 89) but must have worried the authorities. Certainly policy seems to have switched decisively to at least wishing to see a more restrictive stance in this period.

6.3 Willing the End but Fearing the Means? October 1972-July 1973

On 9 October the Bank announced and on 13 October implemented a new method of fixing its basic penalty rate. Bank Rate was abolished and replaced by 'Minimum Lending Rate'. At least this change in nomenclature was sensible. Only one bill had been rediscounted since the Second World War and then, it is said, because the chairman of a discount house was curious to see how the mechanism worked. The Bank lent against the security of bills at a level it determined. (The Bank could and did fix this higher than either Bank Rate or MLR.) At a policy level the change to MLR permitted an increase in the rate without the problems of announcing it too overtly at a time of tricky negotiations between government and unions.

The new rate was fixed at 7¼ per cent, i.e. a 1¼ per cent rise. This level was determined by a formula: the Treasury Bill average rate of discount plus ½ per cent rounded up to the nearest ¼ per cent. This was treated in the press as a move towards a more market-oriented formula – probably with official encouragement, though the 'Bulletin' was careful not to say this. The implicit disclaimer proved to be necessary as the authorities continued to determine the Treasury Bill rate by signals to the discount market and reserved the right to override the formula if its signals were ignored. The Treasury Bill formula offered a fig leaf to cloak policy changes. As Treasury Bills were one of the discount market's major earning assets, it was a logical basic relationship. Policy could then be implemented by lending below, at or above the MLR as seemed appropriate, and by varying it by either of the methods described above. Of these, signals were expected to be the normal method, but the override power had to be used several times, before the formula was abolished in May 1978.

The change, though of interest technically, was more important as a change in policy stance. MLR continued to rise (to 7½ per cent on 27 October, 7¾ per cent on 1 December, 8 per cent on 8 December and 9 per cent on 22 December). This eventually triggered off an increase in the banks' base rate, the key to the method of control, of ½ per cent on 15 December and further increases during January, finally reaching 8½ per cent. MLR then fell back to 8¾ per cent, but base rates rose in February to 9½ per cent.

Thus interest rates had risen by 5 per cent since June, but the tax relief meant that personal borrowing was cheaper than in March 1971. Inflationary expectations had accelerated, as the CBI and FT surveys showed, despite the standstill on pay and prices announced on 6 November. So the rise in interest rates was probably too small to rein back significantly the growth of money and credit, and was certainly too late. The official response to the acceleration in borrowing was so slow that it had taken a year to produce a change in rates, scarcely the response implied by the new approach. Calls for Special Deposits of 1 per cent announced on 9 November (which 'had no significant impact')[12] and of 2 per cent on 21 December contributed to tightness in the money market, and so helped to push up MLR as well as being interpreted as a signal of official wishes.

In the first quarter of 1973 M_3 grew by 5.8 per cent, bank lending to the private sector rose by £1,464m and the Bank acted as a net purchaser of public sector debt from the private sector. In fact the growth would have been even higher but for the large outflow from sterling which cut M_3 by £250m. Thus, judged by their own criteria of the magnitude of credit flows and asset movements, the authorities were not tightening policy. In the second quarter, growth in M_3 accelerated to 7¾ per cent using the banking month series, while on a calendar quarterly basis the increase was 5.3 per cent. By any standards this was excessive, but the discrepancy is a comment on the poor quality of official statistics and (perhaps) on the volatility of arbitrage funds, the merry-go-round discussed in Chapter 7. These problems are partly a comment on the authorities' incompetence and partly a comment on the problems they faced. In the short term policy-making was hampered by poor statistics. The solution lay in the Bank's hands. Financial statistics had been improved since Radcliffe and upgrading them had been continuous. The authorities could and should have pressed the banks to provide better figures sooner.

6.4 Competition and Credit Control in Action, July-December 1973

During the first half of 1973 interest rates had been allowed to fall. MLR had been reduced six times to 7½ per cent and bank base rates fell from their peak of 9½ per cent to 8 per cent. The authorities' policy was strange, given the developments of monetary aggregates and the rationale of competition and credit control. Declining interest rates had enabled large sales of gilt-edged securities to be made in the second quarter, but these had not offset an avalanche of private borrowing from banks. This was the immediate background to the situation facing the authorities in July 1973. On a longer-term basis, bank lending to other financial companies was 175 per cent up, to companies 85 per cent up and to persons 175 per cent up on the third quarter in 1971. Added to this, there was another sterling crisis in July — the pound depreciated by a further 5 per cent between 1 and 4 July (it fell from 89 per cent to 85 per cent of its Smithsonian effective parity). By 6 July it was down to 82 per cent and, after a recovery in the next part of July, it fell to 80.5 per cent on 26 July.

Thus it is not surprising that the authorities sharply changed their policy in July and forced MLR up by 1½ per cent on 20 July and a further 2½ per cent on 27 July, partly by a call for Special Deposits and partly by making its views clear to the market. The changed tone of official policy was very marked and clearly the authorities had accepted the need to let nominal rates rise sufficiently to achieve their goals. Unfortunately, one cannot determine whether it was in response to the pressure on sterling or to domestic developments. It is clear that both were in the authorities' minds. The kindest and most likely explanation is that the response to the immediate problems was determined by the longer-term credit and monetary environment.[13] A cynic might say that the crisis provided an excuse. The cynic with a long memory would have commented that the UK authorities had always responded, like Pavlovian dogs, with higher interest rates when there was a foreign exchange crisis.

Within the monetary policy framework of competition and credit control, the crucial development was that bank base rates rose by 3 per cent (to 11 per cent) between the beginning of July and the end of August. The immediate response of the monetary aggregates was unfavourable. Gilt-edged sales were sluggish, as might have been expected, and bank lending to the private sector continued to surge ahead, by £2,115m in the third quarter (the largest increase in the year so far). Thus M_3 rose by 7.8 per cent in the third quarter, or by 8.5 per cent if one takes the difference in the levels series, rather than the change. Another quirk, which reflects the inaccuracies of official statistics, is that there are separate, inconsistent series for levels and changes. The rise may have been reinforced by arbitrage operations, but not by so much as to change one's assessment of the position.

The authorities reacted with a Governor's letter (11 September)[14] calling for restraint in lending to persons and property companies. Lending to persons (other than for house purchase) was £1,658m in August 1972 (after £767m a year earlier). In August 1973 it was £2,346m on a comparable basis (and £2,943m on a revised basis). The other 'escape clause' in competition and credit control was also invoked − 'Regulation Q' was used to prevent the banks from paying more than 9½ per cent interest on small deposits, i.e. below £10,000. Mortgage rates nevertheless rose to 11 per cent. The rapid rise in interest rates and the use of the escape clauses suggested that competition and credit control was (at last) being used as intended.

However M_3 and bank lending continued to rise − bank lending rose by £1,000m in October alone − and further measures were taken in November when another 2 per cent of Special Deposits were called (13 November) and MLR raised to 13 per cent by the Bank using its override power (16 November). Furthermore, the clearing bank chairmen were ordered to raise loan rates to 13 per cent and complied. However in the fourth quarter M_3 grew by a further 7.3 per cent, and the authorities decided to drop the scheme. The new 'new approach' is analysed in Chapter 8, but it is clear that the authorities felt that competition and credit control had failed.

They felt that it was necessary to control money and credit for both economic and political reasons. They were also unwilling to increase interest rates, or to see their volatility increase. Thus the mechanism of competition and credit control could not be used.

Appendix: Principal Events and Data 1971-3

Principal Events[15]

1971 (10 September) Bank lending rates to be tied to their own 'base
      rate' instead of Bank Rate from 1 October.
      (18 December) Smithsonian Agreement reintroduces fixed
      exchange rates; pound had been floating since 23 August.
1972 (21 March) Expansionary budget: aims at growth in money stock
      that is 'high . . . to ensure that finance is available for the extra
      output'.
      (22 June) Sterling floated.
      (9 October) Bank Rate replaced by MLR.
      (9 November) Call for Special Deposits, first since the
      introduction of the 'new approach'.
1973 (6 March) Budget closes CD tax loophole.
      (17 December) Reintroduction of HP controls.

Financial Statistics

	M_1 (Growth %)	M_3 (−)	Bank Rate/MLR (%)	20-year Bond Rate (%)
1970/1	13.7	12.3		
1971/2	9.3	14.4		
1972/3	10.0	27.3		
1973/4	3.3	25.2		
1971 I	4.0	3.2	7.0	8.9
II	1.3	1.6	6.0	9.0
III	3.3	2.7	5.0	8.5
IV	2.2	5.3	5.0	8.1
1972 I	3.3	4.7	5.0	8.4
II	4.3	7.1	6.0	9.3
III	1.5	4.6	6.0	9.4
IV	4.0	7.2	9.0	9.8
1973 I	−0.3	5.7	8.5	10.0
II	6.7	4.7	7.5	10.2
III	−2.6	8.1	11.5	11.5
IV	2.1	6.9	13.0	12.4

Other Economic Developments

		Inflation (% p.a.)	Growth (real GDP) (% p.a.)	Unemployment (%)	Balance of Payments (£m)
1971	I	8.6	1.5	2.9	141
	II	9.8	0.8	3.3	278
	III	10.1	1.5	3.6	392
	IV	9.2	1.5	3.8	237
1972	I	8.0	1.4	4.0	120
	II	6.2	3.1	3.8	121
	III	6.5	2.1	3.7	−105
	IV	7.7	4.1	3.4	−5
1973	I	8.0	8.6	3.0	138
	II	9.3	4.6	2.7	−32
	III	9.2	4.9	2.5	−235
	IV	10.3	2.3	2.2	−347

References

1. Competition and Credit Control: text of a document issued on 14 May 1971 reprinted in Bank (1971), p. 3.

2. *Bulletin*, vol. 11, no. 2 (June 1971), p. 151.

3. *Hansard*, 30 March 1971.

4. All figures in the text are latest revisions. Initially, published figures were often very different, see MPCC, pp. 173-4 for a comparison.

5. See Bank (1971), p. 14.

6. See Bank (1972).

7. See Bank (1974).

8. *Hansard*, 21 March 1972.

9. *Bulletin*, vol. 12, no. 3 (September 1972), p. 314.

10. E.g. the enormously influential Brittan (1971) had concluded that 'A case could be made for taking a calculated risk and attempting a home based expansion provided there was an ultimate willingness to devalue.' For Brittan's later views see Brittan (1977).

11. Reprinted in *Bulletin*, vol. 12, no. 3 (September 1972), p. 327, see p. 198.

12. *Bulletin*, vol. 13, no. 1 (March 1973), p. 12.

13. 'The sharp tightening of monetary policy was most immediately occasioned by the upward trend of interest rates in foreign countries but has to be seen in the broad context of the state of the economy.' In *Bulletin*, vol. 13, no. 3 (September 1973), p. 277.

14. Reprinted in *Bulletin*, vol. 13, no. 4 (December 1973), p. 445.

15. A full chronology appears in MPCC, pp. 178-83.

7 COMPETITION AND CREDIT CONTROL: AN ANALYSIS

The most striking feature of the era of 'competition and credit control' is the explosion in monetary growth which occurred. Table 7.1 shows this enormous expansion in the growth of M_3 compared to the period before and after. M_3 grew by over 60 per cent in the 27 months of the 'new approach'. Normally such growth would be regarded as grossly excessive in any Western economy, even by non-monetarists. Nevertheless, a number of reasons were offered why it might not be excessive. These ranged from arguments that the statistics were misleading to a view that the nature of the demand for money function justified this growth. These arguments are considered in section 7.1. In section 7.2, consideration is given as to why *competition and credit control* was so unceremoniously dropped. The reasons considered include the technical deficiencies of the scheme as well as the political context at the time of the decision. Finally in this chapter, the effects of the very rapid growth in money are considered. This is done first in a neo-Keynesian framework in which the various possible transmission mechanisms are considered seriatim. These consist of the impact of the money supply on the property market, on the stock market, on inflationary expectations and on the exchange rate. Through all of these routes, as even a diehard anti-monetarist has to admit, the money supply could have increased inflation, or lowered unemployment. Finally, a more monetarist analysis of the impact is presented and considered.

Table 7.1: M_3 Growth Per Cent Per Annum

Old Approach		Transition		New 'New Approach'	
1963/4	7.3	1970/1	12.3	1974/5	10.7
1964/5	5.9	1971/2	14.4	1975/6	8.2
1965/6	9.3	New approach		1976/7	9.7
1966/7	3.6	1972/3	27.3	1977/8	14.5
1968/9	9.6	1973/4	25.2		
1969/70	2.4				

7.1 Defences of the New Approach

7.1.1 'End-Ceiling' Effects and Reintermediation

It was argued that much of the growth in M_3 reflected the effect of the end of ceilings as depositors, and borrowers strove to remove the excess demand for money and credit which had built up in the 1960s. However, one must carefully distinguish two different types of 'end-ceiling' effect. One brings back within the banking sector transactions which had occurred outside it during the era of ceilings – 'reintermediation' as the Bank called it. The other is the satisfaction of previously frustrated demand. The inflationary effects of satisfying the demand for credit are the same whether the demand has existed for one week or ten years. In fact, one of the chief arguments against rationing is that when the control is abolished steps must be taken to remove any excess demand. 'Catching up' in money and credit markets after the removal of ceilings is identical in effect to an increase in the demand for credit (or money) caused by a change in inflationary expectations, or any other factor.

The volume of reintermediation is hard to measure. One must first of all stress that disintermediation is not without economic effect. To take the simplest form of disintermediation: A lends money directly to B rather than A holding a bank deposit and B having an overdraft with the same bank. A may regard a claim on B as less liquid than one on the bank because it is less marketable or has a higher default risk. This is an economic effect of considerable significance – it is part of either a Tobinesque or Friedmanite argument for caring about banks (the money supply) or financial intermediation in general. The intermediation of a transaction obviously yields benefits to the transactors, otherwise it would not occur. These benefits probably include lower transaction costs, but they normally involve either changing the maturity structure of the claim or increasing its marketability. Most financial institutions lend longer than they borrow, thus increasing the 'liquidity' of both sides. The monetarist position stresses the importance of banks in this context, the Tobinesque one stresses that all financial institutions matter – as in Gurley and Shaw's work.[1] However both groups agree that reintermediation may have increased the liquidity, the 'moneyness' of the private sector assets involved. This could be of major significance to economic policy.

The importance of the effect depends on one's view of the transmission mechanism; it is greatest if one takes a portfolio balance approach. Thus the 'reintermediation' argument is more significant if one is an extreme 'Keynesian' arguing that credit matters, rather than money or Tobinesque 'liquidity'. It also depends on how much more liquid claims on banks are than claims on private borrowers. In some cases the change would be small, in others large.

The extent of 'reintermediation' depends on showing that some transactions were switched from one market to another, or at least that the banks' share of some markets rose. It is very difficult to do this precisely because of the poor quality of statistics. It is possible, however, to use the Bank's flow-of-funds figures to make some attempt to do this for loans to the personal sector (see Table 7.2).

Table 7.2

	1970/1 (£m)[a]	1972/3 (£m)[a]
New loans to persons by companies[b]	138 (23.9%)	100 (3.6%)
New loans to persons by OFIs[c]	269 (46.5%)	357 (12.8%)
New loans to persons by banks	171 (29.6%)	2,327 (83.8%)
	578	2,784

Notes: a. Financial years. b. Other items, which include trade credit to public corporations. c. HP lending plus 'other lending'.

It is clear from Table 7.2 that the share of banks had risen dramatically from 30 per cent to 80 per cent, comparing the financial years 1970/1 (the end of the old approach) and 1972/3 (the heyday of the 'new'). Nevertheless, concentration on new personal lending by banks does not distort the picture very much, if expressed as a percentage of the level of M_3 in the first quarter of 1972 (or of personal disposable income or any other relevant magnitude). To know that new credit extended to persons has risen from 2.7 per cent to 13 per cent is no different in its implications for policy than a rise from 0.8 per cent to 10.9 per cent. Moreover, the increase includes the effect of structural change, discussed below, as well as end-ceiling effects.

7.1.2 Structural Change in Bank Behaviour

An argument related to that in section 7.1.1 is that the new approach led to a structural change in bank attitudes whereby they bid more vigorously for deposits and so created a new type of demand for banks' liabilities. It is important to realise that this argument could be presented to argue that the real growth in the money supply was even higher than 60 per cent. The new behaviour of banks may have made their interest-bearing deposits more liquid than before; as, for example, with the growth of Certificates of Deposit (CDs). A three-month CD is almost identical to a three-month wholesale deposit, except that the former is marketable in a vigorous secondary market whereas all one can do with the latter is to use it as security for a loan. This has two additional implications for analysis of statistics. M_1 includes a lot of interest-bearing sight deposits (in December 1976, £2,495m or 13.1 per cent). Any theory of structural change would imply that some of the growth in CDs represented a switch from these deposits, since a marketable interest-bearing deposit is a very much closer substitute for a 'sight' deposit than any previously existing security. More generally, the increased bidding for deposits must have attracted funds from current accounts, if only because some current accounts earned implicit (tax-free) interest in the form of remitted bank charges. M_1 and M_3 are the closest of substitutes for each other at the margin. Cheques can traditionally be written against deposit accounts; much of M_1 pays explicit or implicit interest. Hence a structural growth in M_3 must represent a structural fall in M_1. In any case, one would expect M_1 to grow more slowly than M_3 as transactions balances should grow less fast than output, because of economies of scale, even without this substitution effect. Thus, the slower growth of M_1 (21.1 per cent) can be discounted as proof of monetary orthodoxy.

To analyse the basic proposition — that structural change reduced the impact of monetary growth — it is necessary to see whether any increase in bank deposits represented a change in the composition of liquid assets, or an increase in their level. Increased competition by banks can lead to:

(a) a diversion of the demand for assets from other private sector assets. This would have little effect on the economy except in so far as the bank asset is more marketable or has a lower default risk. The exception is crucial — e.g. of bank compared to finance house deposits;

(b) a diversion as in (a) but from public sector assets. Here the effect is to increase credit but probably not 'liquidity'; money again rises. Liquidity would actually fall if public sector assets were less marketable than private ones. In the UK, a claim on the Midland Bank is probably as highly regarded as a claim on a local authority so this does not matter;

(c) an increase in total liquid or near-money assets.

One can try to see which of these occurred by examination of alternative definitions of the 'money supply'. If the structural change hypothesis is valid there would be substantially less growth in monetary aggregates which are not affected by the change. For example, if bank deposits had replaced Treasury Bills, then a wider monetary aggregate, including Treasury Bills, would show slower growth.

Adding other 'liquid assets' to M_3 does not change the analysis significantly; this aggregate grows by 50.2 per cent, M_3 by 61.5 per cent. Further, the public sector component of these assets grew by only 36.4 per cent, so 'credit' grew even faster than this broad aggregate.

Table 7.3

	End 1971[ab]	End 1973	% Change
M_1	10,790[a]	13,100	21.1
£M_3	19,897[a]	31,540	58.5
M_3	20,411[a]	32,970	61.5
Treasury Bills[c]	54	22	−59.3
Trustee Savings Bank Ordinary Accounts	481	544	13.1
Trustee Savings Bank Investment Accounts	1,636	2,025	23.4
National Savings Banks Ordinary Accounts	507	537	9.9
National Savings Banks Investment Accounts	117	114	−2.6
Local Authority debt 'short term'	1,802	3,026	69.9
Building Society Deposits[d]	491	596	−21.4
Building Society Shares	11,695	16,022	37.0
Public Sector Liquid Assets	4,597	6,268	36.4
All Liquid Assets[e]	37,194	55,856	50.2

Notes: a. Adjusted for breaks. b. As near to the end of the year as statistics permit; all are between 30 September and 31 March, except for building societies. c. March 1971 level plus subsequent changes as shown in 'Bulletin' to give figures for December 1971 and 1973. d. End of financial year for individual building society, probably centred around September. e. This comprises all financial assets with an original maturity of less than 3 months, except for corporate bills.
Sources: *Bank of England Quarterly Bulletin*; *Annual Abstract of Statistics*.

7.1.3 The Nature of the Demand-for-money

The crucial issue discussed in this section is whether monetary policy can be justified on the grounds that it merely satisfied the demand for money. The authorities argued on occasions that it did.[2] They argued that whereas the theoretical arguments tend to assume a real income elasticity of demand-for-money of approximately one, this view was incorrect for the UK as this income elasticity was nearer to two.[3] As this view was abandoned in a later 'Bulletin' article, the econometric issue can be ignored, though its influence on policy was considerable. The high elasticity, it was argued, meant that 'an apparently rapid rate of monetary expansion might actually be restrictive in its effects when associated with a strong increase in output'.[4] There are two issues raised by this.

(a) Did the authorities create an 'excess supply of money'?

(b) Is it proof of a safe monetary policy if the supply of money does not exceed the demand?

The first argument has been put very strongly by Artis and Lewis.[5]

Their proposition is that the 'supply side counterparts', especially bank lending, created an excess supply of money and that this disequilibrium was responsible for the adverse consequences of the new approach. In the more academic of their two papers they develop a useful model to test the workings of the new approach. The supply of money is determined by the interaction between the 'supply side counterparts' (the PSBR and private demand for government bonds and credit). This in turn, together with interest rates, influences GDP, which in turn affects the demand for money. The supply and demand for money are equilibrated over a period by movements in interest rates. They argue that in 1972-3, the money supply consistently exceeded demand with continuing inflationary effects.

The Artis-Lewis model is very powerful and useful, and illustrates the cleft stick in which the authors of the new approach were caught when defending its adoption. The scheme assumed a stable demand-for-money, so if no such function existed the case for the new approach disappears (using 'modus tollendo tollens' for the rigorous-minded). On the other hand, with a conventional, stable demand-for-money function the inflationary consequences of the policy's implementation are clear. However, Artis and Lewis seem to imply there is some normative significance in satisfying the demand for money, just as the Bank argued. That is, both claim that if there had been a structural shift in the demand for money, then this would be sufficient to justify the implementation of the policy,[6] or at least to argue that the inflationary or other consequences of such a policy would only be those attributable to the level of interest rates (which might even be exogenous, fixed perhaps by overseas influences). This argument seems misguided. In one sense, the quantity of money in existence must be demanded, pace Artis and Lewis: 'The view is regrettably heard too often that the stock of money in existence must be demanded. It is important to stress that this is fallacious.'[7] So long as one ignores cheques in the process of clearing and other 'transit items' such as bank notes in the post, the holders of money must be willing to hold it, at least for an instant in the constrained situation they face. There must always be a momentary equilibrium, in that no one is forced to hold money in the way that a shopkeeper holds involuntary stocks, since the nature of money is such that one can always get rid of it. The holder in many cases may intend to dispose of some part of his money balances when conditions alter. Someone living in a village, for instance, may intend to buy goods or financial assets the next time he is in town, i.e. using the neo-classical analysis, when the transaction cost falls. Thus a perfect demand-for-money function would explain why the quantity of money in existence was held. In this sense, money demand and supply would be in equilibrium (albeit temporary equilibrium). However, either of the following might be the case.

(a) The holder plans to dispose of his balance in such a way that only some 'inflationary development' (e.g. a rise in asset prices or nominal GDP) could restore equilibrium. This could occur when there is a relaxation of the constraints inducing the holder to be content to hold his balances, e.g. transactions costs, real or psychological. Alternatively, it might be that his intended reason for acquiring money was to perform some transaction which would put the money market back into a constrained equilibrium, which would involve some other transactor engaging in an inflationary transaction.

(b) The monetary equilibrium might only have been achieved by putting at least two other markets into disequilibrium (thus avoiding violation of Walras' law), and the resolution of these disequilibria would involve 'inflationary consequences'.

The Bank/Artis-Lewis position is valid in the 'comparative static' world of the IS/LM curve. It is true that if the demand-for-money function is

$$D^m = 30 + 1.1 \text{ (output)} + 1.0 \text{ (prices)},$$

output is 110 and the price level 120, in period t, then if one fixes the money supply for ever at 271 (the level demanded) this will not have inflationary effects. However, this result does not apply in a world of continuous adjustment and many markets. The momentary equilibrium in the money market is a result of interaction between the demand and supply curves of all other markets and the whole range of behaviour of transactors involving inter alia adjustment patterns and expectation patterns.[8] There is no normative meaning to a demand-for-money function in this context. Nor can one attribute any such meaning to a longer-term equilibrium level of money demand. In this general equilibrium context one cannot say that that part of money demand which depends on the existing price level is any different to that dependent on, say, the building society being a 20p bus ride away.

7.1.4 Arbitrage and the 'CD Tax Loophole'

During this period, quite large sums of money were on occasion borrowed from banks to lend back to them. It was argued that this made M_3 a meaningless statistic. This bizarre situation arose in two ways. One was that, at a time when bank profits were over 100 per cent up on a year earlier, the banks were prepared to take losses on marginal business to preserve market shares, to avoid the administrative and psychological costs of rate alteration and, especially, to avoid political criticism. Like public utilities in the USA, and banks elsewhere in the 'Old Commonwealth', the clearing banks in particular have been targets for political criticism on many occasions and there have been frequent suggestions that they be nationalised.[9] Thus there was arbitrage to take advantage of overdraft rates being lower than deposit rates, the so-called 'merry-go-round'. It was estimated by City sources that perhaps £600m was involved in such transactions.

The other reason for the redepositing of bank loans was the 'CD tax loophole'. This was perhaps twice as large as the merry-go-round. A Certificate of Deposit was defined as a debt, and, as a result of the 1965 Budget, trading in debts was not taxable (nor losses offsetable against tax) – this provision being enacted to close some loopholes in the tax laws. In consequence, tax was paid on the interest on a CD only if it were held to maturity or the holder was an 'authorised dealer' in securities. This meant that a one-year CD could be bought on 1 January for, say, £100,000 at 10 per cent and sold on 30 December for £109,990 without paying tax. Moreover, one could use the CD as security for a loan and offset the interest on this against tax. At the top UK rate of 98 per cent this meant one could borrow at, say, 12 per cent and pay net only £240. Thus a top-rate taxpayer could make £9,750 on an investment of nothing while his bank was still making a very healthy 2 per cent profit.

These transactions were not without economic effect. Their main effect was probably to allow companies to guarantee that their over-draft facilities ('lines of credit') could not be affected by the reintroduction of a ceiling, discussed further below as 'precautionary demand'. However, these transactions probably had little effect on income, output or inflation. Nevertheless, the size of these factors can be exaggerated. In particular, the CD tax loophole was closed in the 1973 budget but the amount of CDs continued to rise. M_3 grew by 60 per cent in 1972 and 1973. At the end of 1973, CDs were still only 6 per cent of M_3 and had grown by only £1,000m, i.e. 5 per cent of M_3, since 1971. More likely, no more than half of this latter figure (2½ per cent) can be regarded as artificial growth in M_3. Indeed growth of M_3 is not significantly affected even by the exclusion of all CDs – in 1972-3 M_3 less CDs grew by 61 per cent and M_3 by 62 per cent.

The loophole and the merry-go-round complicated control of the money supply because it meant that some part of the growth of the money stock was almost entirely without the economic effects one would normally predict. More seriously, it meant that trends in monetary developments, already obscured by poor statistics, were further complicated because the arbitrage 'money' was a very short-term phenomenon and tended to be concentrated in the one-week money market. Thus the month-to-month pattern of monetary growth was obscured by whether or not the arbitrage was taking place. When it occurred, £600m was created; when the transaction was reversed this £600m disappeared. However, the extent of the problem seemed to be greatly exaggerated by the authorities (in the Deputy Governor's speech, for example).[10] This was a phenomenon which could be monitored by observation of the relevant (relative) interest rates, with the money supply figures adjusted accordingly. This was done, for example, by Gordon Pepper in his 'Greenwell's Monetary Bulletin'. Moreover, as the Bank believed, and still believes, that short-run fluctuations are of little economic significance, it is difficult to use this as a defence for the overall conduct of policy. The CD loophole was a reflection of the problems facing the Inland Revenue in their perpetual guerilla war with tax accountants, and is perhaps an argument for simplification of the tax laws. The 'merry-go-round' existed because of a serious problem of monetary policy — the inability to force base rates up as effectively as had been envisaged. However, it is difficult to see how policy would have been changed significantly if the 'merry-go-round' itself had not existed.

7.2 The Problems of Competition and Credit Control

The basis of the competition and credit control regime was the authorities' willingness and ability to induce whatever change in bank overdraft rates was necessary to achieve the desired level of growth of M_3. This meant that interest rates might have to vary substantially and might have to reach very high levels in nominal terms. The experience of 1971-3 suggested that the authorities had neither the ability to achieve nor the willingness to accept such interest rates.

The authorities had assumed that there was no limit to their ability to achieve whatever level of interest rate they wished the banks to charge on their loans. As the Governor put it:

Of course the extent of the pressure we shall be able to bring to bear on interest rates by our open market policies, backed up if necessary by calls for Special Deposits will be affected by many factors . . .

> However no limitation is envisaged in the Authorities' ability to
> neutralise excess liquidity or to bring about sufficiently strong
> upward pressure on bank lending rates.[11]

The authorities had assumed that banks were short-run profit maximisers. Therefore if the authorities forced up the marginal cost of funds
to banks (wholesale money rates), then the banks would raise their loan
rates such that marginal revenue was equal to the new (higher) marginal
cost. Unfortunately this model was invalid. One can argue that banks
were profit satisficers or pursued long-run objectives, including 'political'
ones – i.e. avoiding nationalisation (7.1.4). Alternatively, one might
argue that an oligopoly model was the relevant one, in which case the
simple result does not follow.[12]

It is clear that the authorities were seriously worried by their inability
to force up base rates when necessary. Thus, in November 1973, the
authorities took special action to ensure that base rates rose by
specifically ordering the banks to raise them. One can see the need for
this by examining the behaviour of the margin between wholesale
money rates, the marginal cost of bank funds and base rates. The general
tendency was for the margin to fall when rates rose.[13] In fact there was
a negative correlation between the margin and the rate of interest
charged.[14] The sort of model the Bank was implicitly using would
predict the opposite.[15] Ironically, this problem was reduced in December
1973 when the banks related the cost of some borrowing to market
rates on wholesale deposits.[16]

Besides and in addition to these technical problems, the authorities
were not prepared to accept the implications of competition and credit
control. The authorities were unwilling to let (nominal) rates rise sufficiently and these never caught up with the rising inflationary expectations, partially generated by the monetary growth itself. Even the 4 per
cent rise in interest rates in July 1973 was too little, too late. Given the
constraints (both economic and political) imposed by mortgagees, sufficiently high nominal rates were not really a practical possibility. The
authorities' commitment to stability in interest rates abated little.
Varying Shakespeare, even if they were willing to wound, they were
afraid to use the knife.

Another example of the retreat from intention to reality involves
official reaction to bank sales of gilts. The Governor's speech stated:
'thus we shall not normally be prepared to facilitate movements out of
gilt-edged by the banks even if these sales should cause the market
temporarily to weaken quite sharply'.[17] Yet in June 1972 this is precisely

what the 'sale and repurchase agreement' had done. Of course the circumstances were abnormal, yet so was the rapid rate of growth of money earlier in the year. One can argue that the Bank should have intervened to avert a banking crisis, but equally that the form of intervention was inconsistent with both the spirit and the letter of competition and credit control. The authorities chose not to inflict any penalty on the banks for the position of their 'books' (which left them without the ability to meet the outflow) which had resulted from the pace of their expansion of credit. If market mechanisms were to be used, then the loan should have been at a penal rate, rather than (effectively) costless.[18] A loan at, say, 15 per cent or 20 per cent p.a. for a fortnight would have been dramatic, but it was demanded by the logic of the system. This would have made the banks much more cautious about their future lending policy. In a reserve base system (like the US), one may avoid the necessity of such action because during crises the banks fall below their minimum ratio and this is sufficient to induce the desired change in behaviour.

One can argue that the authorities were inconsistent, that they would not do what they had said they were prepared to do. There is a valid case both for interest rate stability and the avoidance of high nominal rates. The point was that if these objectives were valued so highly then competition and credit control should never have been introduced. A kinder view is that the authorities had miscalculated the degree to which these objectives had to be sacrificed. They may then have 'only' underestimated the cost of the 'new approach'. Very conceivably, the Bank and Treasury officials had secured the government's consent to the scheme without the politicians being aware of the cost.

Further, one can argue that this unwillingness to raise interest rates revealed a technical weakness of competition and credit control. Changes in interest rates need to be implemented quickly when the need arises, otherwise a vicious circle develops. High monetary growth, directly and indirectly, feeds inflationary expectations and a boom psychology in asset markets. This in turn feeds a very rapid expansion in bank lending and further monetary growth. Equally crucially, inflationary expectations rise and real rates fall. If the authorities now raise (nominal) rates, then this will probably only partly offset the fall in real rates. Hence real rates are lower than they were when it first became necessary to raise them.

In brief, a scheme like competition and credit control will work only if the authorities are skilful enough to detect immediately when rates need to be increased, and are able and willing to act. This may demand a greater degree of ability than it is reasonable to expect, certainly more than has been shown in the UK. The foibles and fallibilities of those operating the system will be reinforced if they lack the necessary information. It must be stressed that both the quality and quantity of statistical data available in this period were very poor. One can cite many examples such as frequent revisions to data which meant that decisions were often made on the wrong basis, and inconsistencies between 'banking month' and calendar quarterly data, besides the notorious 'inter-bank' difference. Furthermore, much necessary data were lacking, such as a breakdown of M, by category of holder or knowledge of interest-bearing deposits in M_1. Finally, much data, such as whether gilts were purchased by banks or non-banks, was only available after a surprisingly long time. Some but not all of these faults were later cured. Nevertheless UK data are still less good and less plentiful than in the US. This situation was deplorable in its own right − and the remedy lay in the Bank's own hands. More significantly, the authorities never considered the consequences this inadequacy would have for the successful implementation of *any* policy.

The authorities were also unable to estimate in any way what determined the demand for credit. Subsequent analysis has not helped to answer the question.[19] Hence, one cannot say why the demand for credit was so large in 1971-3. There are various hypotheses which can be considered, and the answer is important both in itself and in determining the nature of the effects of competition and credit control. Furthermore, it has some implications for the Artis-Lewis analysis of a large demand for credit leading to excess money creation.

One explanation is that it represented pent-up demand frustrated by ceilings. Another is that the very low, in fact significantly negative, real rates of interest induced people and firms to borrow, especially as inflationary expectations soared. Another concentrates on the high rates of return available on property and some stock market investments. All of these imply similar effects on asset prices and consumer spending. Another explanation argues that much borrowing was precautionary, against the return of ceilings. Given prevailing interest rates, the cost of such borrowing, reinvested in short-term liquid assets, was low. It certainly seems that such borrowing was very extensive. One should, however, note that while the corporate sector as a whole was borrowing from and lending to banks on a large scale, this may not have involved individual firms engaging in both transactions. Furthermore, precautionary borrowing of this type would not be without economic impact. 'Liquidity' is increased by both borrowing and lending, even on a short-term basis, as the bank loans were assumed to be of a much longer maturity than the assets. Radcliffean, monetarist and Keynesian could agree that it would be inflationary. However, its effect would be much more diffuse and longer-acting than if it were concentrated, fairly quickly, on financial and real asset prices. Paradoxically, precautionary borrowing is similar in its implications to Friedman's version of the diffuse unpredictable nature of the effects of monetary policy. Ironically the authorities argued that precautionary borrowing was large as an anti-monetarist argument! With regard to Artis and Lewis, this form of borrowing creates its own demand for money, but without any implication that this legitimises the size of the money stock in any way.

Hence competition and credit control 'failed' both because of its technical failings and because the authorities would not do what they had said they would do. By December 1973, it was necessary to do something for political and economic reasons. Westminster gossip alleged that 40 backbench Conservative MPs had threatened to bring the government down unless the money supply was brought under control. Interest rates were too low to do this, especially in real terms. The authorities could not or would not raise them. Electioneering motives are often unfairly ascribed to governments, but the conjunction of four million mortgagees, a mortgage rate that was already at 11½ per cent and a prospective general election was not irrelevant in this decision. (Actually the election was in February 1974, two months away, but at the time it appeared to be about 12 months away.)

7.3 The Effects of Competition and Credit Control

The next issue to be considered is what were the effects of the 60 per cent growth of M_3 in this period. It is virtually certain that 60 per cent was excessive. In fact, one can construct a theoretical case against any acceleration in monetary growth from about 8 per cent p.a. to 20-25 per cent p.a., at least given the level of inflation in the UK. It seems reasonable to argue that inflationary expectations must have been about 6 per cent. If one wished to leave the level of capacity utilisation and employment unchanged, this implies about 9 per cent p.a. growth in money, whatever the theory of how monetary developments affect 'real' ones. The monetarist argument is straightforward. The neo-Keynesian view is that monetary growth should not exceed 9 per cent, unless financial markets are affected by a strong 'bear' mood, when both Tobin and Keynes would have argued that monetary expansion should be used to try to offset this. There was certainly not a 'bear' mood; share prices had risen consistently since the Conservative victory in June 1970 (by 25 per cent). In fact, if anything, the non-monetarist should have argued for less monetary growth in this period. However, the authorities wished to reduce unemployment. It is clear that in a modern economy as rigid as the UK's, it is virtually impossible for output to grow by more than 5 per cent p.a. This implies that capacity utilisation should be rising by about 2 per cent p.a., employment by about 1 per cent in the first year, and unemployment falling by about ½ per cent p.a. in the first year and 1 per cent in the second and subsequent years. This may be an unpleasant fact about the UK economy, but it was accepted by Mr Barber – his policy was to achieve precisely this. Thus, the maximum desirable rate of monetary growth can be calculated so long as one can reach consensus on what rate of monetary expansion is necessary to increase output relative to the capacity ceiling. Unfortunately, monetary theory is least well developed on this subject, and the answer would depend on speeds of adjustment, various income and interest elasticities, and other factors, including the structure of the economy. However, no economist who grants any importance to financial factors has ever argued that such growth should exceed twice the rate of output growth. In the context of 1972-3, this implies, prima facie, a maximum desirable rate of 12-13 per cent, about half that which occurred. In the context of 1971-3, there is little difference between the result of monetarist and Keynesian analyses. Hence, actual money growth was at least twice the desired level which leaves open the question of what were the effects of the excess growth.

7.3.1 The Residential Property Market

For the reasons discussed in Chapter 2, one would expect monetary policy to have a substantial impact on the property market. Both the construction of and purchase of property are largely financed by credit. Furthermore, the attractiveness of property as an investment is more dependent on interest rates than is any other good or asset. Finally, one would expect changes in the money supply to have a direct influence on property through the portfolio balance mechanism. Building society deposits are a near substitute for money, and an increase in the money supply will have a large effect in increasing these deposits. Building societies tend to respond to these flows by increasing their lending. Thus monetary policy will increase the *effective* demand for housing even if it does not influence *notional* demand. Finally, and to a monetarist, crucially, there is probably large direct substitution from money to property.

Hence, it is not surprising that the 'new approach' seems to have had fundamental effects on both the owner-occupied residential property market and on the commercial property market. There was some overlap between the markets as developers bought large older homes for conversion into offices or flats, which were then resold to owner-occupiers. Large blocks of flats were also traded between developers and frequently sold off to tenants or other buyers piecemeal ('flat-breaking'). However, at least outside London, the two markets were distinct.

The residential property market was and is dominated by building society loans, which finance most purchasers. In 1972 these loans amounted to 88.5 per cent of total loans for house purchase. Of the balance, local authorities accounted for 7.9 per cent (£325m), mainly for old properties and/or poorer households, where financing is provided by public bodies in most countries, e.g. by Federal Housing Administration underwriting in the USA. Insurance companies provided 3.7 per cent, mainly in the highest price brackets, where the extra tax advantages of this form of finance sway borrowers. Some borrowers from insurance companies have been attracted by the availability of fixed-rate mortgages but these companies' share of the market was small.

The housing market was dominated by two phenomena.

(a) In 1972 and 1973 house prices rose at an annual rate of 34 per cent and by over 100 per cent in total during the period of the new approach. For comparison, the retail price index rose by 9 per cent p.a. and real personal disposable income by 5.5 per cent p.a. in 1972-3.

(b) The total of building society advances rose from £2,021m in 1970 to £3,649m in 1972 and £3,540m in 1973.

The issue is the causal relationships of these two and monetary developments. Economic theory would suggest that:

(a) the increase in the money supply leads to a reshuffling of portfolios and as a result;

(b) there is an increase in building societies' funds and this leads to an increase in their lending. This probably takes the form of reducing 'equilibrium rationing' as they satisfy previously rationed-out demand by, inter alia, cutting the income/mortgage ratio and raising the loan/house price ratio;[20]

(c) because of (b) there are now more buyers in the market and each has greater purchasing power. This increase in 'effective demand' leads to some increase in new building, but most of the effect is seen in higher house prices.

Certainly developments in the housing market are largely consistent with this picture. In 1971 the number of houses started in the private sector rose by 25.4 per cent (from a very depressed level), but at that time the industry was near its capacity, and starts rose by only 9.5 per cent in 1972 and actually fell by 5.3 per cent in 1973. This is the response one would expect to such an increase in demand, either as a 'St Louis' monetarist predicting an initial increase in output and a delayed price effect or as a more orthodox economist arguing in terms of capacity and relatively inelastic supply.[21]

However, the building societies denied any responsibility for the increase, and tended to blame either costs or rising demand. The first is basically the proposition that there was an exogenous shift in the replacement value of houses which led to a rise in prices. A priori this is unconvincing as it should have led to a fall in the number of houses built, and it is rather bizarre to expect such a sudden shift in building costs. The evidence is that it did not occur – construction costs rose by only 11.2 per cent in 1972 and by 23.5 per cent in 1973. With the upsurge in demand it would be a normal response for wages (and over-time hours) to rise as builders tried to satisfy extra demand. One would expect the economists' 'less suitable resources' to be employed in building, e.g. as unskilled and inexperienced workers were employed.

More of the 'supply side' theorists have, however, concentrated on land prices rather than construction costs. This ignores the point, going back at least to Ricardo, that land prices do not affect the price of houses but are determined by the demand for houses. This would not be the case if, for example, alterations in planning regulations greatly reduced the amount of land available, but this was not the case – and is again inconsistent with the increase in house-building. It was also argued that speculators were responsible for the 61 per cent increase in land prices and so for the rise in house prices. Again, they were given the opportunity to make (very easy) profits by the boom but could not have caused it except, perhaps, by a ring buying up all the available building land and reducing supply, or some other implausible scenario.

Thus it is reasonable to conclude that a shift in demand was responsible for the rise in prices, but it was argued that this was much more a rise in underlying demand than in 'effective' demand, i.e. due to changes in other factors rather than to building-society behaviour. One obvious such factor would be a rise in incomes, but clearly no plausible income elasticity could explain the behaviour of the housing market, whereby a 5 per cent increase in real incomes is associated with a 25 per

cent increase in relative prices. It has been argued that the Housing
Finance Act of 1973 may have switched demand from the local
authority housing sector to the private sector (by raising rents on public
sector housing). This is possible, but there is no evidence for it and the
likely size of any switch is very small.[22] It is very unlikely that any
underlying demographic change would have had such a marked effect in
such a short period, especially as the only major trend (downwards in
the birth rate) might have been expected to produce the opposite result.
New household formation was very high in this period, consisting largely
of an increase in single-person households, but this probably reflects a
response to the low cost of mortgages and the availability of finance
rather than any underlying demographic change.

It should be noted that the low turnover of the housing stock (around
8 per cent p.a.) and the loan-financed nature of the transactions makes
it peculiarly vulnerable to variations in price. Thus the building societies
have a responsibility to try to ensure some stability, which they accepted
by the formation in 1973 of a Joint Action Committee with the
Department of the Environment and the Bank of England.

It is clear that monetary policy and building societies can be 'blamed'
for the rise in house prices. This is not in conflict with Mayes' argument
that building-society behaviour was little different in 1971-3 from
before or since.[23] This is the point of my argument. Given building-
society behaviour, an increase in monetary growth will cause a magnified
rise in house prices. One must note the very attractive nature of housing
as an investment in this period, with mortgage rates of 8 per cent p.a.,
offsetable against tax. A very high rate of return was offered even at the
historic inflation of house prices of 9-10 per cent p.a., let alone when
expectations responded to the acceleration in house prices. The boom,
like any speculative one, was of a self-fulfilling nature. Capital gains on
one house encouraged people to buy bigger ones, and provided the
deposit ('margin' in US market parlance). The rise in prices encouraged
people to bring purchases forward and to buy bigger houses. Prices were
justified on the 'other sucker' theory (i.e. that they could be resold at a
high price) at least as much as on the underlying nature of the house.[24]
The picture of a speculative market is reinforced by the enormous ratio
between cash put up and the effect on the value of houses. The value of
houses probably rose by £60,000m in two and a half years. The amount
of new money is harder to calculate. Total loans for house purchase
were about £13,000m. Applying a 40 per cent ratio of own to borrowed
funds suggests that total own funds were £8,000m and this depends on
a very high ratio: for the new purchasers 15 per cent is a more typical

figure. Some of this £8,000m was provided by the capital gain on a house already owned by those 'trading-up' (who tend to provide the largest share of own capital). Allowing for these factors, perhaps the total of 'new' money was £2,000m, and some of this may have been provided by bank borrowing or borrowing from relations to pay the deposit. Thus this provided the leverage for £60,000m of capital gains. Reported widespread 'gazumping' (breaking a contract to resell at a higher price) and dealings in rights to purchase unbuilt houses reinforce this picture of a speculative market.

The effects of this enormous rise in house prices are hard to judge.[25] The personal sector's financial wealth was about £125,000m at the end of 1971.[26] Net of mortgages, owner-occupied houses were worth about £35,000m and landed wealth was about £25,000m (net of mortgages). Thus the impact was considerable on both the net worth of the personal sector and its composition, and economic theory suggests that these would have some effect on spending and the allocation of savings. Even if one assumes only £60 extra spending on average by each owner-occupier (less than 1 per cent of the gain), this amounts to about £500m.

Owner-occupiers could realise their gains and move: the choice was rented property or a smaller/cheaper house. The former is and was unattractive both on psychological grounds and because of the expected future trend in rents. The demand for housing is probably price-elastic,[27] but there is a countervailing force: the desirability of a house as an asset offering protection against inflation. So while the higher price may reduce the demand for housing (a movement along the demand curve), a higher price will also generate expectation of higher prices and therefore increase demand (a shift of the demand curve). Almost certainly, the latter effect could be large enough to ensure that the effects of rising house prices will exclude the sale of a house and moving.

The increase in wealth could, however, still probably have had significant effects. One would have expected both more spending and some attempt to reallocate wealth away from the non-interest-bearing illiquid form in which a greater proportion of it was now held. Since houses are indivisible, one cannot sell part of them except by borrowing against the security of a house. One way in which this can be done is by means of a second mortgage; certainly increasing housing prices must be at least a permissive factor in second mortgage loans. There are no figures for other borrowing against houses, e.g. borrowing from a bank with a house as collateral. Even for second mortgages, there are no good data since 1968, despite general agreement, for what that is worth, that they have expanded rapidly. In 1968 the Crowther Report quoted both an estimate of £25m by the Association of Finance Agents and an official estimate of £14m, which omitted some significant lenders.[28] In addition, building societies usually lend between about £30m and £35m p.a. in further advances.

Theoretically, a change in the wealth of owner-occupiers is partly offset by a (notional) increase in expenditure on housing. It is possible that this is an accurate representation of how people view an increase in house prices in that they do not noticeably alter their behaviour. But it must be stressed that a wealth effect may only be subconscious – a person may feel better-off because of his house being worth more, and so buy something he otherwise would not buy.

The effects of rising house prices on aggregate demand can be examined from the viewpoint of neo-classical price theory, which separates the income and substitution effects of higher prices. To take the latter effect first: if the rise in house prices reduced the demand for housing, then, if other goods are a substitute, more of them will be bought, and if a complement, less. If, however, more housing is bought for expectational reasons, the demand for complements will rise and that for substitutes fall. At least for this period the latter seems more likely. The income effect is complex for existing owners, but for new buyers and potential new buyers it is clearly negative. To expand this point, they will probably have to save more both to pay an increased deposit and because of greater uncertainty about the size of deposit to be paid. New buyers will also have higher mortgage burdens so gross saving may be higher in future years. Expectations of rising house prices may also, as discussed above, have meant that houses were bought earlier and/or larger houses purchased. If so, the burden of mortgage payments would have risen still further. Hence for new buyers, it seems that both income and substitution effects worked to cut their demand for other goods. In the sense that he will finish up owning a more expensive house than when he started, everyone who 'filters up' is a new buyer. However, it seems reasonable to assume the capital gain on the house sold will cover the higher deposit on the new one, so the effects will be small. As for people in the rented sector, it seems likely that they will suffer from a negative income effect and thus their spending will be lower. This would, at least partially, offset any 'wealth effect' of the type discussed above.[29]

Among other effects a rise in house prices will also affect two other groups directly – builders and landlords. While rent controls restrict the rise in rents, even under 'fair rents',[30] there is probably some direct connection between house prices and rents. In addition, the capital gains can be realised if and when the tenant leaves. During the period, the implicit deflator of the price of housing services rose; the increase was less than half the rise in housing prices, but it is still a considerable increase in income for both property companies and private landlords. The capital gains would be even larger, although perhaps not immediately realisable.

The increase in house prices will also affect builders; the increase may permit them to increase the price of new houses whilst building them. Alternatively, the profit will go to purchasers or speculators. Reports of a premium on options for new houses suggests some of the latter were in operation, but there are no data on this phenomenon. The general result will probably be to increase builders' profits in the short term, and is bound to be to increase them in the long run. The increase in demand and/or profits may also lead to an increase in building wages (as discussed above) and so to an increase in wages generally, therefore bringing about some spillover effects on other prices. This is either a cost-inflationary effect or the monetarist/Tobinesque transmission mechanism at work, depending on how these effects are interpreted. One might also expect some effect on the general level of prices from an influence on price expectations, and a tendency to increase cost pressures if the need to save for higher deposits increased union wage claims. These factors can lead to either a higher natural rate of unemployment, more inflation or, most probably in the circumstances of 1972-3, both; which of these three depends on theoretical and empirical magnitudes. In 1972-3 all plausible theories would suggest similar effects. Thus the qualitative effects of monetary expansion are clear, if not their magnitude.

7.3.2 The Commercial Property Market

The residential property market may have exhibited all the signs of a classical boom but it fails to match the excesses of the commercial property boom in the same period, which must rival the Dutch tulip boom of the 1630s,[31] the South Sea Bubble,[32] and Wall Street in 1929[33] as amongst the great speculative dramas of all time. The UK property market has always had a fringe of somewhat dubious operators, as well as many colourful characters (and multi-millionaires), and has attracted much attention both from politicians and journalists.[34] It is a paradox of markets which has already been commented on[35] — that the riskiest of speculation can offer the safest of security for loans. Certainly banks have been willing to lend on the security of property as the most solid of all security. Under the 'old approach' they lost a lot of business to insurance companies through the workings of the ceilings (see Chapter 5), and, hence, they were very eager to increase property lending. There were plenty of developers and dealers anxious to borrow, as a result of the effects of the controls on London office-building as well as for the reasons stated above.

Thus it is not surprising that the property market was the scene of a sustained boom in which properties were traded on a very low margin; it was very easy to borrow on such security. Such loans generated price increases which generated further loans and so on, if not ad infinitum at least until late in 1973.

At this point the bubble burst and many institutions found that they had overlent to property companies. Many of their assets were unsaleable or insufficient to cover the loan, or both. It is difficult to ascertain movements in commerical property prices but some indication is available from movements in the yields expected on prime property, which were (on an annual basis) 7.5 per cent in 1970, 4.75 per cent in 1973 and 8 per cent in 1974; in the UK, property prices are normally calculated as a multiple of the current rental. This multiple obviously varies according to the nature of the review clause included in a contract, the quality of the tenant, etc. Even these figures understate the volatility of the market in lower-grade properties. Using these yields and the Department of the Environment survey for 'City' rent figures, one derives the price index in Table 7.4, which shows that prices triples, then halved.

Table 7.4: Index of Commercial Property, 1970 = 100

	Price	Yield (%)	City office rents	Factory rents
1970	100	7.50	100	100
1971	134	6.75	120	98
1972	195	5.00	130	105
1973	277	4.75	175	128
1974 (Nov.)	174	8.00	185	140
1975	144	6.50	125	153

It is difficult to ascertain the impact of these operations on the economy. It is clear that by necessitating official action to rescue banks ('the lifeboat),[36] it complicated the task of monetary policy. It almost certainly contributed to the 'inflationary psychosis' of the era. It may even have pushed rent levels upwards and thus increased the cost pressure on companies. The movement of rents lends credence to this hypothesis, especially the large rise in 1973. However, the impact on costs is lessened as neither shops nor factories shared in the boom. It should certainly have made it temporarily easier for companies to obtain funds by a 'sell and leaseback' arrangement – and much harder to do this in 1974. To that extent it must have increased the pressure on resources in 1973 and reduced it in 1974, thus intensifying the amplitude of the cycle.

7.3.3 Share Prices

There has been much written about the impact of the money supply on share prices – it is a favourite transmission mechanism of monetarists because it omits some of the steps in the Tobin mechanism while being close enough to it in spirit to appeal to Tobinesque economists.

Belief in such a relationship between the money supply and share prices seems to be surprisingly widespread in academic and city circles. It is surprising that it survived the year commencing May 1973 in which M_3 rose by 23 per cent and the stock market fell by 39 per cent, measured by the FT-Actuaries 500 Share Index. It is less surprising that it survived the author's attempt to disprove the relationship.[37] Thomas Whitebread, one of the victims of the 'Popish Plot' agitation, complained in 1680 that it was the hardest thing in the world to prove a negative: 'We are to prove a negative and I know 'tis much harder to prove a negative than to assert an affirmative.'[38] Nevertheless it seems very clear that there was no systematic relationship between money and share prices over any 'short period', i.e. less than six years. My study showed that neither spectral analysis nor a modified form of Box-Jenkins analysis could find any systematic relationship (over any measurable period) between share prices and various definitions of the money supply, either monthly or quarterly. Further, none of the US results could be replicated for the UK, nor did previous work on the UK seem to satisfy either economic or statistical criteria, and, finally, their equations all forecast badly. This conclusion still seems valid as far as monetary policy is concerned.

There are some further points to be made. The major one is that problems arise in reconciling systematic relationships and 'efficient' or 'rational markets'. Another is that there may be an unsystematic relationship between the two. This argument might apply with different force at different times. For example, a 'credit effect' may have been powerful in 1971-2 but not at other times. My study found that interest rate movements did influence share prices. Thus, developments in official policy may affect the stock market — it is worth remarking that this relationship, established up to the end of 1972, obviously 'explained' the movement in share prices in 1973-4 much better than a money one. Thus one may accept a relationship between the 'new approach' and the stock market boom of 1972-3 even while accepting that 'empirical work in both the time and frequency domain seems to prove that there is no relationship in the UK between money and share prices'.[39] However the main connection between money and share prices in this period is that both probably reflected the response to 'Barberism' and the mood of the times.

7.3.4 *Inflationary Psychology*

Many observers in the media, especially the American ones, argued that 1972-3 saw a significant shift in attitudes in the UK as an 'inflationary psychosis' took a grip and behaviour changed in response to this new attitude. The relevant theoretical reasoning in this context is Cagan's analysis of hyperinflation, wherein such a change in attitude is the major factor in inflation becoming hyperinflation.[40] Certainly there were many signs of such a change in attitudes in, for example, the craze for purchasing the most bizarre of objects as hedges against inflation, satirised by 'Punch' in a recommendation to buy articles recommending hedges against inflation. However, it is not clear how widespread this was at a popular level, probably much less so than in 1974-5. There is no real evidence of a 'flight from money'. The savings ratio in fact rose in 1972 to 10.1 per cent (from 8.3 per cent) and rose again in 1973 to 11.4 per cent (and rose in 1974 to 14.2 per cent). Uncertainty (partly induced by inflation) and the wealth effects induced by inflation were more important than any 'flight from goods'.[41]

It would seem reasonable to conclude that while monetary growth contributed to the speculative fever which gripped markets, it had little to do with 'inflationary psychosis' in 1971-2, if only because of the little attention given to monetary development by the City and the media.

This changed during 1973 when 'monetarism' ceased to be only an academic theory and started to become part of the conventional wisdom, especially in the City; previously its only non-academic adherents had been two Conservative backbench MPs, Bruce-Gardyne and Biffen. Under the influence of Peter Jay and Sam Brittan, economics editors of *The Times* and *Financial Times* respectively, the respectability of and publicity accorded to monetarism grew steadily to produce a fascinating circle of monetary effects.

High monetary growth led to a belief that interest rates must rise, both in response to a need to cure monetary growth and because of the inflationary effects of this growth; this depressed gilt sales and so led to faster monetary growth. Moreover, both Keynes[42] and Friedman[43] have made the impact of expected interest rates on actual ones a crucial element of their theories. This means that to curb monetary growth the authorities have to raise interest rates above the 'expected level' (Wicksell's natural rate in some analyses). Thus monetary growth meant that the level of interest rates necessary to curb it grew as the authorities' response was delayed; an error fatal both to the 'new approach' and the government.

7.3.5 *The Exchange Rate*

One of the most basic propositions in economics links quantity and price. Thus it is not surprising that the quantity of sterling and its international price, the exchange rate, have been linked. More formally, there is the monetary theory of the balance of payments (see Appendix 2B, p. 50). Hence the effect of monetary expansion on the exchange rate must be considered. Any theory would predict that there would be pressure on the exchange rate as a result of 'Barberism'. Almost certainly, monetary expansion was a major underlying cause of the floating of sterling in June 1972. However, it is also necessary to consider whether it was a proximate cause as well.

There are various methods by which monetary expansion could trigger off a foreign exchange crisis. One is by undermining foreign confidence. Another is that the ease of borrowing in London may facilitate speculation against the currency, as the cheapest method of speculation is normally to borrow sterling and lend dollars or marks. Closer to the theoretical model, accumulations of sterling in the hands of multinational companies may lead to an attempt to restore a normal ratio between currencies by selling sterling — certainly an increase in the amount held of a weak currency would be unacceptable given the pattern of interest rates in 1972.

It is impossible to test these hypotheses but they seem sufficiently convincing to make one believe that both the timing and the extent of the depreciation of sterling were determined by monetary developments.[44] The consequences of this depreciation and its timing are harder to ascertain. The cost-inflationary effects, though, were very large, and in conjunction with the prevalent stance of monetary and fiscal policy probably made inflation inevitable.

The movement of the exchange rate casts considerable doubt on the then government's argument that inflation in the UK was largely caused by world commodity prices in 1970-1. Sterling commodity prices did rise by about 45 per cent in 1972 and 1973, prior to the OPEC increase in oil prices. However, sterling depreciated by nearly 20 per cent in the period. So one can argue that nearly half of the 'worldwide rise in the commodity prices' cited so often by Heath was caused by sterling's depreciation. This assumes that dollar prices of commodities were unaffected by the UK's depreciation (the 'small country' assumption of economics). This does not seem to be wildly unrealistic. Certainly the effect on wheat, copper or soya prices would be very low. For a few commodities the impact would be larger (lamb, for example). The timing of the depreciation was very unfortunate in that it probably maximised the cost-inflationary impact. It was equally bad in its relationship to the incomes policy cycle in the UK. Accelerating inflation in 1973, when 'Phase 3' was being introduced (and the depreciation 'worked through'), was very badly timed indeed. Price increases need to be as low as possible during the defreezing period of incomes policy to minimise 're-entry problems'.

It is interesting to note that in the Bank of England model the impact of changes in the money supply have their major impact through this channel. Monetary policy influences inflation mainly by influencing the exchange rate and so the cost of imported raw materials, semi-manufactures etc. With a conventional 'mark-up' pricing equation incorporated into the model, this feeds through into inflation with a lag.[45] However, other Bank research has cast some doubt on this mechanism.[46] Nevertheless, this neo-Keynesian route was almost certainly of crucial importance in the period.

7.4 The Money Supply and Inflation

The neo-Keynesian analysis presented in section 5.3 suggests that the rapid monetary growth of 1971-3 was probably a major contributory factor to the acceleration of inflation from 6 per cent in 1970 and 8 per cent in 1972 to 20 per cent in 1974, and a peak of 27 per cent in the year to July 1975. However, a neo-Keynesian analyst would find it impossible to put any quantitative measure on the size of this inflationary impact on the UK. Nor has any econometric evidence helped to answer the question. Finally, the neo-Keynesian would put considerable emphasis on supply side developments in analysing inflation in this period, notably the OPEC price increase of November 1973 and the wage explosion which followed the miners' strike in 1974, and the consequent breakdown of the Heath government's incomes policy.

The strict monetarist would, in comparison, be able to present simple and easily quantifiable answers. The monetary expansion should directly cause an increase in nominal GDP of exactly equal size, and so an increase in inflation. Most monetarists would accept that supply side phenomena might influence the breakdown of the increase in (nominal) GDP between price and output. They would see the impact of the OPEC price increase mainly in higher unemployment, lower output and a change in relative prices rather than in an increase in inflation. It is worth emphasising that the squeeze on manufacturing profits in 1974-5 is entirely consistent with this predicted change in relative prices. It is also interesting to note that on a world scale the acceleration of inflation occurred before the rise in OPEC oil prices. The strict monetarist would be interested in the transmission mechanisms discussed above but would not regard them as essential to this case.

The monetarist position depends in part upon two econometrically unexplored issues: the impact of monetary growth on expectations and on wages. It is arguable that a major impact of monetary growth is to enable employers to pay higher wages; an issue discussed below in Chapter 10. However the monetarist case is probably best sustained by emphasising that all the developments in the economy fit in with simple monetarism without any need for further explanation. Both inflation and such developments as the rise in asset prices are in close accord with monetarism. Unfortunately the events of 1971-6 are equally consistent with other explanations.

No work done in the UK has, as yet, proved the case for monetarism, or even established a definite causal link from money to prices or nominal GDP. For example, the attempt to replicate Sims's study for the UK found that while some of the results 'suggest a possibility that there might be unidirectional causality from money to prices',[47] the general conclusion was indecisive. The nature of the arguments about the exogenity of money and the direction of causality is such that they may never be resolved. Virtually any results can be interpreted to fit most of the contending theories. Post hoc ergo propter hoc is certainly not sufficient to settle this dispute. Certainly the econometric evidence is not such as to make any definite conclusions possible.[48]

It is, however, interesting to note the implications of three moderate propositions.

(1) It is true that an increase in the money supply would be a sufficient cause of inflation.

(2) An increase in some monetary aggregate, or in the range of assets used as a means of payment, is necessary for inflation to continue.

(3) A reduction in the rate of monetary expansion is a necessary condition for reducing inflation.

These limited, generally acceptable propositions have important implications for the period 1972-3. In particular, they imply that the government's incomes policy had no chance of succeeding in 1973, given its monetary policy. Thus the drama of the miners' strike of 1973-4 (and the consequent fall of the government) was in one sense irrelevant to the success or failure of the incomes policy, though not to the events of 1974-6. One may consider various ways in which incomes policy is weakened by a lax monetary policy. Most obviously, the choice facing firms between resistance to wage claims and surrender to them is tipped in favour of surrender by easy credit to finance higher wage bills. Nevertheless this is in one sense irrelevant; the pressure would build up somehow or other and wreck the policy.

It is clear that monetary expansion had a significant role in the acceleration of inflation between 1971 and 1974. How much this was permissive and how much causal is less clear. To some extent it does not matter. Certainly the inappropriateness of the monetary policy pursued is clear. Whatever one's attribution of its role in conjunction with other policies in overall economic management, one must accept that the monetary policy pursued was a necessary component of the government's failure to achieve its objectives.

One cannot do more than speculate on what would have happened if the NUM executive had not voted by a majority of one to institute an overtime ban in 1973 to try to break the incomes policy;[49] or if the Arab-Israeli war had not broken out; or again if the incoming Labour government had not decided to postpone the adjustment to the oil price increase, and had not believed that the events of November-February 1974 made it impossible to resist wage claims. One can say with a reasonable degree of confidence, however, that inflation would have continued to accelerate in the UK, at least up to 15-20 per cent p.a., although the contingencies above may have pushed it up by another 10 points.

It is interesting to compare this analysis with Berman's work for the US. His results suggest that the OPEC price increases of 1973 contributed at most 2 per cent to US inflation.[50] Project Link's assessment was 1 per cent for world inflation.[51] These studies seem to suggest that this 'moderate' analysis of the cause of UK inflation is a reasonable working hypothesis until, if ever, better econometric evidence is available. Strict monetarists can justly claim that the whole of the inflation of 1974-5 and its timing were consistent with their theory. The peak of inflation followed the peak of monetary expansion (and likewise the slowdown) almost perfectly in line with Friedman's 18-month lag. However, one could be a non-monetarist and still believe that the monetary expansion was necessary for the acceleration of inflation in the UK, and was a sufficient cause of, at least, the tripling of the inflation rate to nearly 20 per cent, even if other factors contributed to the explosion which reached nearly 30 per cent p.a. at its peak. However, if one blames monetary policy for the rise in inflation, one must also credit it with reducing unemployment from 4 per cent to 2.2 per cent at the cost of a £3 billion balance of payments deficit.

References

1. See Gurley and Shaw (1960).
2. E.g. the Deputy Governor's Speech Does the Money Supply Really Matter? reprinted in *Bulletin*, vol. 13, no. 2 (June 1973), p. 195.
3. See Bank (1972).
4. Ibid., p. 45.
5. Artis and Lewis (1974 and n.d.).
6. For the conventional and opposite view, see e.g. Hamburger (1973).
7. From Artis and Lewis (1974).
8. See Mussa (1977).
9. For a review of this literature see Gowland (1979), Ch. 4.
10. *Bulletin*, vol. 13, no. 2 (June 1973), p. 195.
11. Governor's speech, Key Issues in Monetary and Credit Policy reprinted in Bank (1971), hereafter referred to as Key Issues.
12. See Sawyer (1980).
13. See MPCC, p. 57.
14. Of −0.37.
15. See MPCC, p. 69, n5.
16. *Bulletin*, vol. 14, no. 1 (March 1974), p. 21.
17. From Key Issues in Bank (1971).
18. The banks were allowed to keep the interest accruing on the gilts.
19. See Moore and Threadgold (1980) and their bibliography. The Spencer references are especially useful.
20. See Hadjimatheou (1976).
21. For econometric models of the housing market see ibid.; Mayes (1979); and Pratt (1980).
22. A maximum of 10,000.
23. See Mayes (1979).
24. Ibid.
25. See Taylor and Threadgold (1980).
26. Figures from *Annual Abstract of Statistics* (CSO, London).
27. See references in n 21 above and bibliography in Pratt (1980).
28. See Crowther (1971).
29. As there is no suitable evidence available on differential behaviour of

owner-occupiers and tenants, this section is pure surmise.

30. See MPCC, p. 88, n6.
31. See Mackay (1941).
32. See Carswell (1960).
33. See Galbraith (1954).
34. See e.g. Marriott (1969).
35. E.g. in Galbraith (1954).
36. See MPCC, Ch. 6 and p. 210; also Bank (1978).
37. See Gowland (1975).
38. The case is discussed in Kenyon (1974).
39. From Gowland (1975).
40. See Cagan (1956).
41. See Gowland (1982), chapter entitled Consumption, Saving and Inflation.
42. See Keynes (1936).
43. See Friedman (1969).
44. For a recent review see Saville (1980).
45. See Bank (1979).
46. See Brown, Enoch and Mortimer-Lee (1980).
47. See Williams, Goodhart and Gowland (1976).
48. See also Enoch (1979).
49. See Butler and Kavanagh (1974).
50. See Berman (1978).
51. For an early account of Project Link see Renton (1975), p. 657.

8 THE NEW 'NEW APPROACH'

At the end of 1973, the authorities had to devise a new regime of monetary control very quickly. Competition and credit control was now regarded as a failure. Monetary growth was 30 per cent p.a. The balance of payments deficit was £3 billion p.a. The political and economic pressures on the government were enormous and growing rapidly as the miners' strike and OPEC price increases approached. It was impossible to have the long-drawn-out consultations that preceded changes of regime of monetary control in 1971 and 1980. It was also undesirable to the government as they wished to save face. Hence, the authorities replaced the new approach with a totally different method of monetary control, usually known as the new 'new approach'. Other even less elegant terms are sometimes applied to the new regime such as 'the son of the new approach'. There were various new features about this new regime which were to emerge during 1974. These were also a number of volte-face which meant the total abandonment of the principles of competition and credit control. These included

(a) the reintroduction of ceilings. This time the authorities were to put a ceiling on bank liabilities not on bank assets as in the 1960s, but the effect was the same. This new ceiling, the IBELs ceiling, is discussed in section 8.1. It meant the abandonment of the arguments against ceilings presented by the authorities in 1971.

(b) the development by the authorities of a new method of selling gilt-edged — the Duke of York strategy. This meant that the authorities once more sought to manipulate the gilts market. This new modus operandi is discussed in section 8.2.

(c) the alteration of the PSBR for monetary purposes. From June 1975, all major changes in taxation and public spending were for monetary reasons. By 1977, the idea of an independent fiscal policy was dead. This is discussed in section 8.3.

(d) the authorities, in 1976, accepting the idea of monetary targets; this was of obvious importance in moving towards an explicit and avowed *monetary* policy. The difference between monetary and credit or other types of financial policy is often a mere matter of semantics. In 1976 it was far more significant. This issue is discussed in section 8.4.

8.1 The IBELs Ceiling

One of the most immediately apparent and striking features of the new regime of monetary control was that the authorities had to eat their brave words of 1971 about ceilings. 'Terms control' on hire purchase was also reintroduced.[1] They introduced a new type of ceiling with many new features, but it was a ceiling none the less and subject to all the usual problems (2.4). The new ceilings were imposed on one category of bank liabilities rather than, as in the 1960s, on one category of bank assets. This particular type of control is discussed in section 2.4.2 above. The form of the control was to place a limit on the growth of interest-bearing deposits (IBELs) from the non-bank sector; inter-bank deposits were deducted from the gross total. Non-interest-bearing deposits were excluded from the control because it was thought to be impossible for a bank to reduce non-interest-bearing deposits but it could turn interest-bearing deposits away by offering a lower rate of interest.

One new feature of the ceiling was an explicit penalty for breaking it. This was an obligation to lodge a percentage of the excess amount with the Bank of England as an interest-free Supplementary Special Deposit (SSD). (There is no connection, other than the name, with orthodox Special Deposits.) The percentage lodged rose according to the amount by which the ceiling was exceeded. In the original version, the SSD was 5 per cent of the excess if the excess were less than 1 per cent of the ceiling. The SSD rose to 25 per cent for excesses in the 1-3 per cent band and 50 per cent for an excess over 3 per cent. In April 1974, the bands were changed to 0-3 per cent, 3-5 per cent and over 5 per cent. The SSDs were still calculated as 5 per cent, 25 per cent and 50 per cent respectively. These bands remained unchanged until 1980 when the scheme was dropped. The scheme has some aspects of a 'tax' about it — lodging a 50 per cent interest-free deposit is equivalent to a 50 per cent tax on banking. But while a 5 per cent SSD might act as a tax on banking, a 50 per cent SSD is prohibitive and acts as a ceiling.[2]

The problems of this modus operandi are discussed above (p. 29). The crucial problem is that black markets may develop, which leads to inequity, inefficiency and the distortion of official statistics. In the end the scheme was dropped for these reasons but not before it had been used five times in the period 1974-80. The scheme seems to have been initially quite effective. This was perhaps surprising as one might have expected the old devices used in the 1960s to evade the ceilings on bank lending to be resurrected. The ceiling could have been evaded either by the use of parallel markets or by manipulation of their port-folios by banks. In the former case, the mechanism would have been as follows. The banks were simultaneously turning away deposits (or increasing their margins by cutting the rates paid) and rationing credit, as the whole purpose of the scheme was to avoid rationing credit by price. So, both a supply and demand for funds would be created. Normal economic analysis would suggest that these would create a 'free' or 'black' market at some price higher than would have prevailed in a uniform market cleared by price.[3] One might have expected the money brokers etc. to come back into vogue, or more likely, given that they were under a cloud, the corporate money market to grow.[4] However,

(a) the 'secondary banking' failures in 1973-4 reduced the appeal of evasion, as the necessary agents were less trusted; and

(b) the depression cut the demand for funds.

Both of these are in accordance with elementary microeconomic theory. If black marketeers are not trusted, rationing works. Most of the evasive devices used some financial intermediary. All unconventional transactions and small or less well-established intermediaries were under an (often unjustified) cloud in 1974. Rationing works more easily the less excess demand exists.

In addition, there was one market force which strengthened the scheme. The new scheme deterred banks from bidding for deposits, since growth in interest-bearing deposits was penalised, so the rate paid on deposits fell, relative to other rates. Consequently, short-dated public sector securities became more attractive. The authorities were a vigorous bidder for any diverted funds. Thus, the non-bank private sector acquired £356m of Treasury Bills in the first quarter of 1977, following the reimposition of IBELs ceilings. These reduced the money supply in the same way as any other sales of public sector debt and thus made the ceiling on bank deposits and (indirectly) on credit effective. Of course, the private sector's liquidity was not reduced — if anything it increased, as Treasury Bills are more marketable than wholesale deposits and as marketable as CDs. Issues of economic theory are perhaps more relevant in this area than anywhere else in the practical application of monetary policy.

Over time the scheme became less effective as evasive devices were developed and the factors working in favour of the scheme became less potent. However, the chief reason for the failure of the scheme in the long run is that it was misused. It was imposed too often and the ceiling left on for too long. As an infrequently used, short-term weapon it could have been very useful for a much longer period. In this mode of operation, the costs of evasion would have been too high, relative to the benefits, for black markets to develop. As it was, there was large-scale evasion.[5] One form of evasion was the use of acceptance credits – 'the bill leak'. In essence, the banks performed all their normal functions but the transaction did not count as a deposit. A held a bank-guaranteed security and B obtained credit. In all but name this was the normal deposit/loan relationship. However, B's bill had been discounted (i.e. the acceptance) and A held it. The possibilities of evasion were even greater after the removal of exchange control in November 1979. Transactions could be 'booked' abroad. It is clear that by 1980 the scale of the evasion and consequent distortion was enormous. Transactions equal to over 6 per cent of $£M_3$ were brought back into the official statistics in July and August 1980. Of course the very distortion of the statistics that made the control undesirable in the first place makes it impossible to estimate evasion accurately; how much evasion there was earlier is less clear.

That the banks were able to cut their interest-bearing eligible liabilities by 6 per cent in six months in 1976-7 without apparent damage to the economy suggests that some manoeuvring by the banking sector may have taken place. The *Financial Times* suggested that the large increase in the clearing banks' loans on the inter-bank market may have represented loans by the banks to their subsidiaries that were 'earmarked' for on-lending by the subsidiary to particular customers (the subsidiaries being below their ceilings unlike the parents). However this, and similar deals between banks, would only enable individual banks to keep below their ceilings, not the entire banking sector. In fact, by ensuring that all banks were close to their ceilings, this would help the authorities – in the same way that the Federal Funds market in the US ensures greater efficiency in the use of reserves, and so the workings of monetary policy. The Bank suggested that some evasion might have taken place in 1976 by the use of bills.[6] Banks could also have encouraged switches to current account by remitting bank charges (for services) or by reducing commitment fees on facilities. Imagine a company that had £100,000 on current account and £400,000 in deposit accounts earning 10 per cent interest, and which was paying £25,000 per annum in bank charges and £5,000 per annum as a ½ per cent commitment fee on an overdraft limit of £1m (a 'line of credit' in US or continental jargon). If it switched £300,000 to current account and had the charges remitted neither it nor the bank would be worse off but the bank would be helped vis-à-vis its IBELs ceiling. In the three months following the reintroduction of the ceilings in 1976 M_1 grew by 0.9 per cent and £M_3 fell by 3 per cent. This suggests that some such transactions occurred.

In summary, the control had some genuine (and a substantial cosmetic) effect on monetary growth.[7] This declined over time, although as late as 1978 the device seems to have been useful. The Treasury seems to have welcomed even the cosmetic effect in so far as it boosted confidence in 1977. The control, in short, was a stop gap measure which fulfilled its original purpose well. It was probably right both to introduce it and to remove it, but with more prudent use of the technique, it could have had a longer useful life.

8.2 The Gilts' Market: The Duke of York Strategy

The authorities adopted a new, aggressive method of selling gilt-edged securities, known as the Duke of York strategy. This new technique avoided the problems of 'leaning into the wind' (p. 89) and made it possible to market large quantities of government securities. The new method was not without its problems. The two major ones were that it was not clear for how long the technique would persist and that it probably contributed to excessive variability in monetary growth.

To sell something you need to know why it is bought. The Duke of York strategy was based on a new theory of gilt-edged demand. This was a composite theory which reconciled the economists' and cashiers' theory. It assumed that there were three arguments in the demand function for gilts of the non-bank private sector:

(a) the level of (long) interest rates, with a positive effect as in the economists' theory.

(b) the change in interest rates, with a negative sign as in the cashiers' theory. It was still assumed that the gilts' market was dominated by short-period maximising holders with extrapolative expectations.

(c) the margin between long and short rates. Gilts are usually issued as longer-term securities. Thus the attractiveness of gilts' is increased by the *relative* yield compared to short-term interest rates.

This theory implies that the sales of gilts will be at a peak when long rates are absolutely high, but falling, and long rates are high relative to short-term ones. The 'Duke of York' strategy is to manipulate the market to produce these conditions. This is done by first raising then reducing interest rates, hence the name; interest rates are marched up to the top of the hill and down again. The objectives, furthermore, are achieved without the authorities having to purchase any bonds to set off a selling season, the fatal flaw with 'leaning into the wind'.[8]

The stages of the Duke of York technique work as follows (Figure 8.1):

(1) they increase both long and short rates.

(2) they lower short rates.

(3) the favourable margin induces an increase in the demand for gilts by the private sector. This enables the authorities to sell some bonds.

(4) the increased demand leads to a rise in the price of bonds, i.e. a fall in long rates.

(5) conditions are now ideal for large sales by the authorities; long rates are high but falling and the differential between long and short rates is also favourable.

Thus a brisk selling season follows. This ends at some stage and the authorities wait until they wish to sell some more gilt-edged bonds when the whole game restarts. This manoeuvre was executed on eight occasions between January 1974 and August 1980. On six of these occasions the authorities raised interest rates sharply within three months of the end of the selling season. This generated a sharp fall in bond prices and more than wiped out the gains made while bond prices were rising (stage 5 above). This leads to two, related, puzzles:

(a) why does the market continue to hold extrapolative expectations when official actions are such as to falsify these expectations? The authorities have deliberately induced false expectations. It is puzzling that the market apparently still holds (false) extrapolative expectations where they are not only wrong but lead to heavy losses.

(b) why do people continue to be conned into buying bonds when this activity leads to heavy losses?

This behaviour violates every principle of the rational and efficient markets hypothesis and is very hard to explain. Some possible reasons might be:

(1) operators in the market are stupid and will learn. This seems unbelievable. Most of the 200 or 300 large institutional fund managers who dominate the market are very well aware of the nature of the Bank's manoeuvre.

(2) the technique is not necessary. 'Money burns a hole in the pocket' of the managers and they would buy sometime anyway. At most, the manipulation determines the timing of purchases. This implies that the Bank is stupid, if it carries out unnecessary manoeuvres of this kind. It is again unbelievable that the Bank carries out such a complex operation for no purpose.

Figure 8.1

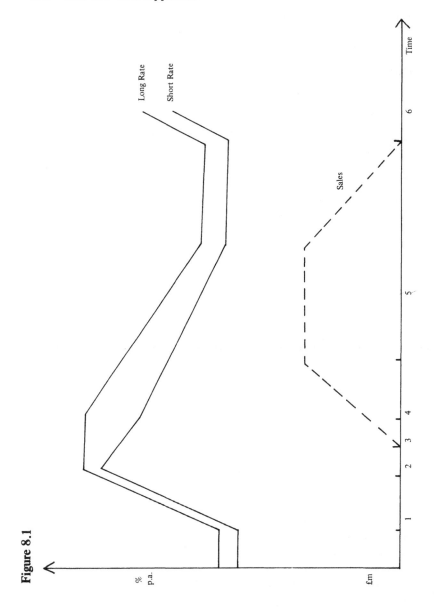

(3) the managers love excitement, like gamblers at a race meeting, and enjoy the thrills of a (normally) losing game. This seems unlikely.

(4) they all believe they are cleverer than the other managers. Thus each time the game is played profits are made by enough players to keep the participants in. This is similar to people who bet on the football pools knowing that on average the punter loses 75 per cent of his stake. This statistic is not relevant if one believes one is sufficiently better than average.

(5) Game Theory suggests the possibility of everyone being locked into a sort of 'super prisoners' dilemma'. An alternative Game Theory explanation stresses the disproportionate size of the participants, i.e. the elephant and chicken game.[9]

(6) the reward structure for fund managers is such that the cost of not making profits far exceeds the benefit of avoiding losses. Following the herd may be a safe strategy for a manager — even if he knows that over the long run his fund would do better if he did not buy bonds. The pay-off matrix in Table 8.1 illustrates this proposition. The top line shows the pay-off to the fund. The expected return is 5 from holding bank deposits, −37.5 from buying bonds. The second strategy has a higher return (and less risk), but if the bracketed figures represent managerial utility, then buying is the right strategy, indeed, it is the dominant one. The reason is that the manager (probably rightly) believes there is no penalty for a wrong, but universal, action and a large penalty for failing to join the herd when it is right.

Table 8.1

	Extrapolative expectations are right ($P = 0.25$)	Extrapolative expectations are wrong (0.75)
1. Buy Bonds	+10	−50
	(+30)	(0)
2. Don't Buy (hold bank deposit)	+ 5	+ 5
	(−50)	(0)

This explanation is based on the concept of a perverse rewards structure among UK financial institutions. The rationale is that fund managers are not adequately rewarded for avoiding mistakes for a number of obvious reasons. Another managerial argument is that managers are risk-averse about their personal position. If one assumes that no one is ever sacked for following the herd but may be either rewarded or penalised for deviating from it, then a risk-averse manager's strategy is clear.

While the growth rate of money was at a defensible level over the period 1974-7 as a whole, the variations from month to month and quarter to quarter were very large — for example, the rapid acceleration and subsequent deceleration in 1976 — although the Bank argues that variability was not excessive.[10] The variability was partly a consequence of the Bank's gilt-edged 'selling season' — a tender method would have ensured a smoother flow (p. 17). It is difficult to assess the direct economic significance of such variability. However it is clear that it affected confidence in both the foreign exchange and gilts' market and so complicated the authorities' task.

8.3 Alterations in the PSBR

A crucial development during this period was that the concept of an independent fiscal policy was discarded by the authorities. They concentrated more and more on the financial effects of tax and expenditure policy. Concepts expressed in money terms, in particular the PSBR, became more important as the 'real' notions of the elementary Keynesian model seemed less and less relevant to economic policy. As a change in attitude to public spending, this was as important as those wrought by Pitt, Gladstone and the famous Kingsley Wood Budget of 1941. In brief, the requirements of monetary policy came to dominate decisions about public spending. This new attitude to public spending meant that the *method* of controlling public spending had to be changed. From the early 1960s public spending was controlled in *constant* price terms by the PESC system.[11] The Treasury were always very successful in controlling this aggregate. However, to control public spending in volume terms was no longer appropriate. The financial cost (i.e. *current* price) of public spending could be billions of pounds above the Treasury's projection and yet the Treasury could (truthfully) claim that public spending was not out of control because *constant* price spending was on target. The system was inappropriate, but the Treasury were not incompetent. They were guilty of faults of design but not of execution. The PESC system was replaced by a system of 'cash limits'. These imposed limits on the current price level of public expenditure; this new system worked well. However, some areas of public spending were uncontrollable — and unpredictable! In 1977/8, public spending was over £2 billion less than the official estimate. Of this, only £300m was shortfall in that part of public expenditure covered by cash limits.

Over £1 billion was the result of interest rates being below forecast, and debt service charges accordingly being lower. The remaining error was the result of unemployment not rising as fast as anticipated. Tax revenues were equally unpredictable. Thus, the authorities control over the PSBR was less than perfect, even after the introduction of cash limits.

This, therefore, was one reason why the government 'cut' public expenditure on at least six occasions between 1975 and 1979, although the term 'cut' is very misleading as total expenditure rose, even in volume terms. This was variously ascribed to incompetence and to gradualism of the sort recommended by Laidler and Parkin. One could take Healey's line that 'salami must be sliced thinly' (i.e. to ensure that the cuts were exactly the right amount) or alternatively, one might view the government as eternally over-optimistic. Either way, its repeated rounds of cuts damaged its prestige. There was a probably justified suspicion that repeated cuts represented the only method by which Healey could push the cuts through against cabinet and PLP suspicion and opposition.

In brief, the government, in an act of major significance, made the PSBR a major weapon of monetary policy. Unfortunately the execution of the policy failed to match the intention, but the government did show enormous courage in cutting the growth of public expenditure. It showed equal courage in eliminating nationalised industry deficits. To eliminate them while inflation was reduced from 25 per cent to 9 per cent in 1975-9 was a major triumph. The Labour government's record on public spending was mixed; henceforth, however, the needs of monetary policy would determine the desired size of the PSBR and thus tax and revenue policy. This was both a highly significant and courageous act of policy.

8.4 Money Supply Targets

Explicit money supply targets were introduced in this period.[12] Although the money supply consequences of a DCE target had been spelt out by Jenkins in 1969, this was an unprecedented step. It is difficult to over-state its significance. The April Budget in 1976 included the first semi-official money supply target in UK history.

> To this end, I aim to see that the growth of the money supply is consistent with my plans for the growth of demand expressed in

current prices. It is became clear that this aim were not being achieved, I would be ready to use the appropriate mix of policies – not necessarily monetary policy alone – to redress the situation. After two years in which M_3 has grown a good deal more slowly than money GDP, I would expect their respective growth rates to come more into line in the coming financial year.[13]

In July the numerical implications of this were spelled out and the target firmed up: 'For the financial year as a whole money supply growth should amount to about 12 per cent.'[14] Further targets followed: 9-13 per cent range for sterling M_3 for the financial year 1977/8 and 8-12 per cent for 1978-9 on a 'rolling basis'. In the UK a 'rolling target' is one which is reassessed regularly, in practice once every six months. In the US, a rolling target means that there is a target to be met every month. As shown in Table 8.2, the government's record in attaining these is not particularly impressive. Nevertheless over a longer period the actual growth of the money supply was close to the targets. The existence of the targets certainly had a significant impact on monetary policy. The government's commitment to the targets was such that it retained them in the teeth of IMF opposition. In 1977 both its exchange rate policy and its DCE policy were in clear contravention of the Letter of Intent.[15] The exchange rate was allowed to rise, rather than be at 'a competitive level'. DCE grew by only 35 per cent of the target agreed with the IMF. Both policies were adopted as part of the strategy to keep monetary growth within the target range. Ultimately the attempt failed, in part because of bad seasonal adjustment of the $£M_3$ data (9.4).

It is important to consider why such a radical change of policy was made. The argument that international pressure forced money supply targets on the authorities can easily be rejected (in particular the advent of the IMF led to a 'de-emphasis on money'): 'our target will now be in terms of DCE not M_3'.[16] Equally, the argument that the government was monetarist seems fallacious. There are three reasons why they might adopt the targets.

(a) Together with 'cash limits', it seemed to be a method of curbing public spending. This is using the 'supply side counterpart' equation yet again. Depending on forecasts for the private sector's desire to lend to the public sector and to borrow from the banks, setting a limit on a monetary aggregate implies a level for the PSBR. However, the PSBR can be cut by sales of assets (e.g. BP shares as in 1977) and by financial transactions whereas those seeking to curb the PSBR are usually more interested in cutting public spending per se.

Table 8.2: Monetary Targets

A: Labour Government

Period	Announced	Variable	Target (%)	Actual (%)
1976-7	July 1976	M_3	12	
1976-7	December 1976	$£M_3$	9-13	10.5
1977-8	April 1977	$£M_3$	9-13	6.5
1978-9	April 1978	$£M_3$	8-12	13.0
October 1978- October 1979	October 1978	$£M_3$	8-12	10.0

B: Conservative Government

Period	Announced	Target[a]
1979-80		
June 1979- April 1980	June 1979 Confirmed November 1979	7-11
1980-81 Mid-February		7-11
1980-Mid- April 1981	April 1980 Confirmed November 1980	

C: PSBR Forecast and Actual (£m)

	Post-Budget Forecast	Actual
1971-2	1,209	1,326
1972-3	3,358	2,855
1973-4	4,423	4,276
1974-5	2,733	7,602
1975-6	9,055	10,773
1976-7	11,962	8,820
1977-8	8,471	5,600
1978-9	8,163	8,162
1979-80	6,881	9,120
1980-1	8,536	13,455

D: Other Targets

DCE (announced December 1976) (£m)

	Target	Actual
1976/7	9,000	4,934
1977/8	7,700	3,772

Note: a. All $£M_3$.

(b) The authorities, especially the Treasury, had come to believe that the financial community is monetarist. Thus, even if monetary factors had no direct impact on economic affairs, money supply targets are necessary to inspire confidence in financial markets.

(c) Finally, it seems the Chancellor, Mr Healey, believed that control of the money supply was a necessary but not a sufficient condition for control of the rate of inflation. The Budget speech of 6 April 1976 gives some credence to this.

> Second, it remains my aim that the growth of the money supply should not be allowed to fuel inflation as it did under my predecessor. To this end, I aim to see that the growth of the money supply is consistent with my plans for the growth of demand expressed in current prices.[17]

This third reason then probably swayed the political authorities while the Treasury and Bank supported them for the first two reasons.

The psychological role of the targets is illustrated by the prolonged arguments over the appropriate base for the targets. The problem was whether the target growth should be added to the previous actual level or the previous target. Say that in Year 1 target growth was 10 per cent which would imply a level of £50,000m. If in fact the level at the end of Year 1 was £48,000m, a policy of 10 per cent growth could be announced and mean two different things. It could mean 10 per cent on the actual level (£48,000m), i.e. a new target of £52,800m, or on the previous target (£50,000m), i.e. a new target of £55,000m. There was much media discussion over the appropriate level. There was an issue of substance involved: namely, whether previous errors be corrected or ignored. Most economic theory suggests the error should be corrected over a period of years; so, in the above example, £1,000m of the error could be corrected by higher growth in Year 2, £500m in Year 3 etc. However, this issue is totally independent of the form of the announced growth rate when this is discretionary. If one wishes to correct a past error this can be added on to the growth rate before it is announced. Thus, in the above example, if one wishes to adjust for the whole of the past error then one could announce a new growth target of 10 per cent, based on the old target level, or 14.6 per cent, based on the actual level. Both imply a new target level of £55,000m. Contrawise, even if one had to announce targets as growth rates based on the old target there would be no need to compensate for past errors. Instead the new target level could be calculated and the appropriate growth rate announced. Hence to care about the number announced indicates that the authorities and the markets treated the numbers as being symbols of policy; implying much more than a new monetary target. The authorities varied the base so as to maintain greater stability in the announced figure. It was never made clear how the targets were determined. They had something of the forecast as well as the optimal about them.

This ambiguity is also revealed in some of the official statements about the reason for the wide band —4 per cent — compared to the US 2 per cent. This was often (e.g. in the Mais lecture)[18] justified as much on grounds of unpredictability of monetary growth as lack of precise control. In both cases the reason given was practical; an *economic* case was never put forward. Such a case could have been for example that the optimal level within the band depended on other factors, or a moderate Keynesian case might have been that small variations in money did not matter.

The case for and against targets is analysed by Foot.[19] There are three principal reasons for the adoption of monetary targets.[20] The first reason is that there should be a greater stability in the economy as a result. In many ways monetary targets are analogous to the automatic stabilisers advocated so strongly by Keynesians in the mid-1960s.[21] In both cases the essence of the concept is that if an economy diverges from the desired path, countervailing forces are set in motion to bring it back, without the need for discretionary government action. For example, if government spending is higher than planned, this would mean that, ceteris paribus, monetary growth would exceed the target. Hence, to meet the target it would be necessary, for example, to raise interest rates above planned levels. Thus the expansionary/inflationary effects of higher government spending would be at least partially offset. In this way the commitment to a monetary target provides a quasi-automatic adjustment device. Friedman has always argued that this would provide the best attainable degree of stability as any attempt to achieve more, by fine-tuning, would end in disaster.[22]

The second argument for a target is to influence expectations and to provide the private sector with the information about government actions necessary for its decision-making and planning. There are obvious gains to both public and private sectors if this is achieved. In some ways this process is comparable to the goals of indicative planning.

Finally, monetary targets are seen by many economists and politicians as a desire to restrict the freedom of government action. In the context of 'economics of politics' models of the political business cycle, this is regarded as highly desirable in order to prevent government manipulating the economy for electoral purposes at a disastrous longer-term cost.[23] This viewpoint is in many ways the successor to the 'discipline school' of advocates of fixed exchange rates. Thus a monetary target is a means of achieving ends previously sought by other routes, involving fiscal devices, planning councils and exchange rates.

There are a number of further points that need to be considered. The first is that it is difficult to see how any rational coherent policy can be implemented without a precise numerical target. Moreover, the decision to publish this seems to be highly commendable. Published targets are a necessary condition for both the accountability of policy-makers and, indeed, for any form of responsible decision-making.

Both criticism in advance and ex post analysis are much easier if such information is published.[24] The advantages to those making financial decisions are also great. It can increase the pressure on the authorities to stick to their targets, not a bad thing but capable of generating both virtuous and vicious circles. High monetary growth can lead to low gilt sales, because higher interest rates are expected, and hence to still higher monetary growth. Thus the pressure on the authorities to pursue a stable, predictable policy is increased. This is something which some may deplore but the author applauds, even though some forms of very fine-tuning are rendered impossible.

An optimist might have hoped that monetary targets would have lowered inflationary expectations, and even wage claims. There was very little evidence of this, but, at worst, money supply targets could not increase inflationary expectations. There are various dangers in monetary targets but the principal one is that it may lead to excessive concentration on one aggregate. The authorities are tempted to use cosmetic controls to 'manage' this series. There are dangers in any case that this statistic will become misleading, as stated in Goodhart's law (p. 4). If this statistic is out of line then corrective action may be delayed. In 1977/8, the acceleration in $£M_3$ seemed to occur much later than in other financial series (DCE, M_1, M_3 and others), possibly because of faulty seasonal adjustment. Because $£M_3$ was the target variable, the authorities ignored the acceleration in the other variables. Thus the mood of complacency (9.5) was intensified and the authorities delayed raising interest rates by at least four months. The authorities should look at a wide range of financial aggregates, stocks and flows, and asset prices, and in the light of these decide on appropriate policy. It seems reasonable for the UK authorities to set a target for a broad monetary aggregate, probably sterling M_3, but to have supplementary targets for alternative definitions and to reappraise policy whenever these are breached or there are sharp movements in equity prices, or other movements in 'confidence'.

Alternatively, one could have various targets of equal standing. The problem is what to do if they move outside the target band in opposite directions, and policies are not available to have the desired effects on the aggregates. Hence it seems desirable to have a principal target and a whole range of supplementary ones. The secondary targets should trigger off a reappraisal of the whole range of targets, or a close examination of what is really happening. It may be that some statistics are becoming distorted (or are simply wrong), or that some crucial assumption on which policy is based is incorrect. For example, if DCE is below target and £M_3 above target, the balance of payments is much more in surplus than desired (or predicted). Hence a reappraisal is necessary. The authorities will have to change their monetary policy, their balance of payments target or both.

Since I proposed such a system of principle and supplementary targets in MPCC, a similar but more formal proposal has been made by various authors, notably Buiter.[25] He suggests an 'open feedback' rule or contingent policy target. The level of the monetary target would depend on other variables. Thus, the rule might be that the £M_3 target is 10 per cent plus 1 per cent for every 2 per cent by which M_1 growth falls below 8 per cent. (This would give a target below 10 per cent for £M_3 if M_1 grew faster than 8 per cent.) In particular, he suggests that monetary targets could depend on exchange rate targets. In Buiter's model such a policy clearly outperforms a fixed target. It is impossible to draw a simple comparison with my proposal, since it would depend on how well one thought the authorities could judge the situation. (Clearly they could always abide by a rule; hence with good judgement they must do at least as well as the rule.) To fall into the monetary economists' vice of analogy, Buiter and I agree that it would be better for a car's speed to vary with the driver's visibility than to be fixed at 30 m.p.h. He suggests the speed should be calculated by a formula using data from a light meter. I am proposing that whenever the light meter shows a different sort of light, the driver should consider changing speed. A sufficiently good driver could always do at least as well as the formula. But he could do worse, depending on his judgement. Buiter's rule has many of the advantages of monetary targets in influencing market reactions. How practicable is it though? It is not clear just what formula should be used, especially if one thinks that more than 2 variables matter. In brief, there is a case for and against Buiter's scheme.

Buiter's argument has been extended by Artis and Currie.[26] They start with the generally agreed premise that *any* nominal variable could be selected as the target variable, including prices such as interest rates and exchange rates as well as quantities such as the money supply. In a steady state economy or a world of perfect certainty the choice of target variable is irrelevant since the choice of a target for any one variable implies a path for each of the remaining nominal variables. Any of these implied paths could have been selected as the target variable and the effect on all given variables would have been identical. Thus the choice of a target variable must depend on the nature of the uncertainties facing decision-makers and on the nature of any 'random shocks' experienced by an economy. Random shocks might include an OPEC price rise, a depression in the US, or some internal development which cannot be predicted by the authorities and so is a 'random event' as far as their models are concerned.

In this respect the Artis-Currie argument is similar to the analyses pioneered by Poole and Waud,[27] who examined interest rate, monetary and money base targets in this context. However, Artis and Currie's analysis is in the context of an open economy and looks at exchange rate targets and monetary targets. Their analysis is also original in that it incorporates the concept of a 'jump' variable into the debate about targets. The proposition is that a shock is likely to affect some variables far more than others in the short term because, say, the size of the real capital stock is virtually fixed in the short term whereas there is virtually no constraint on movements of the exchange rate. Therefore it is necessary to examine the possibility that a shock might be stabilising through its effect on jump variables, and in particular on the exchange rate. Thus they argue that there is an a priori case for allowing large fluctuations in the money supply to stabilise the exchange rate, since they share Buiter's preference for conditional targets.

It is worth pointing out that the arguments put forward by Buiter, Artis and Currie provide a perfect defence for the Conservative government's policy in 1979-80 when the monetary target was overshot by about 100 per cent (a growth rate of almost 20 per cent against a target of 7-11 per cent) at a time when there was an unexpectedly high exchange rate. Buiter, Artis and Currie have, however, made it clear that they are not seeking to defend Mrs Thatcher; indeed, they are amongst her sharpest critics. Artis and Currie also argue that if shocks are predominantly internal the authorities should seek to maintain an exchange rate target and if they are predominantly external, a money supply target. This would seem to strengthen the case for monetary targets in the UK.

There are, however, a number of problems inherent in the work of Artis and Currie, the major one being that it involves some modelling of private sector expectations and such modelling is virtually untestable by present techniques. The equations derived by estimation from rational expectations models are normally also derivable from more traditional models. If there were a fully rational model then there would be none of the dangers suggested by Artis and Currie. In less whole-hogging rational expectations models there is a possibility of an overshoot of the exchange rate.[28] However its impact must depend on how agents in the system react to it. If they assume it to be permanent, then instability is virtually certain. If they treat it as a temporary phenomenon then the costs are much less. Brunner's pragmatic view is pertinent.[29] He argues that theoretically one can improve on monetary targets but that the costs of attempting to do so outweigh the benefits.

In conclusion, it is clear that some form of monetary target is desirable but that there are dangers in excessive concentration on a single target. Hence there is a case for multiple targets or conditional rules. However, it is equally clear that the very considerable benefits of targets may be jeopardised if the targets are either too flexible or too complicated.

References

1. See Credit Control – A Supplementary Scheme in *Bulletin*, vol. 14, no. 1 (March 1974), p. 37 and Credit Notice – Consumer Credit in *Bulletin*, vol. 14, no. 1 (March 1974), p. 40. For full details of maximum permitted growth rate etc., see MPCC, p. 147, n1 and the regulations listed on p. 198.

2. To act as a tax, overdraft rates would have had to rise to 34 per cent.

3. Proof available from author.

4. See Gowland and Pakenham (1974).

5. See various issues of the *Bulletin* for estimates.

6. *Bulletin*, vol. 16, no. 2 (June 1976), p. 197.

7. The cosmetic role is discussed more fully in MPCC, Chs. 8 and 9.

8. See Gowland (1977b) and the references in sections 5.4 and 5.5 above; for the 'flaw' see Chief Cashier in Bank (1971).

9. See Brams (1975) and (1976); see Friedman (1977) for the 'super prisoners dilemma'. The name was invented by Bob Sugden of Newcastle, to whom I express my gratitude for much stimulating discussion on this topic.

10. See *Bulletin*, vol. 17, no. 2 (June 1977), p. 152.

11. For the switch and other issues concerning the control of public spending, see Gowland (1979), Ch. 13.

12. On Money Supply targets, see especially Volcker (1977); Foot (1981) and Sargent's chapter in the same volume; the Governor's main lecture, *Bulletin*, vol. 18, no. 1 (March 1978), p. 210; Boston (1976); Brunner and Meltzer (1980), especially the article by Brunner and Meltzer (p. 1) and Sumner (p. 91). Foot and Sumner both contain very full bibliographies.

13. *Hansard*, 6 April 1976, Col. 237.

14. *Hansard*, 10 July 1976.

15. See *Hansard*, 15 December 1976, Col. 1534 for the letter and Healey's interpretation.

16. Ibid.

17. *Hansard*, 6 April 1976, Col. 237.
18. *Bulletin*, vol. 18, no. 1 (March), p. 210.
19. Foot (1981).
20. See Buiter (1980) for an alternative view.
21. Hansen (1969), Heller (1968).
22. Friedman (1968).
23. See e.g. Tullock (1976).
24. See Sargent's analysis (1975).
25. E.g. Buiter (1980).
26. Artis and Lewis (1980).
27. Waud (1973); Poole (1970).
28. For an interesting model of this type see Dornbusch and Fischer (1980).
29. Brunner (1981).

9 THE LABOUR GOVERNMENT'S MONETARY POLICY

This chapter presents a narrative of the period 1974-9 together with an assessment of monetary policy in the period.

9.1 A New Scheme and a New Government, January-October 1974

In December 1973 the Conservative government announced the new 'new approach', a £1,200m package of public expenditure cuts, and the 'lifeboat'.[1] The government was also facing an overtime ban by the National Union of Mineworkers, in opposition to Phase 3 of the government's incomes policy. Following a pithead ballot (the result was announced on 4 February) the NUM called an all-out strike commencing on 11 February. This led, inter alia, to a three-day working week (on 13 December) and a general election on 28 February, which in turn was followed by a change of government – Mr Wilson heading a minority Labour government with Mr Healey as Chancellor.[2] The new Chancellor introduced his first Budget on 20 March and announced a complex package of tax increases and both expenditure increases and reductions. He forecast a PSBR of £2,700m for 1974/5 against a £4,200m out-turn for 1973/4.

The new government was obviously most concerned with 'getting the country back to work' but the first signs of the working of the new measures were encouraging. The reimposition of terms control on hire purchase had a significant impact. In 1973, the personal sector borrowed £183m net 'on hire purchase'; in 1974 it repaid a net £76m. The swing was £259m, implying that consumers' expenditure was £160m lower in 1974 than it otherwise would have been (p. 86). The September 1973 directive (p. 112) reinforced by the impact of the new method of control had also 'worked'. Loans to the personal sector (other than for house purchase) fell by £253m in the year to November 1974. Loans to property companies continued to rise rapidly into 1974 (as the developers' need for funds rose with the three-day week and other restrictions on building) but in the year from February 1974 rose by only £173m. In this period loans to the 'other-financial' sector fell by £189m. So total loans for property, direct and indirect, were probably constant. As liquidation of loans on a very large scale was impossible in the prevailing conditions, this was as much compliance with the directive as could have been achieved.

In the first quarter of 1974 the money supply (M_3) rose by £1,214m (and DCE by £1,593m). This (3.6 per cent) was a marked deceleration in the rate of growth. The deceleration seemed greater on the initial figures which showed growth of 3.1 per cent; the subsequent revisions were downward (to 2.8 per cent) before the latest figures showed an upward revision; an example of the poor quality of the statistics. The underlying growth was lower, as the Bank bought large quantities of commercial bills in both the fourth quarter (£204m) and first quarter (£118) to smooth the impact of the new measures. The change was even more dramatic on a monthly basis. In the month to 12 December, M_3 grew by 2.6 per cent, in the month to 16 January ('banking December') by 2.2 per cent, in banking January by 1.3 per cent, and in the next two months by 0.3 per cent and 0.4 per cent. In the first (calendar) quarter bank lending to the private sector was £1,267m. As might have been expected, sales of gilts were fairly low (£214m), but other categories of public sector debt were purchased on a large scale, so even after the open-market operations the total public sector offset was £586m. Three-month inter-bank sterling deposit rates had risen from 12.25 per cent on 9 November to 16.25 per cent on 21 December, but fell back. MLR was reduced by a ¼ per cent on 4 January and 1 February and so ended the quarter at 12½ per cent. Base rates were unchanged at 13 per cent. Longer-dated bond yields continued to rise, the Bank's 20-year rate (calculated by yield curve)[3] having been 12.37 per cent at the start of the quarter and 14.69 per cent at the end of it (and 10 per cent in March 1973).

Consequently conditions were ideal for using the Bank's new method of selling gilts. Long rates were high relative to short rates and, so it seemed, absolutely. If they were pushed slowly downwards, a large volume of sales of public sector debt would be generated, which is what happened. During the second quarter of 1975, sales of public sector debt to the non-bank private sector exceeded £1,000m. This included a very substantial unwinding of the open-market operations of the previous quarter but gilt sales were £679m. In consequence, the (seasonally adjusted) growth in M_3 was £685m (2 per cent). DCE growth was much higher, at £1,459m, which was not surprising in view of the UK's balance of payments deficit (£4,000m p.a. at an annual rate). Nevertheless DCE growth was the lowest since the first quarter of 1972 and M_3 growth lower than any quarter since the third quarter of 1971, i.e. since the introduction of the 'new approach'. Interest rates fell during the second quarter; the 20-year rate dropped to 13.6 per cent at the end of May. It rose again to 15.2 per cent at the end of June — the first of several 'selling seasons' in which stocks were sold on expectations of a continuing fall in rates and where the expectations were later falsified. Base rates fell by ¼ per cent in April and by ¼ per cent in May to finish the quarter at 12 per cent, and MLR was cut on 5 and 11 April (by the override power) and on 24 May, by ¼ per cent on each occasion, to 11¾ per cent. During the quarter the government lent £100m to the building societies and promised a further £400m to avoid an increase in the mortgage rate. This can be compared with Mr Barber's subsidy of £15m in May 1973 to achieve the same end.[4]

The Chancellor introduced another Budget in July. He was perhaps encouraged by the slowdown in monetary growth, and by the banks being some 2 per cent below their IBELs ceiling. The worsening state of the corporate sector's financial position may have worried him, their financial deficit being £689m in the first quarter and £957m in the second, but electoral considerations must have been the principal influence on his package of measures, which added £340m to the forecast of the PSBR. In fact the commitments in the two budgets to keeping prices down[5] had created an open-ended drain on the public purse. One justification was the 'threshold' system left by the previous government which meant that wage increases were triggered by rises in the Retail Price Index (RPI).[6] However the policy of buying down the RPI was to prove as disastrous for the size of the PSBR as it had been when Mr Barber tried it.

In the third quarter, M_3 rose by £1,215m (3.5 per cent) and DCE by £2,014m. Compared to the second quarter, gilt sales were somewhat lower (£341m) and there was no longer any significant offset from the unwinding of open-market operations in commercial bills. MLR fell to 11½ per cent on 20 September, but otherwise base rates and MLR were unchanged. Bond rates fluctuated quite sharply but fell nearly ½ per cent over the quarter, to 14.89 per cent.

9.2 Company Liquidity and the Social Contract, October 1974-June 1975

On 10 October there was another general election and shortly afterwards (12 November) Mr Healey introduced a third Budget which inaugurated a new phase of economic management. The Budget included massive tax relief for companies as well as an easing of the price code.

He forecast that the PSBR for 1974/5 would be £6,300m and would have been £5,500m without the package. In March he had forecast £2,750m. Thus the estimate had risen by nearly £3,000m without taking into account the new package. Much of this was unintentional and reflected the impact of the rising rate of inflation on subsidies. The final out-turn was £7,602m. This 200 per cent overshoot of the March forecast is incredible by any standards. Moreover, announced policy changes only accounted for £1,500m of the £5,000m error. As far as monetary aggregates were concerned this was largely offset by a high balance of payments deficit, almost as much in excess of the official prediction as the PSBR.

In the fourth quarter, M_3 rose by 3.1 per cent (£1,107m). The Bank *bought* considerable quantities of debt; bank lending to the private sector was only £416m, nearly £1,000m down on each of the earlier quarters of 1974, and the lowest level since the second quarter of 1971. This was the beginning of a long period of low private demand for credit. The economy was clearly depressed; a very different situation from that prevailing earlier. The overseas impact on M_3 was negative by over £1,400m, so DCE grew by £2,527m. It was a rather unpleasant period for the economy with accelerating inflation and the balance of payments showing a massive deficit. Longer interest rates rose markedly – the 20-year bond rate rising to 17.39 per cent by the end of the year.

As long rates had risen, indeed had been pushed up, absolutely (by 2½ per cent) and relatively to (unchanged) short rates, there was a good chance of selling gilt-edged securities by lowering rates and having all three factors working in the authorities' favour. It worked – spectacularly – and in the first quarter of 1975 purchases of central government debt by the non-bank private sector were £1,659m. As bank lending to the private sector was only £95m, DCE was 'only' £835m – the lowest since 1971. This was despite the Issue Department's purchases of commercial bills (£268m) and a Central Government Borrowing Requirement (CGBR) of nearly £1,500m. M_3 growth was £290m, the lowest in money terms since 1970 and, at 1.1 per cent, in percentage terms since 1969. Interest rates on bonds fell to 13.34 per cent at the end of March but rose rapidly to reach 14.85 per cent at the end of April, so that once more extrapolative expectations had been falsified. Base rates fell to 10½ per cent during the quarter and to 9½ per cent in April. MLR was reduced six times to 10 per cent (on 17 and 24 January, 7 and 14 February, 7 and 21 March).

In the second quarter, MLR fell by ¼ per cent on 18 April. This was a technical fall which was reversed on 2 May. Base rates were unchanged after the fall noted above, and the bond rate drifted down in May and June. In the quarter, M_3 rose by 1.4 per cent (£631m) – bank lending to the private sector was higher at £240m, virtually all of it in foreign currency. Gilt sales were lower (central government debt sales were £556m) but the Bank reversed the Issue Department's bill sales. The overseas impact was heavily negative; DCE rose by £2,778m.

Against this background, the Budget (on 15 April) raised personal indirect taxation sharply and public spending cuts for 1976/7 were announced. The PSBR was forecast to be £9.1 billion against £7.6 billion in 1974/5, and over £10 billion without the Budget changes. This budget included a forecast of 1 million unemployed and no growth. This shows the extent of the change in emphasis since the election. Only after the Common Market referendum on 5 June were the government prepared to introduce an incomes policy. This they did on 1 July, following the foreign exchange crisis of June 1975.[7]

During the first half of 1975, sterling fell from 79.6 per cent of its Smithsonian parity to 71.1 per cent, following remarkable stability in 1974 when it fell but only four points, despite a balance of payments deficit of over £3,300m. This ushered in a new phase of government policy – the era of the most orthodox and conservative economic management since the Second World War despite, or perhaps because of, a Labour government with a vocal left-wing element.

9.3 Labour Conservatism, July 1975-December 1976

In the third quarter, longer-term interest rates drifted downwards, while inter-bank three-month rates rose (by about 1 per cent) to 10.62 per cent. Base rates rose by ½ per cent to 10 per cent in early August, following a 1 per cent rise in MLR on 25 July to 11 per cent. Sales of central government debt were very high (at £1,234m) but a large amount (some £500m) of this was Treasury Bills. This was a by-product of low bank demand for funds; which was partly caused by the IBELs ceiling and partly by a low underlying demand for credit. The margin between base rates and retail deposit rates rose by 2½ per cent to 4 per cent, reflecting similar factors. But an enormous CGBR (at £2,717m) meant that DCE was £1,193m even after repayment of £141m of bank borrowing by the private sector, while M_3 rose by 4.6 per cent (£1,743m) as the external influences ceased to reduce M_3 much below DCE growth.

Sterling also continued to be weak, and a rise of nearly 3 points following the pay freeze was reversed in August and September, and sterling continued to fall reaching 69.9 per cent by the end of the year. In these circumstances it is not surprising that the authorities once more manipulated interest rates – the 20-year bond rate was increased to 14.91 per cent on 5 November (1 per cent up on the level of one month earlier). MLR was forced up to 12 per cent on 3 October and reduced on 14 and 28 November, 24 December, 2, 16 and 23 January, 6 and 27 February, and 5 March: by now it was down to 9 per cent. Base Rate rose to 11 per cent in mid-October and fell in mid-January (10½ per cent) and February (in two steps to 9½ per cent). Thus for the third time the authorities manipulated the gilts' market. In the fourth quarter of 1975 they sold £1,897m of central government debt to the non-bank private sector (virtually all of it medium and long-dated gilts) and a further £1,435m in the first quarter of 1976.

In the fourth quarter of 1975 the private sector repaid a further £56m to the banks and so, despite a low overseas adjustment and PSBR of £2,589m, M_3 grew by 0.6 per cent. In the first quarter of 1976 growth in M_3 was faster at 1.0 per cent (£741m); a larger (negative) overseas adjustment partly offset a £130m increase in bank lending. These figures may have encouraged the authorities a little but the overshooting of the PSBR forecast (by £1,700m) at £10,800m must have depressed them.

The growing importance of cash limits (p. 152) began to ensure control of the money level as well as the volume of public spending. Their introduction in February 1976 was an important step towards the abandonment of 'post-war' demand management, and towards the acceptance of a financial, if not a monetarist, policy. The other feature of the Budget was a conditional package of tax cuts – conditional on the successful negotiation of a Phase 2 incomes policy with the TUC; after this was accomplished, the total effect of the Budget was to increase the forecast PSBR for 1976/7 to £11,962m (instead of £11,237m) compared to £19,773m in 1975/6.

In the first quarter the current account deficit was only £60m but sterling lurched downwards from 70.0 on 2 January (and 69.8 on 27 February) to 65.9 at the end of March. The downward movement continued in April (to 62.5 on 23 April) and May (reaching 58.8 on 4 June). The authorities continually intervened heavily but only to hold the rate for a while and then let it slide again. This was a very strange policy. It almost certainly maximised the cost to the reserves for a given downward movement as the brief periods of stability provided an opportunity for holders of sterling to get out without providing an incentive for them to stay in.

This policy necessitated continuous heavy borrowing. In these circumstances it is not surprising that overseas factors led to a 1½ per cent increase in MLR (to 10½ per cent) on 23 April and a further 1 per cent increase on 21 May — which with heavy intervention and a new loan enabled sterling to remain in the 59-60 range throughout June, July and August. In the second quarter, government bond yields rose by about 0.2 per cent, the 20-year bond rate ending the quarter at 14.03 per cent. In the quarter, M_3 rose by 4.0 per cent (£1,633m). A very large (£2,257m) DCE was partly offset by a large 'external adjustment'. Bank lending to the private sector was very much higher (at £805m), the PSBR higher (at £2,862m), while sales of public sector debt fell slightly (£1,362m instead of £1,600m), but this stability cloaked larger borrowing by local authorities and smaller sales of gilts. On 22 July, a further credit control notice was issued emphasising the need to keep lending to the restricted sector under control.[8] The restricted sector was personal sector borrowing, property company loans and loans to finance 'purely financial transactions'. Further public spending cuts were announced on 22 July.

The third quarter saw another dramatic downward movement in the exchange rate — it fell from 60.4 on 3 September to 55.3 on 1 October. There was no change in MLR during the quarter but the 'override power' was used to force the rate up to 15 per cent on 7 October. The banks' base rate rose to 12 per cent in mid-September (and to 14 per cent by 22 October). Bond rates rose consistently; the 20-year rate was 15.14 at the end of the quarter.

The authorities had to cope not merely with these worrying overseas developments but also with a continuation of the acceleration in monetary growth — M_3 rose by 5.4 per cent (£2,276m) in the third quarter (DCE rose by £3,113m) as a further increase in bank lending (to £1,193m) and lower debt sales offset a lower PSBR. In these circumstances, the increases in rates described above were not in the least surprising, and nor was the Bank's reimposition of the IBELs ceiling on 18 November 1976: this time the permitted growth rate was about 6 per cent p.a.[9] As the 'qualitative guidance' was re-emphasised,[10] it is not unfair to say that these were ceilings on some categories of both bank assets and liabilities.

9.4 The IMF and After, December 1976-June 1977

During the fourth quarter sterling fell again, reaching a low of 52 in late October (at $1.56). At this point the authorities opened negotiations with the IMF, which as always in such matters was partly the agent of the US and German Treasuries. The negotiations were successfully completed on 14 December. This, and the associated public spending cuts, acted like a Good Housekeeping seal of approval in restoring confidence in both the exchange rate and in domestic monetary management, the exchange rate recovering to $1.70 at the end of the year. There was a high level of bond yields both absolutely and relative to short rates: 16.40 per cent on 27 October. All these factors enabled the authorities to inaugurate the most successful gilts' selling-season ever. MLR was cut by ¼ per cent on 19 November and 17 and 24 December. During the quarter, sales of central government debt to the non-bank private sector totalled £2,396m (of which £2,676m was gilts) offset by repayments of other instruments. Lending to the private sector was unchanged (£1,121m), but a fall in the PSBR (to £1,808m) meant that despite a low external adjustment (£220m) M_3 fell by 0.1 per cent (£28m). The authorities' new (IMF-inspired) aggregate — sterling M_3 — fell by £56m.[11]

The gilt-edged selling season continued during the first quarter of 1977 despite attempts to restrain it as M_3 and sterling fell below their target growth rates. MLR was reduced on 21 January (by ¾ per cent), 28 January (by 1 per cent), 4 February (by ¼ per cent), 11 March (by 1 per cent) and 18 March (by ½ per cent) to end the quarter at 9½ per cent. The unusually large reductions (instead of the usual ¼ per cent) reflected both market pressure and some attempt to slow the sales down. Base rates fell from 14 per cent to 10½ per cent. The 20-year government bond rate fell from 15.27 per cent on 29 December to 12.50 per cent on 30 March — the speed of the fall gathering momentum as the authorities refrained from selling.

Nevertheless, purchases of public sector debt amounted to £2,274m in the quarter. The PSBR was £2,037m and sterling bank lending £567m, so DCE (new definition) was £563m. The external influence was heavily positive — £1,013m — so sterling M_3 grew by £104m (0.2 per cent) and M_3 by £417m (0.9 per cent). Thus over the financial year M_3 grew by 9.7 per cent, DCE by £4,808m, sterling M_3 by 7.5 per cent and M_1 by 9.9 per cent. As the IMF limit for DCE was £9,000m and the Chancellor's (July) target for M_3 was 12 per cent, with the target range for £M_3 9-13 per cent (December), these were commendable achievements. During the first quarter the banks readjusted their portfolios to bring themselves well within the IBELs ceiling. They were now 2¼ per cent below the 'base level' instead of 6 per cent above it as in November. Consequently they were 5¼ per cent below the ceiling, which was abandoned on 12 August.

During the second quarter of 1977 sales of gilt-edged stock continued; during the quarter over £1,200m of central government debt was purchased by the non-bank private sector. However, as bank lending to the private sector was £1,031m in sterling and £156m in other currencies, DCE was £1,527 (new definition) and £1,683m (old definition), comfortably below the 'IMF limit' of £7,700m for the year 1977/8. Sterling M_3 grew by £1,483m (3.7 per cent) and M_3 by £1,724m (3.8 per cent). This could either be regarded as a disturbing sign or a necessary correction to the low growth in the two previous quarters. The authorities faced the problem of entering an era of a positive overseas influence on M_3 and an apparent recovery of the private demand for credit. Regrettably they showed complacency in facing this problem.

9.5 Complacency and its Consequences, July 1977-May 1979

This period was in some ways a re-run of the new approach era. The authorities lost control of the money supply — stoking up a boom in house prices and trouble for their incomes' policy. In May 1978 the authorities tried to reassert their control over the situation; again the reappraisal was signalled by a change in the regulations concerning the 'lender of last resort' rate (p. 18). The new 'new approach' showed its merits as the authorities reined monetary growth back and (just) met their monetary target for the year 1978/9.

In July 1977 MLR was 8 per cent, and was reduced during August to 7 per cent and to 6 per cent in September. This was part of one of the 'Duke of York' manoeuvres. During a brisk selling season long-term bond rates fell by about 3 per cent, to 10½ per cent (for 20-year bonds). Sales of central government debt were nearly £2.4 billion, even higher than in the first quarter. The PSBR was low; about £1 billion, the figures being revised several times. In consequence DCE was negative. However, the largest ever positive overseas influence meant that sterling M_3 grew by 1.9 per cent. The original figure was even higher — 2.3 per cent.

The overseas influence was boosted by large-scale intervention to hold the exchange rate down, the effective rate being maintained in the range 61.7 to 62.6. On 31 October this policy was abandoned and the pound rose to 64.6, and by 10 cents against the dollar. This was interesting in its own right as a technique of monetary control. It is very relevant as an illustration of the priority being given to monetary targets. During the quarter, however, sterling M_3 rose by 3.7 per cent (from an original figure of 4.2 per cent). This worried the authorities sufficiently to cause them to raise MLR from 5 per cent to 7 per cent on 25 November. This caused a fall on bond prices which was to wipe out the gains made by those who had bought in the 'selling season'. The 'season' came to an end in October, but sales were still over £2 billion in the quarter. The expansion in monetary growth was caused by a jump in the PSBR from £235m to £1,557m. The authorities had reacted to the surge in monetary growth by letting the exchange rate rise and by raising MLR. This was commendably tough, if perhaps belated.

During the first quarter of 1978 $\pounds M_3$ grew by 5.4 per cent. This continued rapid acceleration in monetary growth meant that the monetary target was overshot. In 1977/8 sterling M_3 grew by 16.2 per cent compared to a target range of 9-13 per cent. During the quarter the authorities did nothing about this massive acceleration, despite the threat it posed to their economic policy and to their control over the economy. This was an act of gross complacency, since it was apparent that something needed to be done, and can be explained partly by the mood of euphoria which had been induced by the rapid turnaround in confidence in 1977. It was partly, too, a consequence of poor statistics. Until April it appeared that $\pounds M_3$ growth for the year 1977/8 as a whole would be about 14 per cent, a figure the government was prepared to tolerate. Then substantial upward revisions were made to the growth rates for earlier in the year. This was largely due to faulty seasonal adjustment.[12] Substantial upward revisions were made to the published growth rate for the banking months ending in mid-February and mid-March. There were also some downward revisions to growth in the fourth quarter, even though growth for the year as a whole was revised upwards. These errors meant that the acceleration in $\pounds M_3$ was hidden. It appeared on the basis of the monthly figures that $\pounds M_3$ was decelerating slightly. Thus both the level and trend of the growth rate were distorted. This was yet another example of the poor quality of UK monetary statistics.

However, the authorities still had sufficient information on which to act. Monetary growth (even of $\pounds M_3$) was too high on the earlier data. Other series were accelerating in a much clearer fashion. The authorities undoubtedly concentrated too much on one series, despite all their warnings on the topic.[13]

In his Budget speech, the Chancellor made it clear that he intended to act to curb monetary growth.[14] A sectoral credit notice was issued on 1 April 1978.[15] The new policy was marked by a switch to overt fixing of MLR by the authorities. They abandoned the 'fig leaf' described above — an act of more symbolic than practical importance. MLR was increased 3 times in April and May (by a total of 1½ per cent). However, as the extent of the acceleration in £M$_3$ became clearer, further action followed. On 8 June, the IBELs ceiling was reintroduced, with minor modifications designed to enable new banks to grow quickly.[16] MLR was raised to 10 per cent on the same day. There were also measures designed to cut the PSBR, notably a rise in the National Insurance Surcharge. It is an interesting illustration of how much the Chancellor's actions were influenced by the new data; there was no other reason to increase taxation within two months of the budget.

These new measures set off a 'selling season' in the gilts' market in June. This helped to cut £M$_3$ growth to 2.9 per cent in the first quarter of the new financial year. This was despite an enormous increase in both the PSBR (to £2.2 billion) and bank lending to the private sector (£1.6 billion). The other main factor in the lower growth rate of £M$_3$ was a swing of £1 billion in the overseas influence, which was negative for the first time since the agreement with the IMF.

In the third quarter of 1978 £M$_3$ grew by 2.4 per cent. Interest rates were unchanged, and there was little that was new or even active in monetary policy. In fact, the government did very little of anything between June 1978 and the May 1979 Election except for its misjudged incomes policy of 5 per cent for Phase 4 in September, and its subsequent renegotiation with the unions at '8-9 per cent plus Clegg'.

In the fourth quarter, £M$_3$ accelerated to 3.7 per cent and the authorities reacted by raising MLR by 2½ per cent on 9 November. This enabled the Duke of York strategy to be used again, and at least £1 billion of gilts were sold in December and £3 billion in the first quarter of 1979 to the non-bank private sector. This massive selling season enabled the authorities to meet their monetary target of 8-12 per cent for the year (reaffirmed in October 1978). The actual growth was over 11½ per cent, but for the first time it was within the target. In the first quarter the PSBR also fell but bank lending doubled — the start of a prolonged period at a high level.

In this period the authorities had lost and regained control of the money supply. The costs of the loss of control were clear in the property market; a 50 per cent rise in house prices in 15 months. It is less clear how much this loss of control contributed to the problems incomes' policy faced in late 1978, but the effect was certainly considerable. The high level of private sector liquidity made both unions and employers in the private sector willing and even anxious to make high settlements. The mini-boom in 1978 probably caused demand inflation in wages and prices in addition to this liquidity effect. In the circumstances it is remarkable that the money supply was brought back under control and that (in consequence?) wages only rose 13 per cent in the year to June 1979.

9.6 Labour's Monetary Policy: An Assessment

It is not easy to assess any government's economic policy without seeming to be either trite or excessively reliant on hindsight. For the period between 1974 and 1979 this is especially true. Monetary policy became ever more central to the government's whole economic strategy and judgements about it ever harder to disentangle from views about the government as a whole. However, it would seem that monetary policy was appropriate to the government's overall objectives. Once the government had decided to let wages 'rip' in 1974, one must conclude that monetary policy helped to mitigate both the effect of this on unemployment (by helping companies) and its impact on inflation, thus helping the 'fight against inflation'.[17] Whether this wages explosion was caused by (Labour) political cowardice in the face of an election or was the result of (Conservative) incompetence in rendering the country ungovernable is an interesting but, here, irrelevant issue.

In a more general sense, one can applaud the government's dedication to control of the money supply. Its success was high — judged over a long period. Monetary growth of about 50 per cent in over five years seems a reasonable level. It is clear, then, that in the context of the period the techniques of monetary control were largely effective. The robustness of the techniques is illustrated by the ease with which the authorities could regain control of the money supply in 1978. The contrast with 1972 is marked. The value of the 'IBELs ceiling' was considerable as a quick-acting corrective even if its long-run impact was small.

One can further applaud the flexibility of the authorities. One problem was the excessive volatility in gilt sales, in part induced by periodic selling seasons. In February 1977 the authorities added to their armoury the interesting new devices of the 'part-paid stock', whereby sales and payments for stocks are separated, which enabled them to reduce this problem. Volatility could occur because of other factors, including misjudgement, but at least this cause was eliminated. The Bank's own evidence suggested that public sector items were mainly responsible, but that fluctuations in the CGBR were even more important than in gilts.[18] The change also increases the appeal of gilts as a speculative instrument, since the (prospective) capital gain is on the total price of the stock, not that part of it paid up. This may increase the demand for gilts in total but its advisability is doubtful.[19] Further proof of flexibility was shown when the authorities introduced a limited experiment with a tender system of selling gilts in March 1979. The first tender on 16 March followed heavy criticism of the chaos surrounding an issue by the conventional method on 22 February which was heavily over-subscribed. This was an experiment and a response to excess demand not the policy advocated by those to use a tender system when bonds would not be sold by the 'tap' system;[20] this point was made in the Bank 'Bulletin' at the time.[21] The Bank set a minimum price and normally they expected that less than the whole issue would be sold at this price. The general performance of monetary policy was appropriate to the government's overall objectives.

But, some caveats have to be entered, the first being that the government and its official advisers committed some appalling blunders. These include the mismanagement of the exchange rate in 1976 and the complacency of 1978. Some of these blunders suggest inadequacies in the machinery of control as much as the use of it. The second caveat concerns the different views about the nature and effects of the high level of the PSBR over the period. The line that a hagiographically minded supporter of the government would take is that the government has had the problem of both maintaining adequate growth of money and avoiding excessive growth. Thus the authorities have had to manipulate public spending, taxation (and so the PSBR) and the market in government bonds to achieve this. The initial increase in the level of public sector borrowing from banks was necessary to offset the very depressed level of private borrowing and so maintain (relative) stability in monetary growth.

The alternative argument is that the authorities were very 'lucky'. They lost control of public expenditure and have been spared hyper-inflation as a result of this only because the depression has reduced private borrowing so much. The frequent changes of policy reflect confusion, cowardice and incompetence, and (possibly) an ill-founded belief in fine-tuning rather than gradualism. The monetary aggregates do not, in any case, reflect the full damage done to the economy as much of the money creation 'leaked' abroad leading to a lower exchange rate. Domestic credit expansion over the period 1974-6 was £20,000m, whereas M_3 grew by only £11,500m. It is not clear what the exchange rate objectives of the authorities were or should have been. The authorities on occasion feared the cost-inflationary effects of depreciation but also believed that it was necessary to retain competitiveness. It seems clear that the (temporary) creation of excess supplies of sterling drove down its international price in 1976; the relative monetary tightness boosted it in 1974 and 1977-8. Judgements about exchange rates are controversial. Certainly the impact of monetary policy was in part through its influence on the exchange rate. One can argue that the exchange rate effect was contrary to the overall stance of policy in 1974 (when the policy was expansionary) and in 1976 (when counter-inflation was accorded priority). Alternatively, though, the authorities may have chosen to use the exchange rate to offset the cost impact of movements in wage claims. When these were low in 1976, the government could afford to let the exchange rate fall to reduce unemployment. In 1974, and between 1977 and 1979, this luxury could not be afforded. This latter view seems the more tenable; if this is the case, then the exchange rate movements generated by monetary policy were what the authorities wanted. As a judgement on the execution of monetary policy no more is required.

Another view concerning the PSBR is that it 'crowded out' private borrowing. The first two views accepted a similar flow-of-funds approach to the analysis of money creation as that adopted by the authorities, differing in whether the high level of bank borrowing by the public sector and low level of bank borrowing by the private sector were associated by a lucky accident or by design. The next view was that the impact of the high PSBR was seen largely in the exchange rate and a negative overseas impact. The final view is that a high PSBR caused a low level of bank lending to the private sector; this was the crowding-out hypothesis much discussed in the media and in financial circles in 1975-8.

9.6.1 Crowding-out

Discussion of monetary policy in the UK and US in recent years has often been concerned with the issue of 'crowding-out',[22] but it was discussed most in the context of the UK between 1974 and 1978. The concept of 'crowding-out' is not clear-cut as there are at least seven different meanings attributed to this concept. However, all forms of 'crowding-out' seem to have as their central idea some form of increased government spending leading to an (undesired) fall in private spending.[23] The first form crowding-out may take is in the goods market at a micro level. The government may, for example, so increase public construction programmes that a shortage of bricks restricts private house-building. This form of crowding-out normally seems to occur only in the labour market — the government, it is frequently alleged, hires too much of various sorts of skilled labour. Research engineers spend time on Concorde and defence products and consequently private research is 'crowded-out'.

Crowding-out in the goods market can occur at a macro level. If there is increased public expenditure on goods and services, this may so increase aggregate demand that it exceeds aggregate supply, and some demand is thereby rendered ineffective. If the public sector can succeed in fulfilling its plans, then private spending must fall in volume terms, and this is sometimes termed, reasonably enough, crowding-out. However, this effect can be achieved by inflation or by rationing, queueing, etc. As a matter of usage, 'crowding-out' is sometimes used to describe the latter but virtually never the former. Nevertheless, logically, either might be termed crowding-out, making three forms of crowding-out in the goods market.

The phenomenon of 'crowding-out' in the goods market may have been a problem in the 1950s and 1960s, for example in the UK in 1955, but scarcely in the period 1974-8 given the amount of spare capacity. So attention must be devoted to crowding-out when there is spare capacity, due to the behaviour of financial markets. The simplest version of this type of crowding-out is when government borrowing (to finance fiscal-expansionary spending) leads to higher interest rates. In models without an accelerator, an increase in public spending must, ceteris paribus, lead to a fall in private investment. This is illustrated very clearly in the IS/LM model, with an inelastic LM curve. A rise in government spending shifts the IS curve to the right, increasing the rate of interest and leaving income unchanged. As total spending (income) is unchanged and public spending higher, then private spending must be lower, i.e. it has been crowded-out.

The importance of this form of crowding-out depends on the impact of interest rates on the demand for investment and credit. However, there is virtually no evidence that this form of crowding-out was significant in this period. This is reinforced if one notes that the real cost of borrowing was significantly negative during the period, if one allows for tax and inflation.

So one must examine those forms of crowding-out which depend on imperfections in the credit and/or money market.[24] One such version draws heavily on the work of Jaffee and the concept of equilibrium rationing.[25] He argues that interest rates are unlikely to clear the market for credit either because of official intervention or because of the constraints imposed by the nature of banking, i.e. that the real and psychological costs of changing interest rates are large. One might add that — as in the UK in 1972-3 — motives other than short-run profit maximising may also influence bank behaviour, as discussed above. The Jaffee model argues that banks then introduce 'equilibrium rationing', that is they vary the other terms on which credit is granted (collateral, etc.) such that they are in a utility-maximising position subject to the constraint. This model then argues that the effect of increased public sector borrowing from banks is that banks tighten the requirements in which private sector customers can borrow, but do not adjust interest rates. In this case the 'crowding-out' is of riskier borrowing, including perhaps smaller loans, and of the expenditure they finance. It is worth emphasising that one might equally expect the opposite response to a larger portfolio with increased holdings of liquid, low-risk public sector assets. Jaffee assumes some form of quantity constraint imposed by the authorities. In any case, credit rationing might be expected to occur in an arbitrary fashion, e.g. first come, first served. This form of arbitrary credit rationing is one of a whole family of forms of crowding-out depending on capital market imperfections. Lack of information, oligopoly, inefficiency or a host of other factors may determine who gets credit and therefore what expenditure is crowded out. It is impossible to assess their importance in recent years.

Both the 'Jaffee' and 'imperfection' forms of crowding-out depend on an external quantity ceiling. This is provided in 'flow-of-funds' crowding-out, which, however, lacks the theoretical rationale of the other forms.[26] This approach uses official policy/actions to constrain some of the cells in a flow-of-funds matrix and from these deduces consequences for the availability of credit. For example, using the usual relationship, PSBR + bank lending to the private sector — non-bank private sector lending to the government = DCE. Given the size of the PSBR and official targets for DCE (or M_3 or sterling M_3), one can then deduce a maximum size of private sector bank borrowing by 'forecasting' the highest or lowest plausible figures for the other items. For example, for 1977-8, someone wishing to predict crowding-out might have argued as follows (by rearranging the supply side counterpart equation):

− PSBR	£8,500m
+ Non-bank private sector lending to the public sector	£5,000m
− Overseas influence on the money supply (overseas sector expected to increase the money supply)	£2,500m
+ Non-deposit liabilities	£1,000m
+ M_3 Target (11 per cent)	£5,000m
Implied change in private borrowing from banks	Nil

This 'forecast' would have implied that the private sector could not increase its borrowing from banks in the 1977/8 financial year. This is implausible so it would be crowded out. It must be stressed that these figures are purely illustrative (based as they are on various stockbroking circulars and published forecasts), and that financial forecasting is not a very well-developed art so one could have varied the figures greatly. This approach assumes an implicit knowledge of the private sector's demand for credit such as to say, either in advance or with hindsight, this point could not have been on it. Furthermore, no explanation is offered as to how the 'crowding-out' (non-satisfaction of demand for credit) affects the economy. However, its operational value is considerable.

In this flow-of-funds form of crowding-out, the views of market analysts and the media differed sharply. The *Economist*, for example, believed that it had been a problem since 1975/6, Greenwell's *Monetary Bulletin* that it became a problem during 1976/7, Phillips and Drew that it would become a problem during 1977/8. A third gilts' broker, Grieveson Grant, seemed to argue that it will not arise until the end of the decade. The Treasury believed that the problem could be averted by public expenditure cuts and that sectoral guidance could ensure that personal spending rather than industrial spending would be crowded out.[27] It seems that crowding-out was not a problem as

(1) the banks claimed to have had excess funds available for lending to industry throughout the period and no one has challenged this.

(2) the figures show that restricting monetary growth has not reduced the availability of funds from the Stock Exchange and financial institutions.[28] Even in real terms, restricting the rate of monetary expansion was associated with at least a threefold increase in funds available to industry.

Appendix: Principal Events and Data 1974-9

Principal Events[29]

1974 (March) Labour government takes office.

(6 August) Introduction of index-linked National Savings.

1975 (28 February) Supplementary Special Deposit Scheme suspended.

(1 July) Incomes policy introduced.

1976 (27 October) Pound falls to $1.57.

(18 November) Reintroduction of Supplementary Special Deposits Scheme.

(21 December) Negotiations completed with IMF.

1977 (11 August) Supplementary Special Deposit Scheme suspended.

1978 (25 May) MLR 'formula' abolished. MLR henceforth to be determined by authorities.

(8 June) Reintroduction of Supplementary Special Deposits Scheme.

1979 (3 May) General Election.

Financial Statistics

		M_1 growth (%)	M_3 growth (%)	£M_3 growth (%)	MLR (% p.a.)	20-year bond rate (% p.a.)
1974	I	−2.7	3.1		12.5	14.5
	II	2.9	1.8		11.75	15.3
	III	3.9	3.7		11.5	14.9
	IV	7.3	3.1		11.5	17.4
1975	I	2.7	1.1	0.8	10.0	13.4
	II	2.7	1.4	2.0	10.0	14.7
	III	5.1	4.6	3.6	11.0	14.2
	IV	2.0	0.6	0.2	11.25	14.8
1976	I	5.4	1.3	0.9	9.0	13.8
	II	3.4	4.0	3.2	11.5	13.7
	III	3.1	5.4	4.6	13.0	15.3
	IV	−0.6	−0.1	0.1	14.25	15.2
1977	I	2.9	0.9	0.9	10.5	12.5
	II	5.0	3.8	2.5	8.4	12.9
	III	7.2	1.2	2.9	7.0	13.0
	IV	5.3	3.1	3.6	6.3	11.1
1978	I	5.1	5.5	5.2	6.5	11.5
	II	3.1	4.0	2.9	8.5	12.6
	III	3.7	2.3	2.7	10	12.6
	IV	4.0	3.4	3.5	11.7	13.1
1979	I	2.0	1.3	2.0	13.2	13.3
	II	2.5	3.7	3.8	12.7	12.1

Other Economic Developments

		Inflation (% change 1 year earlier)	Growth (Real GDP) (% change 1 year earlier)	Unemployment (%)	Balance of Payments (current account £m)
1974	I	12.9	−3.5	2.5	−877
	II	15.9	0.6	2.5	−887
	III	17.0	2.3	2.6	−772
	IV	18.2	1.7	NA	−844
1975	I	20.3	3.6	3.1	−541
	II	24.3	−2.5	3.6	−309
	III	26.5	−4.8	4.2	−579
	IV	25.3	−3.3	4.8	−221
1976	I	22.5	−0.4	5.2	−90
	II	16.0	0.7	5.3	−390
	III	13.7	1.6	5.5	−511
	IV	15.0	2.4	NA	−414
1977	I	16.5	−1.3	5.5	−461
	II	17.4	0.2	5.6	−204
	III	16.5	0.5	5.8	307
	IV	13.0	1.7	5.9	280
1978	I	9.5	2.8	5.8	−194
	II	7.6	3.9	5.8	417
	III	7.9	3.3	5.7	87
	IV	8.1	1.8	5.4	397
1979	I	9.6	0.1	5.6	−692
	II	10.6	2.3	5.4	−192
	III	16.0	0.0	5.2	−189
	IV	17.3	0.8	5.3	−557
1980	I	19.1	2.0	5.7	70
	II	21.5	−3.1	6.2	−88
	III	16.4	−1.9	7.0	870
	IV	15.3	−3.4	8.4	+1885

References

1. See *Bulletin*, vol. 14, no. 1 (March 1974) especially p. 13 and *Hansard*, 17 December 1973.

2. See Butler and Kavanagh (1974) and (1975).

3. See MPCC, p. 147, n10.

4. *Bulletin*, vol. 13, no. 1 (June 1973), pp. 146-7.

5. See Butler and Kavanagh (1975).

6. See MPCC, p. 148, n12.

7. See *The Fight Against Inflation*, Cmnd. 6071 (HMSO, 1975). For a racy account of the crisis see Haines (1977).

8. *Bulletin*, vol. 16, no. 3 (September 1976), p. 307. See p. 198 below for a complete lists of notices issued in the period.

9. See p. 145, n2 above.

10. *Bulletin*, vol. 16, no. 3 (September 1970), p. 307.

11. See *Bulletin*, vol. 17, no. 1 (March 1977), p. 39; also MPCC, Appendix A.

12. *Bulletin*, vol. 20, no. 2 (June 1980).

13. For the warnings, see the statements listed on p. 199 below.

14. *Hansard*, 11 April 1978.

15. *The Times*, 9 April 1978.

16. *Bulletin*, vol. 18, no. 3 (September 1978), p. 357.

17. This is quite close to the official view, e.g. *Bulletin*, vol. 16, no. 4 (December 1976), p. 453.

18. *Bulletin*, vol. 18, no. 3 (September 1978), p. 320.

19. See Dosser, Gowland and Hartley (1981); also Gowland (1977b).

20. See MPCC, especially pp. 162-3, for a fuller statement of the case.

21. *Bulletin*, vol. 19, no. 1 (March 1979), p. 34.

22. The issue was given great prominence in *Greenwell's Monetary Bulletin* and in various ephemera produced by Salomon Bros, the most respected financial analysts in the UK and US respectively.

23. See MPCC, pp. 135-9.

24. See Sargent (1975).

25. See Jaffee (1975).

26. See Hewitt (1977) for the practical problems.

27. See *Public Expenditure*, Cmnd. 5879 (HMSO, 1975).

28. See MPCC, p. 139.

29. A more detailed chronology of 1974-7 can be found in MPCC, pp. 191-200.

10 PLUS ÇA CHANGE?

In May 1979 there was a General Election which returned a Conservative administration led by Mrs Thatcher.[1] The nature of the impact of changes in government on monetary policy is controversial. Some have argued that official domination of policy-making is so pervasive that it does not matter who occupies Numbers 10 and 11 Downing Street, nor to which party they belong. Such views are at best overstated and usually misleading. During the period covered by this book, all three chancellors and all four premiers had a major impact on monetary policy. Furthermore, the change to a Labour government in 1974 coincided with the introduction of the 'new approach'. By May 1979, the continued desirability of this system of control was very much in doubt. The new government both inspired and was associated with the consequent reappraisal of the techniques of monetary control. Moreover, the new government was avowedly 'monetarist' and proclaimed that monetary policy would be its major tool of policy.

There was a new attitude to both the operation and function of monetary policy in both the political and official wings of the authorities. There was a major change of technique in 1979-80. The IBELs ceiling was downgraded and finally abolished in June 1980. This abolition revealed the extent of the evasion, and the distortion of monetary statistics which it had engendered (8.1). The authorities put much more reliance on the impact of interest rates on bank lending, almost in the spirit of competition and credit control. This change of emphasis was seen as an interim step until a new regime could be inaugurated. As in 1971, an elaborate consultative process followed, marked by *Monetary Control*.[2] The aim of the Bank appeared to be to argue that control of the money supply had to be attained via the effect of interest rates on bank assets. They sought to refute those advocates of both direct controls and a reserve base system who believed that they were alternatives to interest rate controls.

The first section of this chapter is devoted to a consideration of the implications of the commitment to 'monetarism'. In particular, a number of contradictions in Conservative thought are presented and their possible resolution discussed. The impact of monetary policy on the economy is also analysed. Section 10.2 is an analysis of the methods of monetary control used between June 1979 and September 1980. This analysis reveals both the extent to which the needs of monetary policy have dominated government policy and the reasons for the government's problems in controlling the money supply. Section 10.3 is a narrative account of the period. Finally, section 10.4 discusses the conclusions drawn from the earlier part of this chapter in the light of the consultative document *Monetary Control* and the authorities' response in 1980-1.

10.1 The Implications of 'Monetarism'[3]

The advent of an explicitly 'monetarist' government was clearly of major importance in the evolution of monetary policy in the UK. However, there were a number of contradictions inherent in the Conservative government's approach. Some of these came from conflicts between the implications of monetarism and the other statements made by Conservative politicians in their election speeches and manifesto. Some of the problems arose from the ambiguity of the term 'monetarism'. The word has a strict meaning but this is frequently not adhered to. Strictly, a monetarist is one who believes that a change in the money supply is both sufficient and necessary for a change in nominal income, and that a 1 per cent change in the money supply will always lead to a 1 per cent change in nominal income.[4] The term is used very loosely in the media, often merely to denote an advocate of reducing public expenditure. Academic usage is frequently guilty of inexact and polemical use of the term. Sometimes additional views are included within the 'monetarist' canon; in particular, views about fine-tuning or the nature of aggregate supply. The Conservative leadership used the term in the precise, narrow sense but many of its followers had a much looser concept in mind.

A contradiction arises because monetarism is an interventionist doctrine whereas there were many advocates of laissez-faire in the Conservative ranks. In some ways monetarism is like the Butskellite consensus of the 1950s and 1960s. The government determines the key macroeconomic aggregate but can let the market system work within this framework. This policy requires very heavy intervention in some markets, especially of course the money market, and interference with many industries, in particular banking. At one time Friedman's monetarism led him to advocate the abolition of banking in its present form.[5] Hayek and others of the Austrian school have regarded Friedman as a socialist because of his monetarist views. The dissatisfaction of the laissez-faire right with the monetarism of the government was made clear in an article in *The Times* signed by leading laissez-faire academic liberals.[6] The government has accepted the interventionist implications of monetarism, but has disillusioned some of its supporters in the process.

In Opposition, the Conservatives frequently preached the virtues of low, stable interest rates. A monetarist policy is likely to lead to a need for high (nominal) rates and for frequent variations in them. This was the first implication of monetarism to be faced by the government. After a delay, monetarism prevailed, but CBI and backbench Conservative Opposition has revealed the problems monetarism causes for a right-wing government.

The problem of reconciling monetarism with Conservative views was faced by Sir Keith Joseph.[7] The particular problem that concerned him was that monetarism does not say anything about the optimal level of public spending. The monetarist proposition is that the money supply determines nominal income and thus, in conjunction with aggregate supply, inflation. This has no implication for the optimal level of public spending. At best, it offers a reason for cutting the PSBR as a means of reducing inflation. Sir Keith Joseph revealed a hankering after the American 'New Right' view that public *spending* causes inflation, even if it does not lead to an increase in the money supply.[8] Clearly, many Conservatives would like to agree with him. Two consequences would follow. One is that cutting both taxation and expenditure would reduce inflation. (Ironically extreme Keynesians, who believe in the balanced budget multiplier, join hands with the 'New Right' in accepting this view.) The other is that tax cuts would not be inflationary. In contrast, relatively pure monetarists like the *Daily Telegraph* leader writers and Enoch Powell argued for substantial increases in income tax in early 1981. Sir Geoffrey Howe went part of the way to meet this viewpoint by not increasing personal allowances in the 1981 Budget and so increasing the real burden of income tax.

It seems clear that many people voted Conservative as an anti-union vote.[9] So it is paradoxical that the government elected by anti-union electors believed in an economic theory that did not ascribe blame for inflation to the unions. The government made no attempt to influence wages directly for the first year of its life. At this point, it seemed to realise that monetarism indeed might not be enough.

Hence, anyone who had predicted or hoped for a union-busting, tax-cutting, low interest rate, laissez-faire policy was to be disappointed, as the commitment to monetarism ruled out all of these. There were further paradoxes in store: for example when the government risked crowding-out private investment by its 'sale of the century' (p. 188). However the most surprising contradiction arose from the government's view of the transmission mechanism of monetary policy. Their view appeared to be that high monetary growth led to high corporate liquidity. High corporate liquidity led to a willingness to meet high wage claims. Thus the government deliberately sought to squeeze corporate liquidity. It welcomed a high exchange rate as a further device to achieve this end.[10] Hence monetarism led a Conservative government to pursue an overtly anti-business policy. The Tory 'wets' rightly emphasised the burdens placed on traditional Conservative supporters. It was indeed paradoxical for a Conservative government to put the burden of fighting inflation onto business, by aiming to squeeze profits so as to restrain the ability and willingness of firms to pay higher wages. This aspect of government policy and its consequences produced howls of anguish from the CBI and the Tory 'wets'. They were indeed the most consistent and arguably the most logical group in politics. Mrs Thatcher put the cost of fighting inflation onto businesses whereas Wilson-Callaghan had put it onto the unions with an incomes policy. The Tory 'wets', and they alone, sought to defend their natural supporters and acted in line with the predictions of interest group politics. There were a number of problems with the monetary transmission mechanism based on squeezing corporate liquidity. A squeezed company could respond in various ways; in particular, it could borrow more or cut its net expenditure, either by selling assets or cutting gross expenditure. Many companies responded to the squeeze by increasing bank borrowing. This negated the policy in all aspects. The growth of the money supply was certainly not reduced and there were no consequences for output and inflation. The authorities should, to be logical, have raised interest rates so as to choke off borrowing and thus prevent the nullification of their policy. Undoubtedly there were sound political and economic reasons why the authorities did not respond in this manner, but another contradiction had arisen.

Not all companies responded by borrowing more and many who did borrow more also reduced their net expenditure. Thus the squeeze was not totally pointless but when it did 'work' further problems arose. Companies could reduce expenditure by investing less, running down stocks or cutting their wage bill. Relatively little of the first occurred as investment held up well but clearly it was not desired and would lead to output falls, not price reductions. Destocking was substantial, and stimulated by detailed tax changes in the 1980 budget and by uncertainty concerning tax and accounting practices following the rather confused debate on inflation accounting culminating in the Hyde guidelines. Destocking contributed massively to the fall in output in 1980 but also slowed down inflation as the dumping of stocks led to its natural supply and demand effect. Finally, companies could respond by reducing the wage bill below what it otherwise would have been. This could be achieved either by lower wage settlements or by reducing the numbers employed. The government undoubtedly misjudged the relative size of these two phenomena. The general ambiguity of monetary or fiscal contraction — does it squeeze output or prices? — stood out in all its starkness with this transmission mechanism.

Non-monetarists had often speculated as to what would happen if a government sought to hold monetary growth at 10 per cent whilst wages rose by 20 per cent. They had suggested that problems would arise in trying to control the money supply. They also predicted that monetary statistics would become distorted. Both of these predictions came true, aided by the breakdown of the IBELs ceiling. They also pointed out that the strict prediction derived from the quantity theory would be a very sharp fall in output. From other theories, a rise in the exchange rate was likely. Both proved correct as the pound rose 40 cents in the government's first 18 months of policy and output fell by 6 per cent. The sceptics had wrongly assumed that no government would tolerate these developments. In fact the elementary, basic quantity theory was a remarkably accurate guide to developments in this period. So were the new theories of the balance of payments,[11] which all said that macroeconomic forces determine the balance of payments, i.e. not relative prices or exchange rates. Events in 1980 seemed to suggest they were right.

However, if the simple quantity theory was correct in its predictions, its limitations were starkly revealed. The inability to determine what price/output mix would fit in with any level of nominal income was a very great restriction on economic management.

10.2 The Techniques Analysed

None of the techniques used in 1979-80 was totally unprecedented in the UK. Nevertheless, there was a considerable element of innovation in the conduct of monetary policy. The innovations were in the range of techniques used, and in the different emphasis placed on them compared to the recent past. For example, the authorities in this period placed considerable reliance on the use of instruments designed to influence overseas flows. Healey had let the exchange rate rise in 1977 for monetary reasons, but, nevertheless, the degree of emphasis placed on overseas factors was unprecedented. In November 1979 the government abolished exchange control. There were a number of reasons for this action but a major one was the hope of reducing monetary growth by provoking a capital outflow, or at least a reduction of net inflows. It seems clear that the timing of the measure was entirely determined by its monetary impact. That is, instead of being a long-term dream, the abolition of exchange control became an immediate action.

To complement this quantity tool, the authorities used a price weapon, the exchange rate. The authorities countenanced a very rapid rise in the exchange rate to minimise capital inflows. On occasion, especially early in 1980, they seem to have bought sterling to reduce the domestic borrowing requirement (DBR) which had the effect of forcing the exchange rate up. The balance of payments swung into surplus on current account but the authorities still achieved a negative overseas impact of £2 billion in 1979-80. There are various problems with vigorous attempts to influence overseas flows in this fashion. The major one is that it is likely to boost unemployment. The other principal one is the 'German problem', i.e. the more this policy succeeds the more desirable the currency becomes, and the more the policy has to be used. The Germans found that as a result they were forced to use inward exchange controls, the Bardepot.

The Conservative government placed as much reliance as its Labour predecessor on the control of the PSBR as a tool of monetary policy. However, they seemed to place much more emphasis on asset sales. This fitted in with both their monetarist and ideological stance. As monetarists, they did not care by what means the PSBR was altered only about its size. As believers in private enterprise, they were pleased to see the size of the public sector reduced. Nevertheless they offended some conservative financiers (of all parties) by seeming to sell assets to finance tax cuts. (The accusation is not entirely fair.) The major criticism levelled at this action was that it could only be short term. This is again not entirely fair. There is an enormous stock of public sector assets and, in any case, the authorities claimed it was a short-term policy. They hoped that other measures would work in the long run.

More serious criticism can be levelled at asset sales, even narrowly regarded as a tool of monetary policy. The first problem is that the purchases may be financed by bank credit. In this case, the impact on the money supply is zero. The purchases may even be financed by loans from the public sector (council house sales in some cases). In this case, there is no net change in the cash flow between the public and private sectors, and so no change in the money supply. The major assets sold in 1979/80 were BP shares and a miscellany sold directly by BNOC. In both cases one can argue that they were very likely to be substituted for public sector assets in private sector portfolios. BP shares were very likely to displace National Savings and gilts in private sector portfolios, especially in view of the way they were marketed. Some of BNOC's asset 'sales' were actually borrowing by BNOC. A BNOC debt and a public sector one are very close substitutes. Finally, in order to calculate the monetary impact of asset sales one has to deduct any purchases by banks and foreigners from the gross total. To summarise, the *net* effect of asset sales on the money supply will be much smaller than the quantity of assets sold since one has to deduct:

(a) purchases financed by bank credit.
(b) purchases financed by public sector loans.
(c) purchases which are substituted for purchases of public sector debt.
(d) purchases by banks.
(e) purchases by foreigners.

In addition, there was one element of contradiction in the policy. One reason cited for preferring PSBR cuts to other means of monetary control was that it avoided 'crowding-out'. But if BP shares displace holdings of private sector assets, especially equities, then crowding-out is more intense with this policy than any other. A priori, one would expect that the assets sold would be substitutes for private sector assets to the extent that they had any net effect on the money supply. A BP share, or a British (Airways) one, is more obviously a substitute for a Shell share, or even a factory, than for a loaf of bread or a washing machine. Yet the government assumed the opposite.

The authorities clearly relied heavily, if a trifle belatedly, on the impact of interest rates on bank lending. All of the old problems were present, a point made clear by the Moore-Threadgold study.[12] The problems of this method of control have been discussed above in section 2.4.3 and on p. 123. All that need be added is the Bank's official view from the *Bulletin*, which states that 'even sharp increases in interest rates may have little impact on the money supply'.[13]

The final supply side counterpart to be considered is that of non-bank private sector lending to the public sector. The conventional 'Duke of York' strategy enabled the authorities to make enormous sales on a rising market between November 1979 and the end of January 1980. Similar tactics were used in the Spring of 1980 and July-August of the same year. The policy continued to work, but the authorities made further experiments with tender gilts. They also twice expanded the scale of index-linked securities: in December 1979 and, announced in August, November 1980. This seems to suggest that the authorities recognised the limitations of their previous strategy and were perhaps making some preparations for the eventual collapse of the present system. The flexibility shown in the 1974-9 period (and expressed in the June 1979 *Bulletin* article) continued.[14] Two other innovations are discussed below (p. 191). On purely technical criteria, gilts' management has probably been the most successful area of monetary policy in the UK. Mistakes have been made and problems have arisen, but the authorities have never totally lost control and have endeavoured to solve the problems which have arisen.

Other controls can be dismissed briefly. The authorities fought a determined campaign to avoid a reserve base system. They abandoned the IBELs ceiling. Thus the techniques used were a broad spectrum of measures designed to work via the asset side of the banks' balance sheet. Given the problems inherent in all these controls, it is not surprising that the authorities had such problems in controlling the money supply.

10.3 The Monetarists in Action, May 1979-September 1980

In this period the authorities struggled to control the money supply. They never clearly won this battle, but neither did they suffer total defeat. Their major problem was not only how to control the money supply, but also a division of the rise in nominal income between price and output that disappointed or dissatisfied many. The money supply/ nominal income relationship worked with unbelievable precision. However, a 20 per cent rise in prices and a 5 per cent fall in output was not what had been hoped would accompany 15 per cent monetary growth.[15] It is worth emphasising that this result was not surprising, indeed would seem almost inevitable to any Friedmanite.

The new government proclaimed its intentions in the June 1979 Budget. A money supply target of 7-11 per cent was announced. The reduction from 8-12 per cent was largely symbolic. In fact, it was virtually the same as 8-12 per cent growth from the end of March, as the money supply had been growing rapidly since then and the extra growth was added to the base of the target. MLR was raised from 12 to 14 per cent. £M$_3$ rose by 3.8 per cent in the second quarter, so vigorous action was needed. The reasons for the acceleration were a combination of the largest-ever quarterly level of the PSBR (£3.4 billion) and a continuation of the high level of bank lending (£2.3 billion). In the third quarter the authorities did very little, except occasional intervention on a large scale to hold money market rates down. Sterling M_3 grew by 'only' 2.8 per cent. The PSBR was even higher than in the second quarter, and there was little change in the other aggregates. Monetary growth would have been much higher except for a huge negative overseas contribution of £1.6 billion. In addition, the Bank of England estimated that there was at least £750m of evasion of the IBELs ceiling.[16] In these circumstances, inaction seemed surprising, and still seems surprising. It is even more surprising as the then available data suggested more rapid growth of $£M_3$ than later revisions. Nevertheless, the inaction continued until November. By then the monthly money supply statistics were showing signs of very rapid acceleration. On 16 November MLR was raised to 17 per cent, and the IBELs ceiling was renewed.[17] As this was the period when it had clearly started to breakdown, it is odd that it was neither dropped nor any attempt made to strengthen it. Outward exchange controls were abolished as a further contractionary device. Since this made the IBELs ceiling totally unenforceable, it seems even stranger that this was not abandoned. In the fourth quarter $£M_3$ grew by 3.9 per cent. Only the overseas influence was at all different from third quarter levels; the PSBR, gilt sales and bank lending were all at historically very high levels.

Throughout the period from November 1979 to September 1980 the authorities had to intervene very frequently to stop interest rates rising still higher.[18] They used a whole range of tactics to do this. One method was new – a 'sale and repurchase' arrangement for banks. They sold their gilts to the Bank but arranged to buy them back at a specified price and time. Such arrangements had been used on rare occasions before, especially in June 1972, but this was the first time they were used as a regular tool of policy. The authorities for the first time ordered the government broker to reduce the 'tap' price of gilts ahead of market pressure. To lead the market downwards had hitherto been condemned as 'spitting on the flag'. The Bank had been prepared to prod the market to reduce gilt prices but not to anticipate their action. The Bank did not make a regular practice of reducing tap prices in advance of market forces but it was no longer unthinkable.

Thus at the end of 1979 the government had nailed its colours to the mast. A 17 per cent MLR, reinforced by a plethora of less important devices, would be relied on to curb $£M_3$ growth. The authorities were in the position that their predecessors had occupied in November 1973 and May 1978. They were trying to restrain monetary growth which had accelerated to unacceptable levels. On all three occasions corrective action was too late. The government showed more courage than its predecessors in increasing MLR, but did not support this with an effective direct control. It remained to be seen how the new stance worked, and how quickly. The authorities, or at least the Bank, expressed some scepticism.[19]

The figures for the first quarter of 1980 were encouraging. £M$_3$ grew by-only 1.8 per cent. Bank lending rocketed, to £3.2 billion. Gilt sales were also lower. The overseas influence was virtually nil, having been negative in the fourth quarter. Thus, the whole of the improvement arose from the elimination of the PSBR, which fell from over £3 billion to between £100m and a surplus of £100m (as usual it was the hardest statistic to measure). It is impossible to ascertain how much the fall was a genuine change and how much another blunder by those collecting and seasonally adjusting the data. There were major problems in assembling the data in this period because of the increases in VAT and PRT in the June 1979 Budget. Nevertheless, the seasonally adjusted series had a higher variance than the unadjusted one, indicating that the series might be misleading. In addition several hundred more millions of IBELs evasion occurred in this quarter.

In the Budget on 11 March the government announced a new money supply target − 7-11 per cent but relating to February 1980-April 1981. It also introduced a medium-term financial plan (p. 151). On 26 March the end of the IBELs ceiling was announced, but the sectoral guidance (of 11 April 1978) was re-emphasised. Otherwise the government's policy was 'wait and see'. In the second quarter, £M$_3$ grew by 5.7 per cent. DCE was at an all-time peak at nearly £5 billion. Very high levels of both bank lending to the private sector (£2.7 billion) and PSBR (over £4 billion) more than offset over £2 billion of gilt sales. In the third quarter the statistics were distorted as the IBELs ceiling evasive devices were unwound. Much of the £M$_3$ growth reflected the reinclusion of 'black-market' transactions in official statistics. Nevertheless the growth in £M$_3$ was still 4.5 per cent. Bank lending was over £3 billion, the PSBR £4 billion and debt sales nearly £3 billion.

Largely in response to political pressure MLR was reduced by 1 per cent at the beginning of July. The authorities still had to take steps to bring the monetary system fully under their control. It is necessary to see what the implications of 1979-80 were for the conduct of monetary policy. The first was that the new 'new approach' was no longer viable.

Abuse of the IBELs ceiling meant that this weapon was no longer available, and without it the authorities seemed incapable of correcting errors in monetary policy. Even a relatively short lag before moving to offset acceleration in late 1979 made the situation almost uncontrollable, as inflationary expectations accelerated to the point where real rates were actually lower at the end of 1979 than in May. Without any direct control the other two prongs of the strategy are just not sufficient, even when reinforced by high (nominal) bank base rates.

Thus, yet again, the techniques of monetary control had to be reappraised. It was hard to shrug off a feeling of 'déjà vu'. One difference was that the authorities recognised the need to act earlier than in the past. However, the *Consultation Document* seemed to propose the same message as competition and credit control. Only changes in interest rates could control the money supply. The Bank argued in both 1971 and 1980 that no other technique would work, or at least could work only by causing changes in interest rates. This coherent, rigorous argument is maintained despite the Bank's own scepticism about the impact of interest rates on bank lending and about the long-term prospects for gilt-edged sales. It is also maintained despite the possibility that a reserve base system, or direct controls, might, at the least, reduce the magnitude and speed up the impact of interest rate movements. The Bank argument is cogent and persuasive, as in 1971. The Bank may very well be right but the implication for the long-run control of the money supply, however defined, is depressing.

The wheel had turned full circle and Hegel's words seem appropriate: 'What experience and history teach is this — that people and government never have learned anything from history, or acted on principles deduced from it.'

10.4 The Official Response, September 1980-June 1981

In the latter part of 1980 the government felt political pressures to lower interest rates despite economic arguments to the contrary. Adjusted for the distortions caused by the end of the IBELs ceiling, £M$_3$ was growing at an annual rate of over 20 per cent, twice the official target. In the fourth quarter, £M$_3$ grew by another 4.9 per cent. A higher PSBR and a temporary lull in the rate of bank lending approximately offset each other.

Against this background the government's actions were interesting and rather paradoxical. In what amounted to the monetary policy equivalent of a budget, the Chancellor, Sir Geoffrey Howe, took a variety of actions on 24 November 1980. He cut MLR by 2 per cent from 16 to 14 per cent. He reaffirmed his commitment to 7-11 per cent monetary growth, this time for the period ending in mid-April 1981. These two actions seemed inconsistent but were reconciled with the statement that the target would not be met![20]

The longer-term measures announced by the Chancellor were more interesting, but all of them were tentative and of an interim nature. He announced that monetary base control would not be introduced but that steps would be taken to try to see if there were a meaningful monetary base, and to collect statistics on this aggregate and to monitor it. It was hinted that the authorities would experiment to see if they could control the aggregate and that in the long run this might be equivalent to a non-mandatory base system. The Bank produced several alternative definitions of base.[21] On the whole, the decision was sensible but offered no immediate solution to the authorities' problems. The Chancellor announced the phasing out of the 12½ per cent reserve assets ratio. The ratio would be reduced to 10 per cent from 7 February. Given the limited role of the ratio, this was another prudent decision, but again offered no solution to the Chancellor's problems. Another group of measures concerned dealing methods and statistics, and were all preliminary to a number of policies announced in the March 1981 Budget.

Before the Chancellor rose to make his Budget speech on 10 March, it was clear that monetary growth had not slowed as much as the Chancellor had hoped, indeed at 4½ per cent it was little different from the later quarters of 1980. In fact this development continued in the second quarter when monetary growth was y per cent. A larger PSBR cancelled out the slowdown in bank lending perceived by some of the more optimistic observers.

The Chancellor announced a new monetary target of 6-10 per cent from February 1981-April 1982 and a 4-8 per cent target for 1983-4. He thus announced that his medium-term strategy would continue as before and that there would be no action taken to offset the overshoot in 1980-1. MLR was reduced by another 2 per cent to 12 per cent. The reserve assets ratio was cut to 8 per cent. Following the hints given in November, it was announced that a new series of monetary figures — M_2 — would be collected. This would include, like its American counterpart, currency, demand deposits and retail (small) time deposits; Friedman's preferred definition of money. This was one of a range of new definitions of money introduced in 1980-1. The very broad PSL_1

and PSL$_2$ (Private Sector Liquidity) also joined the range of statistical series during this period. Furthermore, the authorities would change their dealing strategy in the money markets in an American direction, again as foreshadowed in November.[22] The authorities would no longer deal at predetermined prices in securities with more than seven days to mature. Instead, they would respond to offers of the Treasury Bills concerned at a price (i.e. interest rate) within a narrow band, which would be unpublished — in effect, a move towards caring about quantities as well as prices. Sir Geoffrey Howe ultimately hoped to phase out MLR and replace it with an unpublished and more variable intervention or discount rate.

Furthermore, the clearing banks were relieved of the obligation to keep a sum equal to 1½ per cent of their liabilities (deposits) on interest-free deposit at the Bank. The main effect of this had been to guarantee Bank profits, as the deposits were notionally on loan to the government who paid interest on them. Instead all banks would have to hold an amount equal to ½ per cent of their liabilities on the same terms. The change was in response to clearing-bank pressure and restored equity between all the competing banks. The Chancellor also introduced a retrospective 'windfall' tax on clearing banks of £250m. None of these measures was of earth-shattering importance; all meant that a final decision on monetary base had been postponed.

Finally, the Chancellor showed his continued wish to sell debt to the personal sector by announcing 'oil bonds' and more widely available index-linked securities. (The SAYE limit rose from £20 to £50 per month and 'Granny Bonds' could now be held at the age of 50, instead of at the age of 60 for women and 65 for men.) This limited move towards indexation was reinforced in May by an issue of £2 billion of indexed gilts to the pension funds. These offered a 2 per cent real return instead of the 0 per cent offered to the personal sector. None of these measures affected the crux of the problem. The basic dilemma remained. The control of the money supply by direct controls required draconian measures unacceptable to the government. Monetary base control was viewed as 'an interest rate in disguise'. Interest rates were never, perhaps could never, be raised sufficiently quickly or sufficiently high. Thus monetary policy was crucial to economic success, but long-run control of the money supply seemed impossible.

The new system of monetary control announced by Sir Geoffrey Howe in his Budget speech was introduced in stages of which the last and most dramatic was the abolition of MLR on 20 August 1981. This replacement of MLR by an intervention rate described above had two motives. One was a wish to have changes in interest rates regarded as technical operations rather than highly publicised political acts. The changes in 1972 and 1978 had had similar goals. Events since, notably the relatively muted treatment accorded by the press to increases in the intervention rate in September which triggered off a four per cent rise in base rates, suggest that the Bank has partly succeeded in this objective. The other motive for the abolition of MLR was to enable a more flexible and frequent variation of the intervention rate. This was both desirable in its own right and necessary to facilitate the new policy of putting less weight on the stability of short-term interest rates and more weight on the control of short-term quantities. The authorities continued to put increasing reliance on personal sector lending to the public sector, e.g. abolishing the index-linked bondage limit in September and raising the maximum holding in October to £5,000. Asset sales continued — over £220m was raised by a controversial and mismanaged sale of Cable and Wireless shares in October. Despite all these and a substantial rise in interest rates in September (and fluctuations thereafter) monetary growth continued unabated; the target for the whole year being exceeded in the first seven months. The medium-term financial strategy looked ever-less credible and there was press speculation that monetary targets had been abandoned in favour of an exchange rate policy. Sir Geoffrey denied this although admitting that the level of exchange rate was an influence on the stance of monetary policy. In brief, the government had failed to solve the essential problems of monetary control.

Appendix: Principal Events and Data 1979-81

Principal Events[23]

1979 (12 June) Sir Geoffrey Howe's first Budget. VAT raised to 15 per cent and income tax reduced.
    (26 November) Exchange control abolished.
1980 (10 May) *Monetary Control* published.
    (24 November) Chancellor's statement on monetary base control.
1981 (10 March) Budget. New monetary arrangements announced together with tax increases.
    (20 August) Abolition of MLR.

Financial Statistics

		M$_1$ growth (%)	£M$_3$ growth (%)	MLR (% p.a.)	20-year bond rate (% p.a.)
1979	III	2.6	3.5	13.2	12.4
	IV	1.9	3.0	12.7	14.1
1980	I	−0.1	2.7	17	14.5
	II	2.6	5.7	17	14.0
	III	−1.0	4.5	16	13.3
	IV	2.6	4.9	14.7	13.3
1981	I	4.1	1.9	13.3	13.8
	II	3.9	4.6		
Financial Years				PSL$_1$	PSL$_2$
1979/80		6.5	13.2	11.7	10.9
1980/1		8.4	18.0	16.4	18.4

References

1. See Butler and Kavanagh (1980).

2. Bank (1981).

3. A version of this section has been given to various academic and student seminars since 1979, both as forecast and then analysis. I am grateful to all who have commented on it, especially the staff seminar at Lanchester Polytechnic.

4. See Gowland (1979), Ch. 5.

5. See Friedman (1956).

6. *The Times*, 8 February 1980.

7. See Joseph (1976).

8. Ibid., for the American 'New Right'; see also Gowland (1979), Ch. 5, Appendix A.

9. See Butler and Kavanagh (1980).

10. The comments of Mr Biffen, Chief Secretary to the Treasury 1979-81, were especially revealing.

11. See Gowland (1979), Ch. 2.

12. See Moore and Threadgold (1980).

13. *Bulletin*, vol. 20, no. 2 (June 1980), p. 173.

14. The Gilt-Edged Market in *Bulletin*, vol. 19, no. 2 (June 1979), p. 137.

15. Figures as of Autumn 1980.

16. *Bulletin*, vol. 19, no. 3 (September 1979), p. 262.

17. *Bulletin*, vol. 19, no. 4 (December 1979), p. 391.

18. See *The Times*, Friday 5 September 1980: How Bank of England Tried to Keep Interest Rates Down.

19. *Bulletin*, vol. 20, no. 2 (June 1980), p. 173.

20. *Bulletin*, vol. 20, no. 4 (December 1980), p. 390.

21. *Bulletin*, vol. 20, no. 4 (December 1980), p. 428; also The Monetary Base: A Statistical Note in *Bulletin*, vol. 21, no. 1 (March 1981), p. 59.

22. *Bulletin*, vol. 21, no. 1 (March 1981), pp. 38-41.

23. A more detailed chronology can be found in the *National Institute Economic Review*.

11 CONSERVATIVE MONETARY POLICY

11.1 Introduction

This chapter has a number of objectives of which the first is to update the account of monetary policy given above. This is provided in section 11.2 which covers the period from the autumn of 1981 until the end of Mrs Thatcher's first term of office in June 1983. During this period the exchange rate twice came under sustained downward pressure. This produced a potential conflict between the internal and external targets of policy which had been absent for several years. Moreover, the authorities were no longer satisfied with a single monetary target as their major policy weapon for other reasons. Indeed this unhappiness had been apparent since the autumn of 1980, but it intensified in the period under review. One response was the adoption of 'multiple targets', similar to those advocated above, in the 1982 Budget and to considerable emphasis being given in official speeches to a range of 'considerations' besides money which affected monetary policy. Such references were common from the autumn of 1980 onwards, the first being in the Chancellor's speech referred to on p. 194. Hence for a number of reasons the intermediate target of monetary policy was subject to continuous review. The issues underlying this are analysed in section 11.3. During the period major changes in the techniques of monetary control occurred in the field of debt management. These were evolutionary rather than revolutionary in that they continued the innovative and imaginative policy which had been adopted for several years. Nevertheless the overall effect of these changes was great. In his 1983 Budget speech, Sir Geoffrey Howe claimed that these were among the major achievements of his period as Chancellor, second only to the reduction of inflation. These changes are discussed in section 11.4.

During the period much more attention was paid in the media to changes in the Bank of England's *modus operandi* in short-term money markets. Whilst of less intrinsic importance than the changes in debt management policy, these innovations are nevertheless of considerable interest. The changes stemmed from two sources, the changes involving the abolition of MLR on 20 August 1981 described above, pp. 195–6, and 'over-funding' during this period. Over-funding occurs when non-bank private sector lending to the public sector exceeds the PSBR so that the public sector contribution to monetary growth is negative.

To avoid total disruption of short-term money markets the authorities had to respond in some way. Their response is described and analysed in section 11.5. During this period the authorities must certainly have felt themselves the victims of that ancient Chinese curse, 'to live in interesting times', since besides the problems so far mentioned they faced the consequences of reaction of what to some eyes were the most significant changes in the structure of the financial system in the twentieth century. These stemmed not so much from the technological changes in banking brought about by electronic gadgetry as from less spectacular evolution in the nature of financial institutions (section 11.5).

Throughout the period there was much debate about whether or not the Conservative government was or was not pursuing an ideological policy. Critics and defenders alike sought evidence that the government had abandoned monetarism – ranging from the *Daily Telegraph* City editor in the autumn of 1981, to Mr Heath in the 1983 election campaign – Mrs Thatcher 'had abandoned her monetarist policies, which was a very good thing'. Such a debate can easily become semantic but it does conceal a serious issue, which is considered in section 11.7. Finally an overall assessment of Conservative policy is attempted in section 11.8.

11.2 Choices Galore: Monetary Policy September 1981–June 1983

In the autumn of 1981, sterling M_3 was growing at an annual rate of about 20 per cent, compared to the target announced in the 1981 Budget of 6–10 per cent per annum for the period February 1981–March 1982 (detailed statistics appear in the Appendix). In addition the exchange rate was falling – at the end of 1980, the pound had been worth $2.33, whereas by the middle of September 1981 the rate had fallen to $1.79. Its effective exchange rate against all major currencies had also dropped, by over 10 per cent. Especially when the rate of decline of the exchange rate accelerated, both domestic monetary indicators and external ones showed there to be a powerful case for raising interest rates to try to stem monetary growth. In the autumn the pressures seemed overwhelming so the authorities decided to raise interest rates, and forced bank base rate up from 12 per cent in early September to 16 per cent in early October.

This decision proved very controversial and many dissenting voices were raised, notably by Congdon in the influential *Messel's Weekly*

Economic Monitor. He and others referred to the dangers of killing an incipient recovery in economic activity at a time when unemployment was 2.75 million and rising at about 40,000 per month. The latter argument was really an argument against monetary targets and there can be no doubt that it was *consistent* to raise interest rates. The role of monetary policy in causing unemployment is considered below, but one of the strongest arguments for monetary targets is that the money supply is a better indicator of the impact of monetary policy than interest rates. Counter-arguments either cited monetary aggregates other than $£M_3$ or argued that $£M_3$ was distorted by special factors. The former arguments seem bogus. All measures of the money supply were accelerating to apparently excessive levels. Even the aggregate growing least quickly, M_1, was rising by 11 per cent at an annual rate and so was above the Chancellor's target for $£M_3$ even though theoretically it should grow less fast than $£M_3$. Broad measures other than $£M_3$ were growing at rates between 15 and 25 per cent *per annum*.

One special factor concerned the impact of the civil service pay dispute, as a consequence of which the civil service unions had called out a few key workers who handled large-scale receipts by the central government. Public sector cash flow was adversely affected in the first half of 1981/2 by about £4½bn. Nevertheless it would seem that monetary growth was probably little affected because most of those who would have made payments to the government reduced their bank borrowing. In any case the strike was settled in August and it then became clear that $£M_3$ was growing very rapidly whatever it had been doing earlier.

Another special factor concerned the entry of the banks into the mortgage market. This is discussed below but it must be stressed that while it may have caused some extra monetary growth this is not necessarily an argument for arguing that the monetary growth would be different in its effects. Indeed there are powerful arguments for the opposite view.

The decision about whether or not to raise interest rates must have proved agonising to both the Cabinet and the Bank of England. Nevertheless the arguments analysed above would suggest that it was correct. It is not clear, however, how much exchange rate as opposed to money supply considerations swayed the authorities, although the Bank *Bulletin* suggested that domestic considerations were only of secondary importance. Nevertheless some commentators claimed to detect substantial differences between Bank and Treasury statements on the issue. In a sense the issue is moot as monetary and exchange rate considerations were not in conflict; but many commentators saw this action as an abandonment of monetarism in favour of exchange rate targets. By skilful use of the new money market techniques bank base rates were forced up from 12 per cent in early September to 16 per cent in early October. The Bank proved adept at both inducing banks to raise their rates and at putting an end to the period of rising rates in October. Indeed they were able to put some downward pressures on rates and in mid-November base rates settled at 15 per cent. This operation can be judged a success on both technical grounds and on broader criteria. The exchange rate recovered to end the year at $1.91 (and to regain about 5 per cent on a trade-weighted basis). Sterling M_3's growth abated such that it grew by 13 per cent over the financial year, i.e. well above target but much less than had seemed likely earlier. But by this stage the authorities faced a further problem: bank lending was clearly exploding. It is difficult to pinpoint the date at which the acceleration occurred because of the Civil Service dispute, since the underlying rise in the demand for bank credit was masked by the reduction of borrowing caused by not having to make tax payments. Nevertheless by the end of 1981, the underlying rate of growth was about 30 per cent, per annum, and an incredible £6bn was borrowed in the first quarter of 1982 – of which only £1bn was for house purchase. This occurred despite the higher level of bank base rates; although base rates drifted down during this period to 13 per cent, they were still higher than in September 1981.

The authorities responded by massive sales of debt to the non-bank private sector, over £11bn in 1981/2. Gilt sales in late 1981 benefited from a 'Duke of York operation' but the high level of sales was only made possible by the innovative approach discussed below. The major changes involved indexation. The last step in the brilliantly successful policy of creeping indexation was taken in the 1982 Budget when all limits on holding indexed gilt-edged securities were removed. Nevertheless this combination of heavy debt sales and accelerating bank lending caused considerable problems in short-term money markets, discussed below. On the other hand it facilitated a steady fall in interest rates which lasted until late in 1982. The flexible debt management policy almost certainly contributed to the notably successful handling of financial markets by the authorities during the Falklands war, in April–May 1982.

In the 1982 Budget, the Chancellor responded to this background by relaxing monetary policy in that his new target for $£M_3$ was 8-12 per cent growth (for February 1982-April 1983), 2 per cent above his target for 1981/2 although below the out-turn. He also announced that the same target would also apply to M_1 and PSL_2, a narrow and very broad aggregate respectively. This common level of target no doubt reveals that the arguments for the multiple targets were seen as pragmatic rather than theoretical (see p. 204 below).

In 1982 there was a prolonged bull market in gilt-edged securities during which yields on long-dated stocks fell from a peak level in October 1981 of 16.8 per cent to a low in October 1982 of 10.3 per cent. During the period bank base rates fell, to 9 per cent, and mortgage rates to 10 per cent (to take effect on 1 December 1982). A stock market boom had also taken place such that share prices had risen by about a third. It was very clear that this reduction in interest rates was a major objective of government policy. In part this was because it was perceived of as a device to promote economic recovery but it was often presented as an objective in its own right, conceivably for electoral reasons. As was made clear in the 1983 Budget speech, long-dated gilt-edged securities were deliberately withheld from the market so as to maximise the fall in interest rates (and to encourage corporate borrowing). It may also have a relevant consideration that official estimates of inflation were below market ones so that future debt service would be reduced by this policy of the government were right. Other types of debt were marketed vigorously so that monetary targets could be met with the lowest possible level of long-term and mortage interest rates. Indeed all three targetal monetary variables were within the 8–12 per cent band, so official actions were defensible. On the other hand, the authorities did seem to be going too far too fast to many observers in the autumn of 1983. Monetary growth was showing signs of acceleration. After a temporary slow down bank lending was rising as fast as ever and the PSBR was rising. In these circumstances internal considerations suggested that a more cautious approach was desirable.

However, the bubble of official complacency was punctured by movements in the exchange rate which led the authorities to perceive a conflict between external and internal targets. The fall was largely triggered by oil price developments but undoubtedly the belief that monetary policy had been eased was a contributory factor. The pound had fallen slowly throughout 1982, from $1.91 at the beginning of the year to $1.63 at the end of October, and by about 3 per cent on a trade-weighted basis. During November a major slide started which reduced the effective rate by 4 per cent in 3 days, the dollar rate falling to $1.57. The authorities responded as of old by raising interest rates. The process culminated in a rise in base rates on 26 November. This induced what the Bank *Bulletin* called a period of quiet trading but after an initial increase the exchange rate continued to fall. In all the effective exchange rate fell 14 per cent from November to January. In January, a further increase in interest rates was engineered. During this period the Bank's precise role in interest rate changes was obscure. Some commentators felt that interest rates were being fixed by the clearing banks or market forces more generally rather than by the Bank — a view encapsulated in a cartoon which showed a Bank official saying 'I'll ring Barclays to see what our policy is'. On the other hand others saw this period as one of successful camouflage by the Bank, which escaped some of the responsibility for provoking interest rate changes. Mrs Thatcher added to the confusion by comments which were interpreted as showing opposition to the January changes, after a 36-hour journey returning from a visit to the Falklands. Following an apparently successful OPEC meeting in May, sterling thereafter recovered, and by May half of the earlier fall had been reversed. Indeed by 9 June the effective rate was 85.9, against a low of 79.1.

The significance of this episode was that the authorities had been forced to accept higher interest rates in an attempt to stabilise the foreign exchange market. The first change in interest rates was arguably desirable on domestic criteria but was certainly not caused by internal monetary developments. The second change did not seem even to be consistent with domestic criteria.

Ironically as the Chancellor reviewed 1982/3 in his Budget speech he showed that the Government had met its monetary targets for the first time in the first year in which he had not given them priority. He set new monetary growth targets of 7-11 per cent for 1983/4. Some thought the new target too high and more important it was not clear that the new target would be met. Scepticism was increased by an apparent loss of control of public spending. In the Budget (15 March) the Chancellor forecast a PSBR of £7.5 billion for the year ending 5 April. The out-turn was £9.2 billion. To be so inaccurate after 49 weeks of the year have elapsed is even more than anything Mr Healey accomplished. An appallingly high Central Government Borrowing Requirement in the first month of the new financial year reinforced this concern, because it seemed to refute the suggestion that the PSBR misforecast was due to bringing 1983/4 expenditure into 1982/3.

11.3 Monetary Targets

Monetary targets were introduced by Mr Healey (pp. 153 ff above). Sir Geoffrey Howe added to them early in his term of office when he introduced a longer-term monetary target called the medium-term financial strategy which set targets for the money supply ($£M_3$) and the PSBR for the next five years. He continued to produce these figures but they attracted considerable scepticism because they clearly bore no relation to what the targets would be when the year in question arrived. For example in the 1981 Budget the Chancellor reaffirmed his target for 1983/4 as 4-8 per cent growth in $£M_3$. In the Budget of 1983 it was announced as 7-11 per cent. Indeed missing targets and upward revision of their short-term level was the *leitmotiv* of Sir Geoffrey Howe's Chancellorship. He originally announced a 7-11 per cent target for 1979/80 (targets henceforth usually covered the period February year n to April year n + 1). This was symbolic gesture – it was effectively the same as Mr Healey's 8-12 per cent target but was made to seem lower and so tougher by choice of a suitable base date – February instead of April (see p. 190 above). The out-turn was over 13 per cent growth, at annual rate. Not discouraged, in March 1980 the Chancellor announced a 7-11 per cent target for 1980/1 (for $£M_3$) and his first medium term financial strategy. The out-turn was that $£M_3$ grew by over 18 per cent at an annual rate. In November 1980, Sir Geoffrey simultaneously reaffirmed his target *and* said that he would not try to hit it (p. 194 above). He announced a 1981/2 target of 6-10 per cent. In the autumn, as described in the above section, interest rates were raised, at least partly in response to overseas factors. Thereafter, both the Governor and Chancellor stressed that monetary policy was not determined solely by the need to satisfy a monetary target but by a number of 'considerations'. These could have been culled from an eclectic survey of macroeconomic and monetary textbooks. They included the exchange rate, asset prices, the rate of inflation, the level of real activity, the level of interest rates, other financial aggregates and the corporate sector's perceived financial position. Whatever else such a list did, it did not make it easy for the private sector to form expectations about future official actions, nor did it seem to restrict the scope for official discretion, i.e. it removed two of the arguments for monetary targets. In the 1982 Budget, targets were set for three aggregates, see p. 153-61 for a discussion of the case for multiple targeting.

In late 1982, the authorities openly accepted that interest rates were being used with the major objective of influencing exchange rates.

However, some confusion remained – e.g. Mrs Thatcher's remarks on returning from a trip to the Falklands in early January 1982 seemed to dissent from official policy. Even more oddly on 24 March 1982, a Treasury Minister (Bruce Gardyne) claimed that interest rates were fixed by an assessment of domestic monetary conditions – a statement totally irreconcilable with other official speeches or observed behaviour. The final irony was that the 1982/3 targets were actually met, at a time when the authorities were not trying to meet them.

The actual path of monetary growth may have been desirable, e.g. as argued above the government's policy can be defended as following the lines of its critics such as Currie, Buiter and Miller (see p. 160). Nevertheless the record of monetary targets does not at first sight seem to fulfil any of the ostensible purposes of a monetary target – seemingly neither was useful information provided nor could the private sector easily predict official actions nor shocks be stabilised (not at least as a result of sticking to the target).

However, a defence of the role of the value of missed targets had been made, by Fforde (a prime architect of monetary policy throughout the 1970s) and Minford (in his comment on Foot (1981)). Fforde distinguishes the 'political economy' of monetary targets from their 'practical macroeconomic' or 'operational significance'. Accepting that the latter role has been minimal he defends them on the former ground. These include the value of a flow-of-funds approach to macroeconomic policy as a means of achieving a coherent and consistent policy. However, he emphasises the 'vitally important' role of targets 'to signal a decisive break with the past' 'to enable the authorities to stand back from output and employment', (i.e. abandon a commitment to full employment). Minford put this case succinctly; the objective was 'to show the government meant business' about inflation.

The case for this starts with the Keynesian argument that full employment existed in the 1950s and 1960s not because of the direct effect of policy but because of the indirect effect of the commitment or rather the belief in it.[1] This led businessmen to invest more (in expectation of higher sales) and so produced full employment. Unfortunately, all would agree, the commitment also produced malign effects especially in that it convinced trade union leaders (and the underlying *apparatchiki* of shop stewards) that no action of theirs could price their members out of a job. These malign effects made inflation and inflationary expectations so endemic that the commitment had to be abandoned (Graham *et al.* use this as an argument for incomes policy, Beckerman (1972)). Indeed *perceived* abandonment of the commitment was necessary if inflation were to be reduced.

The most obvious course of action would have been for the government to announce that it aimed to ensure price stability *irrespective of the cost in terms of unemployment*. Fforde argues that this would not have been politically possible. Indeed a very large part of his argument rests upon this point, that a government would not say 'we have abandoned full employment' but could say 'we are monetarist'.[2] This is possible but many Tory wets concentrated on the illogicality of a commitment to a financial aggregate. Commitment to price stability at any price might have been easier. Moreover both Mrs Thatcher and Sir Geoffrey Howe made statements very similar to this. Similarly, 'there is no alternative' and 'the lady's not for turning' influenced (and were meant to influence) opinion to believe that the government would press on to the bitter (or sweet) end. However, the essential point is that the Fforde-Minford case depends upon the impact on private sector expectations. Otherwise the government could merely pursue its policy. The argument is much more sophisticated than the argument that money supply targets are *directly* taken into account in formulating, say, wage claims. Nevertheless it still depends upon the effect on expectations. It is in this respect that the case is weakest. It would seem that only the *fact* of large-scale unemployment has changed expectations. The role of an announced target would be to reduce the (unemployment) cost of an anti-inflationary policy. Indeed following the Fforde-Minford argument, the failure to hit monetary targets may have increased the unemployment cost of eliminating inflation by reducing government credibility. Mrs Thatcher's credibility was restored by her behaviour during the Falklands crisis and thereafter the problems caused by missing targets were much reduced.

It may have been desirable to eliminate perceptions of full employment; indeed it almost certainly was, the relevant question is 'was it worth it?', to which responses legitimately differ. Nevertheless, monetary targets do not seem to have contributed to this goal. Experience in the period has strengthened the case for targets that are not merely set but observed in that (to quote Buiter's (1981) statement of the elements of the case for targets that he cannot refute) – they eliminate 'uncertainty about current and future policy instrument values' and avoid 'authorities (who) either pursue the wrong objectives or pursue the right objectives in inept ways'.

11.4 Debt Management

Without doubt, innovations in debt management policy have been the major changes in the practice of monetary policy in the UK in recent years. The consequence has been a resourceful and flexible approach to the marketing of official securities in marked contrast to the rigidity of the early 1970s. This new style has made it possible to sell enormous quantities of securities (see Table 11.1). Almost certainly this has been the most successful arm of monetary policy, whether judged purely technically or by its contribution to macroeconomic goals.

Table 11.1: Sales of Public Sector Debt to the Non-bank Private Sector

	National Savings	Gilt-edged Securities	Other	Total
1973/4	-10	1,474	1,547	3,011
1974/5	128	2,290	1,761	4,179
1975/6	500	3,860	997	5,357
1976/7	997	5,785	439	7,221
1977/8	1,094	4,908	599	6,601
1978/9	1,618	6,179	623	8,420
1979/80	967	8,327	-168	9,126
1980/1	2,241	8,891	-259	10,873
1981/2	4,224	7,098	-138	11,184
1982/3	2,458	4,637	2,494	10,089

In the eyes of any economic theorist the most substantial change has been the gradual introduction of index-linked securities. The details of this tortuous process are set out above, starting with the first timid step of introducing an index-linked contractual saving (Save As You Earn) scheme. The two final steps occurred in September 1981 and March 1982 when all investors were allowed to hold index-linked savings certificates and gilt-edged securities respectively (previously the certificates were restricted to older investors and the marketable bonds to pension funds).

There are enormously powerful arguments on grounds of both economic efficiency and equity for indexation. Almost certainly the authorities were convinced by the more pragmatic argument that it increased the sales of their debt. Creeping indexation had a number of advantages for the authorities. It minimised any potential disruptive effects on financial markets and in particular avoided the advantages and disadvantages of widespread adoption of indexation in other financial markets. This was, however, also a consequence of the timing of the introduction of indexation when inflation was falling, not entirely fortuitous but not entirely planned either. Moreover creeping indexation meant that the authorities could boost debt sales by creeping a bit further at their time of choice. Undoubtedly this was perceived to be a major benefit of the introduction of indexation by the authorities. As proponents of indexation had long argued it made possible much more control of the timing of gilt-edged sales by the authorities since indexed securities were most attractive when conventional securities were least attractive. Moreover, it not only made it possible to avoid excessive reliance on the Duke of York technique, but also made possible the authorities' ability to meet their debt targets in 1982/3 without issuing long-dated conventional gilt-edged. This both facilitated the Chancellor's desire to reduce interest rates as much and as rapidly as possible and made it easier to try to resurrect the corporate bond market (see p. 215 below). Unlimited availability of index-linked securities may well prove in the long run to be one of the most important of all the changes brought about by Mrs Thatcher's first government – certainly this would be Freidman's view.

> I know of no other (expedient) that holds as much promise of both reducing the harm done by inflation and facilitating the ending of inflation.[3]

More modestly, it is undeniable that it has greatly assisted the execution of monetary policy.

Another change of enormous import has involved National Savings which have become a key instrument of monetary control. In the early 1970s National Savings were trivial in size, and, as the Page Report (1973) put it, regarded as a social service not an instrument of economic policy. Ironically it was only in the late 1970s that, for the first time for a generation, National Savings did fulfil their social function of enabling small savers to transfer resources from one period of their life to another. Official attitudes first started to change in 1977. Mr Healey revived National Savings as a tool of economic policy in that he sought to maximise their sales. This, however, was a blunt instrument in that the authorities felt that they had little control over the size or timing of sales. From 1980, however, the authorities started to 'fine tune' sales of National Savings. They pursued a more vigorous marketing policy from September 1980 and started to offer an ever-wider range of new types of security – both index-linked and orthodox, such as the income bond in 1982. The National Savings Bank started to offer competitive rates. The authorities felt that National Savings could be used flexibly, by the timing of innovations and by varying NSB and National Savings Certificate terms. Indeed from 1980/1 onwards targets were set, although not revealed until the 1981 Budget when a 1981/2 target of £3 billion was announced. As the target was later raised to £3½ billion the authorities apparently felt confident of their ability to fine-tune the level of sales, or perhaps that their real objective was still to maximise sales – certainly this is consistent with the out-turn of £4.2 billion. Targets of £3 billion were set for 1982/3 (and achieved, the out-turn was £2,958m) and 1983/4. The only return to old habits was shown in late 1982 when National Savings terms were altered with the blatant objective of influencing mortgage rates rather than to achieve any level of debt sales.

The use of National Savings as a tool of monetary policy replete with explicit targets is important. Nevertheless its exact significance depends upon how the targets are derived. One possibility is that the figures are plucked out of mid-air or represent estimates of sales. A more likely and charitable explanation is that the authorities now aim at a level of National Savings equal to half of gilt sales so as to maintain what the Bank *Bulletin* called 'a more diversified pattern of funding'.[4] Another possibility is that the authorities forecast a personal sector's financial surplus and then deduct from this contractual saving and the desired increase in money holdings. The balance, more or less, is divided between National Savings and building societies. The National Savings target can be derived as a residual by calculating the net inflow into building societies consistent with the authorities' objectives for the housing market.

Another aspect of the authorities' debt management strategy revealed in Table 11.1 is the virtual disappearance of instruments other than gilts or National Savings. This reflects in large part a decision to inhibit local authority borrowing, another revolution of the circle induced by the authorities' schizophrenic attitude to this (see pp. 88-90). The considerations discussed above were reinforced by the additional consideration that local authorities were turning more and more to bank finance – hence local authority borrowing was often no longer even a form of non-bank private sector lending to the public sector. This led, in August 1982, to considerable improvement in the terms on which Public Works Loan Board finance was made available.

The authorities' innovative approach to gilt-edged marketing described above continued. To variable rate stocks (p. 154), part paid issues (p. 175), tenders (p. 175) and various minor changes (p. 191), the authorities added two new devices. One was the convertible stock of which the first was issued in June 1982.[5] A convertible stock is usually issued as a short-dated gilt with the holding having the right to convert to a longer-dated security on pre-specified terms at various prescribed dates. This means that the purchase will reap a capital gain if interest rates fall but is insured against a capital loss if they rise. It thus appeals to the risk-averse and at times of extreme uncertainty. These features render it saleable when other securities are not attractive and the authorities can borrow more cheaply, since purchasers have been prepared to pay a risk premium. The authorities broke new ground in May 1983 by offering a part paid index-linked security by tender convertible into an orthodox gilt – thus demonstrating by how much their attitudes have changed in seven years, since in 1976 any of these features seemed inconceivable. Indeed the indexation and tender proposals in *MPCC* seemed iconoclastic in 1978 whereas in 1983, even in combination, they were the purest of orthodoxy. Another innovation, in May 1982, was the decision to create relatively small amounts (dubbed tranchettes by the Bank) of a number of different stocks rather than issuing a single tap stock.[6] In July eight different long-dated gilts were issued amounting in total to £1200 m rather than a single long-dated 'tap stock' as would normally have been the practice. The impact of this was hard to judge as the bull market in gilts would almost certainly have swallowed a conventional tap as easily and thereafter the authorities abstained from long-dated issues, except of indexed securities.

In summary, nothing has happened to change the conclusion reached above (p. 190) – debt management policy has been the most successful part of monetary policy.

11.5 Lender of Last Resort

Bank of England policy and tactics in short-term financial markets were the subject of considerable change in this period because of two distinct factors, the first being the reforms formally inaugurated on 20 August 1981 with the abolition of MLR (p. 195 above), the other, 'overfunding'. The reforms represented a continuation of the Bank's desire for a flexible, depoliticised intervention rate which had motivated the move from Bank Rate to MLR in 1972 and from MLR mark 1 to MLR mark 2 in 1978. Their ideal would be for interest rate changes to be viewed as technical operations not as major acts of economic policy.

Moreover, while in the 1950s the authorities had welcomed the publicity surrounding a change in Bank rate because they relied heavily on 'announcement effects' as a tool of policy, the fanfare was felt to be counter-productive in the 1970s. Instead the Bank wanted a world in which changes in its dealing rate, whatever its name, had the same newspaper coverage as Australian rules football results – and were similarly ignored by all but a tiny band of devotees. To a considerable extent these goals were achieved. Changes in the intervention rate were frequent and never received the banner headlines of old. It would seem that political constraints on dealings were also lessened. Nevertheless, an important caveat has to be entered in any comparison of new and old systems in that more information is available about the new regime. It is possible that the old system was more flexible than it seemed, especially as the Bank could make the penalty rate as lender of last resort exceed MLR. However, the new system seemed to work more smoothly in the eyes of observers as well as participants.

The Bank certainly obtained more freedom in regard to the other objectives of the reforms; the price/quantity dilemma. Basically the 'lender of last resort' is a monopolist lending money to the banking system, usually in the UK, via the Discount Market, either by buying securities or making loans. The new system involved less emphasis on loans against the security of bills and more on purchasing them, but the change is of no economic significance. The Bank faces a downward sloping demand curve, Figure 11.1(a). According to the elementary textbook it can choose either price or quantity but not both. Nevertheless the choice of either automatically determines the other. Hence it would not matter in Figure 11.1(a) whether the authorities announced a willingness to lend q_1 or to lend at a rate of r_1. However, in the real world the demand curve is not known with certainty, as illustrated in Figure 11.1(b), which illustrates the simple case of two demand curves with equal probability. The stochastic element may be state contingent, for example D_1 might apply if the exchange rate were $1.60, D_2 if it were $1.55. Alternatively it might be purely random and D_1 would be the case on some days and D_2 on others. The problem is that on any day in advance the authorities do not know which will apply and can only operate on the basis of the expected demand curve D_d the average of the other two. Traditional Bank policy was to fix the interest rate and allow quantity to be market-determined. Hence in Figure 11.1(b), the rate would be fixed at r_D, implying that q_D was the preferred quantity. Nevertheless, the actual quantity would be q_1 or q_2 depending upon which demand curve was operative.

Figure 11.1: Lender of Last Resort

a) **Theory**

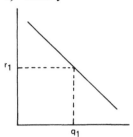

b) **Bank pre 1981**

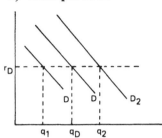

c) **Friedman-Griffiths**

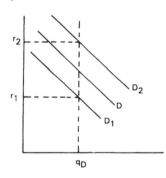

d) **Fed Policy**

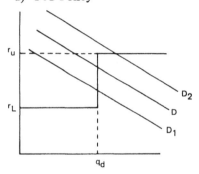

e) **Bank 1981-**

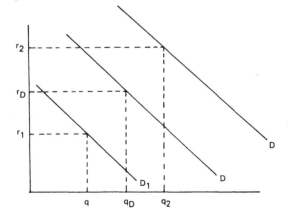

Griffiths, in a witty sally, said that this was being a lender of first resort rather than of last resort. This criticism in substance uses the same as Friedman's critique of the Federal Reserve. It has two elements, that the authorities should care much more about quantity than price and that the implicit perfectly elastic supply curve encouraged undesirable bank behaviour. His preferred system, like that of Friedman and most other monetarists is illustrated in 11.1(c). The authorities fix the quantity at q_D and let the price fluctuate according to which demand curve is operative. Other possibilities include that sometimes practised by the Fed. prior to November 1979 (11.1(d)). They determined a target range for r (the Fed. funds rate) and fixed quantity within this range so the implicit supply curve is stepped (with r_u and r_L the limits of the range).

The Bank responded to the critics and sought its own goal of maximum flexibility in two ways. One involved categorising securities according to the time remaining to maturity. The resulting categories were called bands – band 1 being less than 14 days, band 2, 15-33 days and so on up to band 4 – 64-91 days. The Bank stated that it possessed the right to refuse purchase or lend against bills at any price. In American parlance it might 'close the window' and so the certainty of obtaining funds which had been the object of Griffiths' and his allies' critique disappeared. The other was not to name its price until it had elicited information from the Discount Houses about their desired borrowing. In effect, as illustrated in Figure 11.1(e), the Bank waited until it knew the demand curve prevailing and then allowed both price and quantity to diverge from the optimal level, but price by less than the monetarist solution and quantity by less than the old Bank method. In practice, the system is made more complex still by having two rounds of dealing. Price is fixed after the first so the Bank has not complete information about demand but it has much more than in other systems.

The major change in the period, however, was the growth of the commercial bill market and the Bank's enormous purchases of them – £87 billion gross in the year to October 1982 (by comparison they had been trivial in previous years, e.g. £50 m in 1977/8[7]). The commercial bill market had been growing fast for a number of reasons. One had been the use of bills as a means of circumventing lending ceilings as bank lending in the 1960s and, more importantly, the IBELs ceiling in the late 1970s (p. 145-8). Another had been the consequence of Discount Houses seeking to compete with banks for some types of industrial loan demand. The new arrangements probably increased the desirability of bills to banks. In traditional terminology, the changes reduced the availability of primary liquidity so the banks desire for secondary liquidity increased – if there was a risk of the Bank refusing to provide finance as lender of last resort, banks needed more saleable assets. Despite the attention paid to this fact by some commentators it was almost certainly of much less importance than the Bank's deliberate decision to use the market as a vehicle for its operations in preference to the overnight inter-bank market.[8]

Finally, however, the role of 'over-funding' is crucial. When non-bank private lending to the public sector exceeds the PSBR, the non-bank private sector is a net payer of funds to the public sector. This debt can be settled by a reduction in currency holdings or by cheque in which case bank liabilities (the payer's deposit) and assets (their claims on the public sector) fall – a process described in detail above (p. 39). This is indeed just one of the primary causes of changes in the money supply. However, the operation does present certain technical difficulties when one examines which claims on the public sector the banks cease to hold. The logical possibilities are cash, Treasury Bills or gilt-edged securities. Cash holdings, whether in terms of currency or central bank deposits, were far too small and in any case a major fall in bank holdings of cash would cause massive disruption to the operations of banking, indeed it would make it impossible for banks to function and such disruption would be undesirable for both long-term structural and short-term monetary control considerations. Indeed the Bank had promised not to create or permit such a squeeze.[9] The normal response would have to reduce the banking sector's holdings of Treasury Bills. However, these were too small – at the start of 1981/2 bank and discount house holdings of Treasury Bills were only £1000 m whereas in 1981/2 'over-funding' was over £2,500 m. Moreover other factors increased the net drain on banks' holdings of public sector assets to £4.75 billion (for example, increased currency holdings by the non-bank private sector). This could not be met even by the elimination of the entire stock of Treasury Bills. Moreover even if sufficient this would have been very undesirable as it would have reduced official leverage in short-term money markets and administered an unnecessary and unpredictable shock to the banking system. Hence the authorities chose to purchase private sector assets from the banks, commercial bills. To summarise, the normal effect of a purchase of public sector debt by the non-bank private sector is a fall in the money supply accompanied by a fall in bank claims on the public sector. Instead the process led to a fall in bank claims on the private sector.

The logic of this process is obvious but the scale was incredible. The authorities at one point held over £10 bn of commercial bills. In the circumstances it is difficult to conceive of an alternative that was practicable in the short term, given the scale of bank lending if monetary growth was to be restrained to any reasonable figure. It is possible to devise schemes involving the overseas sector but the consequences are incalculable and certainly even more risky than the acquisition of a bill mountain. Yet, however inevitable, the policy was not liked by the authorities or indeed by anyone else. The root of the problem stems from the corporate sector's desire to borrow being satisfied with loans whose matching asset was a bank deposit. If instead the company had borrowed directly from the personal sector or the claim had been intermediated by a non-bank, the problem would not have occurred. The authorities, logically enough, therefore sought to encourage the growth of the commercial bond market so as to achieve this end. As it was originally the victim of inflation (Gowland, 1979) the timing seemed propitious as inflation fell steadily in 1982. A number of initiatives were taken to encourage corporate bonds.[10] In addition it was one motive for the failure to issue long-dated gilts, to reduce the competition faced by corporate bonds. On the other hand, firms clearly liked the flexibility of bank finance. If banks have a comparative advantage in intermediation in general, or in tailoring loans to corporate requirements, it would be undesirable to interfere with market forces – interference normally aims to make it easier, not harder, for firms to expand. Another option is to encourage banks to have non-money liabilities, e.g. five-year deposits or bond issues (advocated in *MPCC*, p. 186) but again there are snags. In summary the problem is another variant of the old tale, structural efficiency conflicts with short-term policy objectives.

A final Bank initiative concerned the Discount Houses. While the changes had little effect on monetary policy, they were an interesting example of the Bank's increasing sophistication and reliance on rational theory rather than *ad hoc* empirical judgement. Discount houses' gross assets were previously restricted to 30 times 'own resources', owners' capital less fixed assets. The new regulations introduced a limit of 40 times their assets *weighted by risk* where assets carried weights ranging from 1 to 4. In practice a further category of asset had an effective weight of zero ('mop-up' Treasury Bills being the cited example). Risk was calculated to allow for default risk and forced sale risk as well as the potential variability in market prices of fixed interest rate assets.

11.6 Innovations in Banking

There may well have been more change in the financial structure of the UK within the last decade than at any time in the twentieth century. Among the more important developments in the last few years have been the entry of the big four banks into the mortgage market in 1981 and the innovative activity of building societies, which culminated in two building societies advertising interest-bearing cheque accounts in late 1982 (Halifax and Abbey National). Building societies also offer a bewildering array of special accounts whereby a higher rate of interest was paid in exchange for longer notice or a withdrawal penalty; these accounts were not new in conception but both expanded rapidly in 1981–2 and became more attractive as the penalties became less prohibitive. The banks also started to offer interest-bearing cheque accounts, such as Lloyds 'cash flow', and Midland's 'save and borrow' account and the Natwest Cashwise scheme. The larger depositor interested in this facility could also use the Money Market fund account, pioneered by Tyndall. Effectively, these countered the banks' differential interest rates in favour of large depositors by aggregating medium size deposits (£2,500 upwards). Large investors could also use currency funds which were in essence bank accounts located off-shore and easily convertible from one currency to another. Add this to the bill revival discussed above, and the ever-growing role of CDs, and it is easy to see why monetary policy became ever more complex in such a turbulent and ever-changing world.

Moreover these developments reversed a long-standing trend in the UK financial system, the growth of ever more specialised institutions, a development that persisted from the late seventeenth century until the late 1960s. Until then 'merchant princes' like Gresham, Cranfield and Heathcote engaged in every aspect of banking and finance as well as trading and even manufacture. Specialisation reflected both the advantages of the division of labour and less desirable aspects. One was that imperfect competition through quality and product differentiation prevailed rather than price competition (partly because of cartels and other restrictions on competition). Another was government, or Central Bank policy. Sometimes this was a conscious decision, e.g. the split between banks and licensed deposit takers in 1979, which stemmed from the 1979 Banking Act where the object was to protect the innocent from the less reputable bodies but let the well-informed use their judgement. At the other extreme, hamfisted direct controls on banks in the 1960s spawned a whole variety of new institutions designed to be banks in all but name (p. 22 above). The Bank of England had traditionally inhibited price competition (for good and bad reasons), and so encouraged further differentiation. By contrast there is a less rich range of institutions in the US. Over the last decade there have been signs that this trend towards specialisation has been reversed. In fact there has been much discussion of the emergence of so-called financial supermarkets who would provide a whole range of financial services including (brokerage for shares and commodities). This process has been more noticeable in the USA. For example, the world's largest stockbroker (Merrill Lynch, the 'thundering herd') has devised a cash management account which has led to competition with banks. Take-overs — like the (US) Prudential of Bache and Philbro's of Saloman brothers have produced institutions which in their range of services are 'financial supermarkets'. There have been signs of similar developments in the UK. In particular banks and building societies are becoming less distinct. While it would be easy to overestimate the scale of the changes, they have been large enough to affect monetary policy.

The effects of changes in financial structure are complex but more important consequences stem from the normal conflict between the two functions of the Central Bank, monetary control and structural efficiency. This conflict arises in many guises, the most fundamental of which concerns that most ancient of central banking aims, a sound banking system. This means that it is capital of withstanding shocks and being able to continue to provide customers with the services they require. However, the role of monetary control is to administer shocks to the system such that banks are compelled to change their behaviour. In all sorts of ways, this conflict arises. A minor example is the payment of interest on cheque accounts. This is highly desirable on structural grounds (Friedman, 1969; Goodhart, 1976) and so that 1981/3 moves in this direction were welcome as increasing economic efficiency. On the other hand, the macroeconomic effect is hard to calculate but probably inflationary.

A clear disadvantage of such innovation in financial markets is that it renders statistics misleading. Such structural breaks in a series render econometric studies impossible in theory and difficult in practice even when theoretical niceties are ignored. More seriously, targeting becomes a less straightforward exercise when the targeted variable is changing its nature. More generally any rational policy requires information and the greater the changes that occur the less knowledge policy makers have and so, *a priori*, the less soundly based their policies are. The problems caused by a fluid structure probably cancel out the benefits obtained by the Bank's laudable efforts to improve the quality of UK monetary data in recent years.

However, the worst problem caused by structural change is that it brings to the surface problems of economic theory that it is normally possible to ignore. Alternative intermediate macroeconomic targets, money, credit, liquidity, etc. cease to move in line so it becomes crucial to face questions of which financial variables matter and through which transmission mechanisms. This problem is graphically illustrated by the banks' invasion of the mortgage market in 1981-2. They briefly made loans equal to about one third óf total mortgage lending but seemed satisfied with a long-term share of about 10 per cent of the market (or with the equivalent proportion of mortgages in their portfolio). As they both concentrated on groups discriminated against by building societies (old property, frequent movers, short-term mortgages and large borrowers) and induced various improvements in building society practice this development was highly desirable from a microeconomic perspective. Its macroeconomic effect is entirely dependent on one's school of thought.

A simple-minded Keynesian analysis is as follows. Banks have attracted both depositors and borrowers from building societies. This transfer of business will have no macroeconomic effects because the effect of monetary policy is via the effect of credit, on consumption, saving and investment. As no more credit has been extended, merely extended by a different intermediary, there are no effects. A monetarist should disagree (or argue for a redefinition of money). His analysis depends on the effect on money of the holder, and someone holds money who previously did not. In consequence, he is likely to switch out of money into real assets such as consumer durables so increasing either their price or their output. A moderate neo-Radcliffean Tobinite might argue that he cared about $£M_3$ as a proxy for the private sector's overall liquidity. A switch from building society balances to bank deposits increases liquidity but by much less than the increase in money. His use of, say, $£M_3$ as a target variable depended upon an unchanging ratio of bank deposits to building society deposits. More sophisticated analyses are possible if the total of lending for house purchase rises in which case the obvious effect is to induce a rise in house prices, relative to other asset prices and probably absolutely. The Bank of England *Bulletin* article argued for a straightforward monetarist portfolio effect. Rising house prices had caused an increase in the proportion of housing in the personal sector borrowing. Bank mortgages were a means of reducing the net stake in housing and so of moving into other assets with consequent effects upon their price and quantity and so of output and inflation. This may be right or wrong; the point is that analysis is dependent on theory. Often in practice alternative economic theory yields the same result so that policy maker can be content to know what should happen without caring why. This is impossible when structures change.

11.7 'Danger: Ideologues at Work?'

The Conservative government during its first term of office was frequently criticised for its dogged commitment to monetarism, which to quote one opposition speech had allegedly done more harm to British industry than Hitler. On the other hand the House of Commons Treasury Committee's all party report could argue that experience had revealed that monetarism had proved too difficult to implement, not that it had failed. Throughout the Conservative's first term, its abandonment of monetarism was hailed. Besides the quotations above from the *Daily Telegraph* and Mr Heath, Lloyds Bank *Economic Bulletin* were more picturesque, but not at all atypical in its comment:

> (The April 1982 Budget) has been hailed as the death of monetarism. It might be more prudent to regard monetarism − in the UK at any rate − as the Sleeping Beauty, now laid to rest in some citadel of academic purity, to be studied with reverence by her admirers, but not destined to awake and return to the real world for many a long year.

As the best operational definition of a monetarist administration is a government which believes in monetary targets, adheres to them and is prepared to pay a high price to achieve them, it is easy to see why Mrs Thatcher's monetarism rhetoric is viewed as no more than words by so many commentators. Any argument that monetarism has been influential has to look at either the wider aspects of monetarism or to argue that, even if not successful, the commitment to monetary targets was such that the Conservative policy was distinctive. Alternatively those wishing to argue for the pernicious effects of ideology have to argue that better means (direct controls) were rejected for ideological reasons.

Most monetarists do seem to believe that inflation should be the primary target of monetary, indeed of all economic, policy − a view shared by Keynes. There is no logical or obvious connection between a belief that monetary factors are predominant in determining income and a belief that inflation should be eliminated. Nevertheless, as Mayer[11] pointed out, the two are almost always linked. This view is founded on a convincing argument that inflation causes both un-employment and a regressive and inequitable redistribution of income and wealth. The evidence for these propositions is very powerful indeed and so the consequence seems to follow, that in the long run it is impossible to have full employment without something approaching price stability. (Unfortunately the converse may not apply, price stability may eventually lead to higher demand but not necessarily or immediately to low unemployment.) Clearly Mrs Thatcher and Sir Geoffrey Howe are committed supporters of this view and so are the monetarist 'Solons'. Nevertheless the view is not ideological − it is on the contrary argued in a utilitarian framework of costs and benefits. It is the case that assessments of (short-term) costs and mainly (long-term) benefits differ when analysing the case for making inflation 'public enemy number one' but this difference is scarcely ideological. The government may have miscalculated these costs − almost certainly it did − but ideological dogmatism again seems an inappropriate tag.

Arguments for ideology are more persuasive when it is argued that the choice of means to reduce inflation has been ideological, and that the cost of reducing inflation is therefore higher. Many would cite incomes policy in this context − on the grounds that it has not yet been proved to fail and would yield so many benefits if it worked. The rejectionist argument is equally clear − after nearly 40 years of diligent effort, the lack of clear proof of success is sufficient to damn incomes policy − especially in view of the malign effects on expectations discussed on p. 205 above.

The Conservative policy of reducing inflation by deflation seems, then, to be arrived at by pragmatic calculation rather than ideological prejudice. However, it has been argued that alternative methods of deflation would have been preferable and were rejected on ideological grounds. The usual theme of this case is that the high exchange rate, which was both an effect and a means of deflation and monetary control, could have been avoided by fiscal deflation. Scott's[12] analysis suggests that this is not so. Moreover, one can scarcely argue that a government is wedded to monetary deflation when it lets its preferred monetary target grow at 20 per cent, per annum. Furthermore, the most monetarist act of Sir Geoffrey Howe's Chancellorship was the tax increases in the 1981 Budget. However, while Sir Geoffrey's *motive* was monetarist (to reduce the PSBR and so money and so inflation) a Keynesian deflationist would not have acted differently. Ironically, the most ideological act of the government was the income tax cut and VAT increase in 1979. This almost certainly increased the unemployment cost of reducing inflation very substantially. (Indeed it also increased inflation in the short-term view its effect on expectations.) Yet whatever else this act was, it was not monetarist.

Nevertheless, virtually all of the government's policies can be fitted into a monetarist framework. With one major exception, the VAT/ income tax switch in 1979, every major act of economic policy can be, and was, viewed, at least in part, as a means of reducing monetary growth within the flow of funds framework set out above. In this sense it was monetarist − in that most decisions were viewed in a monetary framework. It might be argued that the selection of means was ideological in that asset sales and the abolition of exchange control were imperfect techniques of monetary control. Direct controls or import deposits were probably impracticable in the early 1980s. Lack of a *desire* to cut the PSBR was scarcely a fair criticism of the Conservatives. Interest rate changes were less inhibited by political constraints than ever before. Debt management was technically brilliant. Hence, while ideological influences were not absent, the techniques of control were not really at fault in 1979-83.

On balance, then, it would seem that Mrs Thatcher's policy should be judged on whether the costs of her (resolutely pursued) desire to reduce inflation exceeded the benefits and on the competence with which it was executed. Monetarism was the aspect of policy on which she was most ready to compromise − monetary targets were anything but sacrosanct.

11.8 Conclusion

Any general conclusion to a work of this kind is bound to seem both patronising and superficial. Nevertheless, two conclusions seem worth stating. One is that despite the ever more difficult environment the technical competence of the authorities seems to be growing. However, it would still be a rash person who could say that the problems of monetary control in the UK have been solved.

Appendix: Definitions of Money

When first introduced in 1976, monetary targets were set for M_3. From December 1976, they were set in terms of £M_3. In 1982 targets for M_1 and PSL_2 were added. Since 1979, two other series have joined the ranks of monetary data – M_2 and PSL_1.

M_1 is defined as notes and coin held by the non-bank private sector plus non-bank private sector sight (demand) deposits. Some of these deposits pay interest so if these are deducted, *non-interest bearing M_1* is derived.

The present M_2 series is totally different from a series of the same name used in the 1960s which was a precursor of M_3. The new series was introduced in 1981 but its definition was radically changed in 1983 to add to the confusion. It is called 'transactions balances' by the Bank.

Its 1981-2 definition was Freidman's preferred definition of money; non-interest bearing M_1 plus retail sterling time deposits, those of less than £100,000. In 1983, NSB ordinary accounts and building society deposits (unless more than one month's notice of withdrawal was required) were added to the *mélange*.

£M_3 is the non-bank private sector's holdings of currency, all their sterling bank deposits (including CDs) and public sector deposits. M_3 is £M_3 plus non-bank private sector holdings of foreign currency deposits with UK banks.

Financial Statistics

		M_1 Growth (%)	£M_3 Growth (%)	PSL_2 Growth (%)	Base Rate	20 year Bond Rate
1981	III	1.1	4.0	3.0	12.2	15.45
	IV	0.4	2.3	1.3	15.1	15.65
1981	I	2.5	2.8	3.3	13.9	14.28
	II	2.5	2.1	1.5	12.9	13.70
	III	1.2	1.4	1.4	10.5	11.91
	IV	5.1	3.2	2.3	10.5	10.89
1983	I	3.5	3.9	5.5	10.8	11.35

Financial Years

	M_1 (Growth %)	£M_3 (Growth %)	PSL_2 (Growth %)	PSL_1
1981/2	5.1	13.8	11.6[a]	11.5[a]
1982/3	13.9	12.1	8.8[a]	8.8[a]

Note: a. Calendar Year.

Private Sector Liquidity (*PSL₁*) is £M₃ *less* public sector deposits and private deposits with an original maturity of more than two years *plus* non-bank private holdings of bank and Treasury bills, local authority deposits and certificates of tax deposit.

PSL₂ is PSL₁ plus building society deposits and short-term national savings (excluding Building Society term shares and netting out building society holdings of £M₃).

In effect PSL₂ is £M₃ with building societies redefined as banks and some short-term public sector liabilities redefined as currency (e.g. Treasury Bills). In both cases, supply side counterparts and DCE can be calculated, as in Chapter 3 above.

References

1. E.g. in Graham, A.W.M. (1980), 'Demand Management in Changing Historical Circumstances' in Currie, D.A. and Peters, W. (eds.), *Contemporary Economic Analysis*, Croom Helm.

2. In Meek, P. (ed.) (1983), *Central Bank Views on Monetary Targeting*, Federal Reserve Bank of New York.

3. Friedman, M. (1974), *Monetary Correction*, Institute of Economic Affairs, Occasional Paper No. 41.

4. See *Bank of England Quarterly Bulletin*, vol. 22, no. 3 (September 1982), p. 350.

5. One convertible stock. of a less flexible kind, was issued in 1973.

6. The switch was gradual, e.g. three tranches of £250 m were issued in November 1981. The text date was selected because it was the first issue of a tranche as small as £100 m.

7. See the article in *Bank of England Quarterly Bulletin*, vol. 22, no. 1 (March 1982), p. 86: 'The Role of the Bank of England in the Money Market'.

8. Source as note 7.

9. Source as note 7.

10. Summarised in the Chancellor's 1983 Budget speech, see Hansard or *The Times*.

11. Mayer, T. (1978), *The Structure of Monetarism*, Norton.

12. In Sinclair, P. and Eltis, W. (ed.) (1982), *Money Supply and Exchange Rates*, Blackwell.

BIBLIOGRAPHY

Credit Control Notices and Regulations

Credit Notice: Bank and Finance House Lending (30 March 1971) in
Bulletin, vol. 11, no. 2 (June 1971)

Competition and Credit Control (text of a Consultative Document
issued on 14 May 1971) in *Bulletin*, vol. 11, no. 2 (June 1971),
p. 184 reprinted in Bank (1971)

Credit Notice: Bank and Finance House Lending (30 June 1971) in
Bulletin, vol. 11, no. 3 (September 1971)

Competition and Credit Control: The Discount Market (21 July 1971)
in *Bulletin*, vol. 11, no. 3 (September 1971), p. 316 reprinted in
Bank (1971)

Reserve Ratios: Further Definitions in *Bulletin*, vol. 11, no. 4
(December 1971), p. 435 reprinted in Bank (1971)

Bank Lending: The Governor's Letter to the Banking System (7 August
1972) in *Bulletin*, vol. 12, no. 3 (September 1972), p. 327

Competition and Credit Control: Further Developments in *Bulletin*,
vol. 13, no. 1 (March 1973), p. 51

Competition and Credit Control: Modified Arrangements for the
Discount Market in *Bulletin*, vol. 13, no. 3 (September 1973), p. 306

Credit Notice: The Governor's Letter to the Main Banking Associations
(11 September 1973) in *Bulletin*, vol. 13, no. 4 (December 1973),
p. 445

Credit Control: A Supplementary Scheme (17 December 1973) in
Bulletin, vol. 14, no. 1 (January 1974), p. 37

Credit Notice: Consumer Credit (17 December 1973) in *Bulletin*, vol.
14, no. 1 (January 1974), p. 40

Credit Notice: Supplementary Deposits (30 April 1974) in *Bulletin*,
vol. 14, no. 2 (June 1974), p. 161

Credit Control: Notice, 28 February 1975 in *Bulletin*, vol. 15, no. 1
(March 1975), p. 40

Credit Control: Notice, 17 December 1975 in *Bulletin*, vol. 16, no. 1
(March 1976), p. 35

Credit Control: Notice, 22 July 1976 in *Bulletin*, vol. 16, no. 3
(September 1976), p. 307

Credit Control: Notice, 18 November 1976 in *Bulletin*, vol. 16, no. 4
(December 1976), p. 434

Credit Control: Notice, 12 May 1977 in *Bulletin*, vol. 17, no. 2 (June 1977), p. 169

Credit Control: Notice, 11 August 1977 in *Bulletin*, vol. 17, no. 3 (September 1977), p. 309

Credit Control Notices (8 June 1978 and 17 August 1978) in *Bulletin*, vol. 18, no. 3 (September 1978), p. 357

Credit Control: Notice, 3 April 1979 in *Bulletin*, vol. 19, no. 2 (June 1979), p. 136

Credit Control: Notice, 12 June 1979 in *Bulletin*, vol. 19, no. 2 (June 1979), p. 136

Credit Control: Notice, 15 November 1979 in *Bulletin*, vol. 19, no. 4 (December 1979), p. 391

Credit Control: Notice, 26 March 1980 in *Bulletin*, vol. 20, no. 2 (June 1980), p. 153

Methods of Monetary Control (24 November 1980) in *Bulletin*, vol. 20, no. 4 (December 1980), p. 428

Monetary Control: Next Steps (12 March 1981) in *Bulletin*, vol. 21, no. 1 (March 1981), p. 38

The Liquidity of Banks (12 March 1981) in *Bulletin*, vol. 21, no. 1 (March 1981), p. 40

Statements of Official Policy and Attitudes Towards Monetary Policy (Referred to in the Text)

The Operation of Monetary Policy Since the Radcliffe Report in *Bulletin*, vol. 9, no. 4 (December 1969), p. 448

Monetary Management in the U.K. in *Bulletin*, vol. 11, no. 1 (March 1971), p. 37

Key Issues in Monetary and Credit Policy in *Bulletin*, vol. 11, no. 2 (June 1971), p. 195, reprinted in Bank (1971)

Competition and Credit Control: Extract From a Lecture by the Chief Cashier (Sykes Memorial Lecture, 10 November 1971), reprinted in Bank (1971)

Does the Money Supply Really Matter? (Deputy Governor's Address, 11 April 1973) in *Bulletin*, vol. 12, no. 2 (June 1973), p. 193

Speech by Governor of Bank, 21 October 1976 in *Bulletin*, vol. 16, no. 4 (December 1976), p. 453

Speech by Governor, 17 January 1977 in *Bulletin*, vol. 17, no. 1 (March 1977), p. 49

An Account of Monetary Policy (The Governor's Mais Lecture) in

Bulletin, vol. 18, no. 1 (March 1970), p. 31
The Gilt-Edged Market in *Bulletin*, vol. 19, no. 2 (June 1979), p. 137

Studies of UK Monetary Policy

Artis in Blackaby (1978)
Davis and Yeomans (1971)
Dennis (1980)
Goodhart (1973) and (1981)
Grant (1977)
Pepper and Wood (1976)
Posner (1978), especially chapter by Goodhart
Smethurst (1979)
Tew in Blackaby (1978)

References

Alford, R.J. (1968) 'Bank Rate, Money Rates and the Treasury Bill
    Rate' in *Essays of Money and Banking in Honour of R.S. Sayers*,
    OUP
Allard, R.J. (1974) *The Impact of Hire Purchase Restrictions*,
    Government Economic Service Occasional Paper no. 9
Artis, M.J. and Currie, D.A. (1980) *Monetary Targets and the Exchange
    Rate: A Case for Conditionalizing*, Mimeo
Artis, M.J. and Lewis, M. (n.d.) *The Demand for and Supply of Money*,
    unpublished mimeo
Artis, M.J. and Lewis, M. (1974) 'The Demand for Money: Stable or
    Unstable?' in *Banker* (March)
Ascheim, J. (1961) *Techniques of Monetary Control*, Johns Hopkins,
    Baltimore
Bagehot, W. (1965) 'Lombard Street reprinted in *Collected Works*,
    Economist Newspaper
Bank (1971) *Competition and Credit Control*, Bank of England
Bank (1972) 'Demand for Money in the U.K.: A Further Investigation'
    in *Bank of England Quarterly Bulletin*, vol. 12, no. 1 (March), p. 43
Bank (1974) 'Demand for Money in the U.K.: Experience Since 1971'
    in *Bank of England Quarterly Bulletin*, vol. 14, no. 3 (September),
    p. 284
Bank (1978) 'The Secondary Banking Crisis and Bank of England

Support Operations in *Bank of England Quarterly Bulletin*, vol. 18, no. 2 (June), pp. 230-9

Bank (1979) *Bank of England Model of the U.K. Economy*, Bank of England Discussion Paper no. 5 (September)

Bank (1980) *Monetary Control*, a Consultation Paper by HM Treasury and the Bank of England, HMSO, Cmnd. 7858

Bank (1982) 'Composition of Monetary and Liquidity Aggregates, and Associated Statistics' in *Bank of England Quarterly Bulletin*, vol. 22, no. 4 (December), p. 530

Bank (1983) 'Changes to Monetary Statistics' in *Bank of England Quarterly Bulletin*, vol. 23, no. 1 (March), p. 78

Beckerman, W. (ed.) (1972) *The Labour Government's Economic Record 1964-70*, Duckworth

Berman, P.T. (1978) *Inflation and the Money Supply in the United States 1956-77*, Lexington Books, Lexington, Mass.

Blackaby, F.T. *et al.* (1978) *British Economic Policy 1960-74*, CUP

Boston (1976) *Controlling Monetary Aggregates*, vol. 2: Implementation, Federal Reserve Bank of Boston (June)

Boughton, J.M. (1972) *Monetary Policy and the Federal Funds Market*, Duke University Press, Durham, N.Ca.

Brams, S.J. (1975) *Game Theory and Politics*, The Free Press (within Macmillan), New York

Brams (1976) *Paradoxes of Politics*, The Free Press (within Macmillan), New York

Brechling, F.P.R. and Lipsey, R.J. (1974) 'Trade Credit and Monetary Policy' reprinted in H.G. Johnson (ed.), *Readings in British Monetary Economics*, OUP

Brittan, S. (1965) *The Treasury under the Tories 1951-64*, Secker & Warburg and Penguin

Brittan, S. (1971) *Steering the Economy*, Penguin

Brittan, S. (1977) *The Economic Consequences of Democracy*, Temple Smith

Brown, A.T. (1955) *The Great Inflation 1939-51*, OUP

Brown, R.N., Enoch, C.A. and Mortimer-Lee, P.D. (1980) *The Inter-Relationship Between Costs and Prices in the U.K.*, Bank of England Discussion Paper, no. 7 (November)

Brunner, K. (1981) 'Monetary Policy' in *Lloyds Bank Review*, no. 139 (February), p. 1

Brunner, K. and Meltzer, A. (1980) *Monetary Institutions and the Policy Process*, Carnegie Rochester Conference Series vol. 13, North Holland

Buiter, W. (1980) *The Superiority of Contingent Rules over Fixed Rules in Models With Rational Expectations*, British Discussion Paper 80/80

Burrows, H.P. (1980) *The Economic Theory of Pollution Control*, Martin Robertson

Butler, D. and Kavanagh, M. (1974) *The British General Election of February 1974*, Macmillan

Butler, D. and Kavanagh, M. (1975) *The British General Election of October 1974*, Macmillan

Butler, D.E. and Kavanagh, D.A. (1980) *The British General Election of 1979*, Macmillan

Butler, D.E. and Pinto-Duschinsky, M. (1971) *The British General Election of 1970*, Macmillan

Cagan, P. (1956) 'The Monetary Dynamics of Hyper Inflation' in M. Friedman (ed.), *Studies in the Quantity Theory of Money*, University of Chicago Press

Cagan, P. (1965) *Determinants & Effects of Changes in the Stock of Money 1875-1960*, NBER Studies in Business Cycles, no. 13, Columbia

Cagan, P. (1972) *The Channels of Monetary Effect on Interest Rates*, NBER

Carswell, J.P. (1960) *The South Sea Bubble*, Cresset

Coghlan, R.T. (1980) *Theory of Money and Finance*, Macmillan

Courakis, A.J. (1973) 'Old Wine in New Bottles' in *Economica*, vol. 40 (February), p. 73

Crowther (1971) *Consumer Credit: Report of the Committee*, HMSO, Cmnd. 4596

Culbertson, J.M. (1972) *Money and Banking*, McGraw Hill

Davenport, J.R. (1980) 'Why Can't He Hit His Monetary Targets?' in *Fortune* (6 October)

Davis, D. and Yeomans, K. (1971) 'Competition and Credit Control: The Rubicon and Beyond' in *Lloyds Bank Review*, no. 108 (March)

Dennis, G.E.J. (1980) 'Money Supply and its Control' in W.P.J. Maunder (ed.), *The British Economy in the 1970s*, Heinemann Educational Books

Dornbusch, R. and Fischer, S.C. (1980) 'Exchange Rates and the Current Account' in *American Economic Review*, vol. 70 (1980), p. 960

Dosser, D., Gowland, D.H. and Hartley, K. (1981) *Collaboration Amongst Nations*, Martin Robertson

Enoch, C.A. (1979) *The Direction of Causality Between the Exchange*

Rate, Prices and Money, Bank of England Discussion Paper, no. 7 (November)

Foot, M.D.K.W. *et al*. (1979) 'Monetary Base Control' in *Bank of England Quarterly Bulletin*, vol. 19, no. 2 (June), p. 149

Foot, M.D.K.W. (1981) 'Monetary Targets: Their Nature and Record in the Major Economies' in B. Griffiths and G.E. Wood (eds), *Monetary Targets*, Macmillan

Ford, A.G. (1962) *The Gold Standard 1880-1914: Britain and Argentina*, OUP

Friedman, M. (1956) *Studies in the Quantity Theory of Money*, University of Chicago Press

Friedman, M. (1968) The Role of Monetary Policy in *American Economic Review*, vol. LVIII (March), p. 1

Friedman, M. (1968a) *Dollars and Deficits*, Prentice Hall

Friedman, M. (1969) *The Optimum Quantity of Money and Other Essays*, Aldine, Chicago

Friedman, J.W. (1977) *Oligopoly and the Theory of Games*, North Holland

Friedman, M. (1969) *A Theoretical Framework for Monetary Analysis*, NBER, reprinted in Gordon (1974)

Friedman, M. and Schwartz, A.J. (1963) *A Monetary History of the U.S. 1867-1960*, NBER Studies in Banking Cycles, no. 12, Princeton University Press

Gaitskell, H.T.N. (1933) 'Four Monetary Heretics' in G.D.H. Cole (ed.), *What Everyone Wants to Know About Money*, Gollancz

Galbraith, J.K. (1954) *The Great Crash*, Hamish Hamilton (English Edition), also published by Pelican (1961)

Goodhart, C.A.E. (1972) *The Business of Banking, 1891-1914*, Weidenfeld & Nicholson

Goodhart, C.A.E. (1973) 'Monetary Policy in the U.K.' in K. Holbik (ed.), *Monetary Policy in Twelve Industrial Countries*, Federal Reserve Bank of Boston

Goodhart, C.A.E. (1976) *Money, Information and Uncertainty*, 2nd edition, Macmillan

Goodhart, C.A.E. (1981) 'Problems of Monetary Management' in A.S. Courakis (ed.), *Inflation, Depression and Economic Policy in the West*, Mansell and Alexandrine Press

Goodhart, C.A.E. and Gowland, D.H. (1977) 'The Relationship Between Yields on Short and Long-dated Gilt-edged' in *Bulletin of Economic Research*, vol. 29 (November)

Goodhart, C.A.E. and Gowland, D.H. (1978) 'The Relationship

Between Long-dated Gilt Yields and Other Variables' in *Bulletin of Economic Research*, vol. 30 (November)

Gordon, A.J. (1974) (ed.) *Milton Friedman's Monetary Framework*, University of Chicago Press

Gowland, D.H. (1975a) 'Money Supply and Share Prices' in M. Parkin and A.R. Nobay (eds), *Current Economic Problems*, CUP

Gowland, D.H. (1975b) *Is The U.K. Gilts Market Efficient?*, Mimeo

Gowland, D.H. (1977a) 'Techniques of Monetary Control: The U.K.'s Choice', *Economic Policy Analysis Group Discussion Paper*, no. 1

Gowland, D.H. (1977b) *Debt Management and Monetary Control*, paper delivered to City University, 'Seminar of Debt Management and Monetary Control 21-23 November 1977'

Gowland, D.H. (ed.) (1979) *Modern Economic Analysis*, Butterworths

Gowland, D.H. (1981) *Issues in Monetary Control*, mimeo

Gowland, D.H. (1982) *Modern Economic Analysis II*, Butterworths

Gowland, D.H. and Pakenham, K. (1974) 'The Control of the Money Supply' in *R.I.B. Monthly Review*, no. 1 (February), Section B

Grant, A.J.K. (1977) *Economic Uncertainty and Financial Structure*, Macmillan

Gresham, Sir T. (1949) *Gresham on Foreign Exchange*, edited by R.A. De Roover, Howard UP, Cambridge, Mass.

Gurley, J. and Shaw, E. (1960) *Money in a Theory of Finance*, Brookings Institute

Hadjimatheou, G. (1976) *Housing and Mortgage Markets,* Saxon House

Haines, J. (1977) *The Politics of Power*, revised edition, Coronet Books

Hamburger, M.J. (1973) 'The Demand for Money in 1971: Was There a Shift?' in *Journal of Money, Credit and Banking*, vol. 5 (May)

Hansen, B. (1969) *Fiscal Policy in Seven Countries*, OECD, Paris

Heller, W.W. *et al.* (1968) *Fiscal Policy in Balanced Economy*, OECD, Paris

Hewitt, G.E. (1977) 'Financial Forecasts in the U.K.' in *Bank of England Quarterly Bulletin*, vol. 12, no. 2 (June)

Hicks, Sir J.R. (1952) 'Monetary Policy Again' in *B.O.U.J.S.*, vol. 14, p. 157

Hutton, J.P. (1977) 'A Model of Short-term Capital Movements, the Foreign Exchange Market and Official Intervention in the U.K. 1963-70' in *Review of Economic Studies*, vol. 53

IEA (1980) *Is Monetarism Enough?*, IEA Readings no. 24, IEA

Jaffee, D.W. (1975) *Credit Rationing and the Commercial Loan Market*, Wiley

Johnson, H.G. (ed.) (1974) *Readings in British Monetary Economics*,

OUP

Joseph, Sir K. (1976) *Is Monetarism Enough?*, Centre for Policy Studies

Kenyon, J. (1962) *The Popish Plot*, OUP

Keynes, J.M. (1936) *The General Theory of Employment, Interest and Money*, Macmillan (also in vol. VII of his collected works)

Keynes, J.M. (1971) *A Tract on Monetary Reform*, reprinted in *The Collected Writings*, Macmillan for the RES

Keynes, J.M. (1972) *Essays in Persuasion*, in *The Collected Writings*, Macmillan for the RES, vol. IX

Lewis, M. (1980) 'Is Monetary Base Control Just Interest Rate Control in Disguise?' in *Banker* (September), p. 35

Mackay, C. (1941) *Extraordinary Popular Delusions and the Behaviour of Crowds*, Bentley, reprinted NEL (1952); also abridged edition published by Unwin (1973)

Macmillan (1931) *Report of Committee of Enquiry into Finance and Industry*, HMSO, Cmnd 827

Marriott, O. (1969) *The Property Boom*, revised edition, Hamish Hamilton

Mayes, D.G. (1979) *The Property Boom*, Martin Robertson

Miller, E with Lonie, A. (1980) *Microeconomic Effects of Monetary Policy*, Martin Robertson

Minty, L. Le (n.d.) *The Law Relating to Banking and Foreign Exchange*, New Era

Moore, B.J. and Threadgold, A.R. (1980) 'Bank Lending and the Money Supply', *Bank of England Discussion Paper*, no. 10 (July)

Mundell, R. (1968) *International Economics*, Macmillan, New York

Mussa, M. (1977) *A Study in Macroeconomics*, North Holland

OECD (1975) *Monetary Policy in France*, OECD, Paris

Page, H. (1973) *Report of the Official Committee on National Savings*, HMSO, Cmnd. 5273

Parkin, M. (1970) 'Discount House Portfolio and Debt Selection' in *Review of Economic Studies*, vol. 37 (October), p. 37

Pepper, G.T. and Wood, G.E. (1976) 'Too Much Money − ?', *Hobart Paper 68*, Institute of Economic Affairs

Polak, J.J. (1951) 'Monetary Analysis of Income Formation and Payments Problems', *I.M.F. Staff Papers*, vol. 6

Poole, W. (1970) 'Optimal Choice of Monetary Instruments' in *Quarterly Journal of Economics*, vol. 84, pp. 197-216

Posner, M. (ed.) (1978) *Demand Management*, Heinemann Educational Books

Pratt, M.J. (1980) *Building Societies: An Econometric Model*, Bank of

England Discussion Paper, no. 11 (August)

Radcliffe (1959) *Committee on the Workings of the Monetary System*, HMSO, Cmnd. 827

Renton, G.A. (ed.) (1975) *Modelling the Economy*, Heinemann

Saville, L.D. (1980) *The Sterling-Dollar Rate in the Floating-rate Period: The Role of Money, Prices and Intervention*, Bank of England Discussion Paper, no. 9 (March)

Sawyer, M.C. (1980) *Theories of the Firm*, Weidenfeld & Nicholson

Schwartz, G. (1959) *Bread and Circuses, The Sunday Times*

Smethurst, R.G. (1979) 'Monetary Policy' in D. Morris (ed.), *The Economic System in the U.K.*, 2nd edition, OUP

Taylor, C.T. and Threadgold, A.R. (1980) *Real National Savings and Its Sectoral Composition*, Bank of England Discussion Paper, no. 6 (October)

Tobin, J. (1969) 'Deposit Interest Ceilings as a Monetary Control' in *Journal of Money, Credit and Banking*, vol. II (February)

Treasury (1980) *The Treasury Monetary Model*, Treasury Working Paper

Tullock, G. (1976) *The Vote Motive*, Hobart paperback

Turner, P.J. (1979) *Time for Monetary Reform*, James Copeland Co.

Volcker, P.A. (1977) 'A Broader Role for Monetary Targets' in *F.R.B.N.Y. Quarterly Review*, pp. 23-8 (Spring)

Wadsworth, J.E. (ed.) (1972) *Banks and the Monetary System in the U.K. 1959-71*, Methuen

Waud, R.N. (1973) Proximate Targets and Monetary Policy in *Economic Journal*, vol. 83, no. 1 (March), p. 1

Williams, D., Goodhart, C.A.E. and Gowland, D.H. (1976) 'Money, Income and Causality' in *American Economic Review*, vol. 90 (June)

INDEX

accelerator 177
acceptance credits 147
aggregate demand 133, 177
aggregate supply 177, 184-5
Alford, R. 103n37, 200
Allard, R. 86, 102n10, 200
American 'New Right' 185
Arab-Israeli War 141
arbitrage funds 111-12, 122-3
Artis, M.J. 119-21, 126-7, 142n5, n7, 159-61, 162n6, 200
Ascheim, J. 20, 51n1, n4, 75n8, n15, 200
Association of Finance Agents 133
Australia 3, 52

Bagehot, W. 11, 19n14, 200
balanced budget multiplier 185
balance of payments 7-8, 43-51
 passim, 78, 87, 107, 187; capital flows 47-8, 107, 188; current account 101, 168, 181, 188; deficit 43, 142, 144, 166-8; monetary theory of 43-4, 50-1, 138; statistics 45, 101, 114, 181; surplus 43, 159, 188; target 7, 43, 159; *see also* open economy, overseas influence
Bank of England (Bank) 18-19, 75, 77, 80-4, 91-114 *passim*, 131, 156, 161, 191, 193; banks 83-4, 95, 97-9, 108, 125, 145, 147; case against a reserve base system 64, 67-71; discount market 94, 98-9; gilt-edged market 91-4, 98, 101, 104-5, 108, 149, 152, 175, 191; model 16, 139; statistics 111, 117, 126
Bank Rate 3, 81-2, 101, 106, 113; replacement by MLR 3, 109, 113; statistics 113; *see also* interest rates, minimum lending rate (MLR)
banks *passim*; assets, 5, 9, 13, 23-31 *passim*, 49, 52, 55-6, 63, 85, 87, 105, 118, 169, 183, reserve assets 52-60, 63, 65, 74, 97-8, 100, *see also* ratios; Banking

Act 1979 5; borrowing 8, 23, 26, 42, 46, 60-1, 85, 88, 108, 110, 121, 124, 126, 132, 175-9 *passim*, 186; charges 118, 147; competition 10, 29, 31, 65, 76, 78, 84, 95, 118; crisis 108-9, 125; definition of 5-6, 64-7, 77; deposits 28-31, 49, 60, 64-6, 77, 117-18, 144-8, 195, *see also* Certificate of Deposit (CD), deposits, Special Deposits failures 78, 146; interest rates 3, 13, 28, 31, 35-6, 55, 61, 71-6 *passim*, 88, 108-9, 123-4, 183, 189, 193, base 70, 109-13, 124, 164, 166-70, 192, deposit 28, 31-2, 76-7, 95, 112, 122, 167, loan 13-14, 31, 35-6, 61, 64-5, 77, 100, 123, overdraft 31, 67, 72, 88, 100, 122-3, 147, 161n2, wholesale money 88, 124; lending 3, 8-9, 13-14, 23-39 *passim*, 52, 55, 60-4 *passim*, 72-3, 77, 85, 88, 105, 108-12, 117, 120, 125, 167-8, 171, 173, 176, 178-9, 183, 189, 191-4, price controls 31-3, 88, quantity controls 5, 34-8, 82-4, 87, 101; liabilities 5, 9, 21, 23-31 *passim*, 49, 60, 87, 117, 144, 169, 195, eligible liabilities 13, 49, 97-8, 144-8, non deposit liabilities 49-50, *see also* interest-bearing eligible deposits (IBELs); London Clearing Banks 105, 195; money creation 22-4, 57-8, deposit creation 22-3; nationalisation of 3, 124; nature of 178; political criticism 122; profits 23, 49, 53, 61, 63, 121-2, 124, 178, 195; reserve bases 53-67, 72-4, 125; tax on banking 10, 55, 65, 76-7, 145, 161n2, 195; transactions 86, 98-9, 116, 122, 147
Barber (Lord), A.P.L. 20, 101, 128, 165
Barberism 106-7, 137-8
Bardepot 16, 188
Baumol model 63

For Product Safety Concerns and Information please contact our EU
representative GPSR@taylorandfrancis.com Taylor & Francis Verlag GmbH,
Kaufingerstraße 24, 80331 München, Germany

Batch number: 08151759

Printed by Printforce, the Netherlands